ARMOURED CRUISER
CRESSY

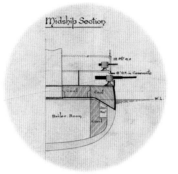

6 inch Armour

ARMOURED CRUISER
CRESSY

detailed in the original builders' plans

ANDREW CHOONG

2 inch Nickel Plating

NATIONAL
MARITIME MUSEUM
GREENWICH

Seaforth
PUBLISHING

Half title image: Midship section from 'Outline Design for New Armoured Cruiser' 1897. (© National Maritime Museum, Greenwich, London. Detail from M1573)

Frontispiece: Part of outboard profile from 'Outline Design for New Armoured Cruiser' 1897. (© National Maritime Museum, Greenwich, London. Detail from M1573)

This edition first published in Great Britain in 2020 by
Seaforth Publishing,
An imprint of Pen & Sword Books Ltd,
47 Church Street,
Barnsley
South Yorkshire S70 2AS

www.seaforthpublishing.com
Email: info@seaforthpublishing.com

Published in association with Royal Museums Greenwich,
the group name for the National Maritime Museum, the Royal Observatory, the Queen's House and *Cutty Sark*

British Library Cataloguing in Publication Data
A catalogue record for this book is available from the British Library

ISBN 978 1 5267 6637 3 (Hardback)
ISBN 978 1 5267 6638 0 (ePub)
ISBN 978 1 5267 6639 7 (Kindle)

Typeset and designed by Stephen Dent
Printed and bound in China

CONTENTS

THE PLANS

The centrepiece of *Cressy*'s plans are the eight highly detailed and beautifully executed drawings completed by the draughtsmen at Portsmouth Dockyard in October 1901. It should be noted that these are not the builders' plans used by Fairfield and based on the original Admiralty designs, but the 'as-fitted' post-completion general arrangements drawn up following a survey of the ship and her fittings. As a reference for the finished product, equipped and ready for sea, this makes them a very useful record of what was physically there as opposed to the theoretical concept of the ship. Furthermore, fascinating details of the equipment, machinery and fittings are present, whereas these would generally be absent on a design drawing. At the impressive scale of 1:48, the plans are easy to interpret – if slightly challenging to handle – and aesthetically they are fine representations of the exceptional draughtsmanship of the late Victorian era. They are on linen-backed cartridge paper and combine inked lines with colour washes to highlight certain areas and bring out detail such as yellow for special castings and forgings.

The as-fitted general arrangement plans comprise an inboard profile, six deck drawings and hull sections. In addition to these, there are four plans that record the ship's brief design evolution, eloquently demonstrating how little changed between White's original concept and the ship that entered service. Eleven further drawings complement the Portsmouth general arrangements. These relate primarily to structural details, but there are also plans relating to the rigging and the arrangement of watertight compartments. Unsurprisingly, a number of these plans also pertain to *Aboukir*, the only other *Cressy* class ship built by Fairfield. Last but by no means least are the 181 drawings from the Admiralty 'B' material which relates to the class as a whole. These cover a range of topics from structural features such as the minutiae of riveting plating and armour to the hull and incorporation of the wood backing and sheathing, to piping and ventilation systems in both diagrammatic and as-fitted formats, and plans to illustrate reports on vessel condition. Two examples of the latter are comparative drawings showing propeller erosion and defective boiler tubes. A handful of drawings also exist in the Vickers Collection, most notably a complete machinery arrangement and the design for the Vickers-supplied 9.2-inch gun mountings.

Impressive as these survivals are, they are not without their limitations. In contrast to the very detailed focus on the ship in her design and completed state, neither the general arrangements nor most of the various other drawings for *Cressy* reflect any of the alterations carried out during the ship's thirteen-year life span. While these alterations were relatively few in *Cressy*'s case, the implications for the class as a whole are significant, as *Cressy*'s general arrangements were the only set retained by the Admiralty as a record of these ships. For the remainder of the class, the remaining drawings provide useful but isolated pieces of information, examples being a set of drawings showing *Bacchante*'s altered masts and rigging circa 1908 and improvements to the magazine cooling arrangements of the *Euryalus* in 1910. Fortunately, the class was heavily photographed over the course of their service lives and there is a large extant body of useful visual references of their later appearance.

ABBREVIATIONS USED ON THE PLANS

BL	Breech Loading	SV	Stop Valve
CS	Coal Scuttle	SVNR	Stop Valve, Non-Return
DB	Double Bottom	SW	Steel Wire
Do	Ditto	UD	Upper Deck
EL	Electric Light	WC	Water Closet
ERA	Engine Room Artificer	WO	Warrant Officer
ERT	Engine Room Telegraph	WS	Wash Stand
ES	Exhaust Scuttle	WTAS	Watertight Armoured Scuttle
FW	Fresh Water	WTB	Watertight Bulkhead
HP	High Pressure	WTD	Watertight Door
LP	Low Pressure	WTH	Watertight Hatch
MP	Medium Pressure	WTL	Watertight Ladderway
PO	Petty Officer	WTM	Watertight Manhole
QF	Quick Firing	WTS	Watertight Scuttle or Watertight Skylight
Std	Starboard	WTT	Watertight Tank

ACKNOWLEDGEMENTS

The creation of this book has been a terrific team effort. I am grateful to Rob Gardiner of Seaforth for the opportunity to contribute to this series, and Steve Dent for his excellent design work. Also to my colleagues at the National Maritime Museum who provided much good-natured and patient support. Jeremy Michell, Bob Todd and Alex Grover bought me time to work on the book by covering some of my other tasks, and read through early drafts of the text. The Pictures and Studio teams endured a barrage of scanning requests from me, all of which were promptly actioned. In my time at the Museum I have been fortunate to meet many learned people, a number of whom I am now privileged to call my friends. Those who found themselves victimised as sounding boards for *Cressy* are too numerous to list here, but have my warmest thanks for their advice and help. Any errors are of course my own. Last but by no means least, deepest appreciation to my wife Claire and daughter Anna for all their love, support and understanding.

INTRODUCTION

HMS *Cressy* was the lead ship of a class of six cruisers launched between 1899 and 1901. She was the first to commission, in 1901, and was soon followed by four of her sisters, HM Ships *Aboukir, Bacchante, Hogue* and *Sutlej* in 1902. The last ship – HMS *Euryalus* – suffered accidents including a major fire during construction and did not enter service until January 1904. The brainchild of Sir William White, the ships were ordered as a single batch under the 1897–1898 Programme. They were virtually identical, the most significant (and largely invisible) difference being the fitting of four-bladed screws to *Aboukir, Bacchante* and *Cressy* while the remainder had three-bladed propellers and they underwent comparatively little alteration for almost a decade. Although capable of operating as an homogeneous squadron, they were dispersed around the globe on their first commissions. *Cressy* went to China between 1901 and 1905, *Euryalus* to Australia, *Aboukir* and *Bacchante* to the Mediterranean while *Hogue* and *Sutlej* were assigned to the Channel Fleet. In 1907 the four cruisers which had been on overseas duties were sent to the North America & West Indies station. *Cressy* served in those waters for nearly two years before being recalled to Britain. The rapid pace of development in naval technology had by this time reduced the class to obsolescence and by 1913 all six were being considered for disposal. The outbreak of war in August 1914 granted them a new lease of life, patrolling the Broad Fourteens to shield the eastern flank of ships transporting the British Army from England to Belgium and France. On 22 September 1914 *Cressy, Aboukir* and *Hogue* were attacked and sunk by the German submarine *U9*. The surviving ships were immediately reassigned to other duties which were relatively out of harm's way, where they continued to give good service for the rest of the war. All three were sold for scrap in 1920. Over two decades of service the *Cressy*s had proven to be useful ships, and it is unfortunate that some subsequent perceptions of this class have been coloured by the notorious 'Three Before Breakfast' incident.

CLASS ORIGINS AND DESIGN EVOLUTION

The considerations which led to *Cressy* came from the traditional requirements for ships capable of guarding the British Empire's far-flung trade routes. While smaller cruising ships had gradually increased in size, speed and gun power in the 1890s, to meet this role the larger British first-class cruisers had been designed somewhat more reactively in response to foreign developments. The *Diadem* class, on which *Cressy* was based, were being heavily criticised for their primary armament of 6-inch guns and their protective arrangements, both of which were believed to be inferior to those of foreign equivalents. These criticisms were somewhat misplaced in terms of the role conceived for the *Diadem*s but they had some validity in that these cruisers were rather under-armed and under-protected for their size, with hull dimensions greater than those of contemporary battleships.

The Admiralty's dilemma was that unlike every other major naval power, Britain had to have large cruisers powerful enough to hold their own against their foreign counterparts while also having sufficient numbers in service to effectively guard their global interests. Given the extent of the British Empire in the 1890s, this amounted to a formidable number of vessels. Even with increased naval spending that followed the formal adoption of the Two Power Standard under the 1889 Naval Defence Act, the Royal Navy could not have both. The *Diadem*s represented a compromise towards numbers and cost effectiveness to suit their role as large detached service cruisers. *Cressy* would represent a compromise of a rather more ambitious nature.

A proactive Director of Naval Construction (DNC), White made a habit of preparing new designs on his own initiative to present to the Board of Admiralty. A contemporary naval officer observed that the DNC 'would point out that time was getting on…and that action was necessary in the shape of a decision. In order to assist their Lordships to reach this decision he submitted a design. Faced with a fait accompli the Board would usually agree with White.' While Commander Hall was likely exaggerating White's influence, it is true that he often got his way in these matters. By his own admission, the inspiration for *Cressy* came to White while he was away on his holidays between 1896 and 1897. At least one of these was while he was ostensibly away to recover from illness. During these 'breaks' he took the opportunity to visit various naval establishments in France, Italy, Germany and Russia, paying particular attention to the Italian *Vettor Pisani* and *Garibaldi* class armoured cruisers. His travels also enabled him to gain useful first-hand perspectives on the French *Jeanne d'Arc*, Germany's *Furst Bismarck* and Russia's *Rossia*. At the time of his visits three of these ships were still under construction and the rest existed only on the drawing board, but in most instances White appears to have been given very privileged access to the designs and the ideas that spawned them.

Impressed particularly by what he had seen in Italy, White drafted a concept for a new large cruiser, first expressed in a letter dated 29 April 1897 and developed into a more detailed report for consideration by the Naval Members of the Board of Admiralty a mere week later. While outwardly similar to the *Diadem* class, this new cruiser took inspiration for its armament from the earlier *Powerful* class cruisers, replacing four of the *Diadem*'s 6-inch guns with two 9.2-inch mounts in commanding positions forward on the forecastle and aft at upper deck level. Most significantly, White introduced side armour to the design, the first time such a feature had been applied to a British cruiser since the mid-1880s. This marked a major improvement, one made possible by developments in the manufacture of hard-faced steel armour. Specifically, White benefited on this occasion from the availability of the new Krupp armour to British manufacturers from 1896. Krupp plates represented a significant improvement on the Harvey

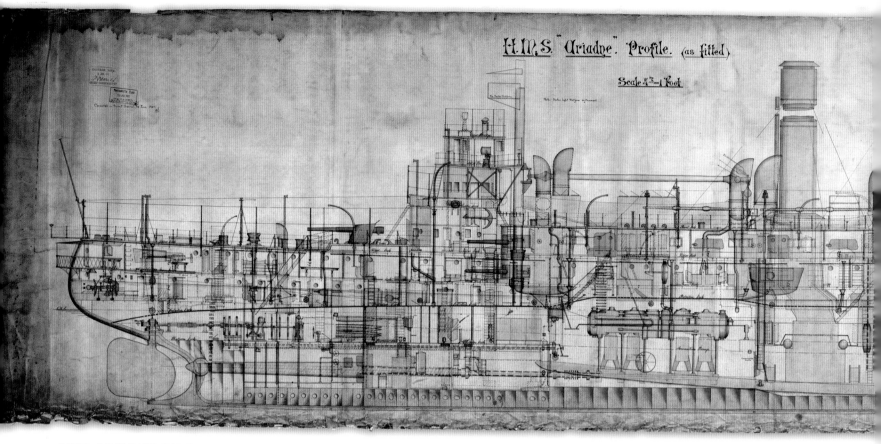

HMS *ARIADNE*, INBOARD PROFILE

This plan shows the protected cruiser *Ariadne* as completed in considerable detail, and includes the alterations carried out up to 1907. The similarities between the *Diadem* and *Cressy* classes are striking, and it is easy to see how much the latter owed to their predecessors in terms of design continuity. The 6-inch guns on the forecastle and aft end of the upper deck are clearly visible, and were mounted in pairs abreast each other. The considerable deadwood in way of the propellers and rudder is evident, and makes for interesting comparison with *Cressy*'s hull form. An alteration in yellow ink near the mainmast illustrates the gunnery spotting position that was added; curiously, this feature is not reflected in *Cressy*'s plans despite her having received this upgrade in 1907 as well. An odd feature not implemented in the *Cressy*s is the retractable boom at the bow which functioned as a short bowsprit. (M1757)

type which had first been employed by the Royal Navy in 1894. This innovation proved timely for *Cressy*, as parallel advances in shells and QF (quick firing) guns made effective side protection a necessity rather than a luxury. In designing his protective arrangements, White transplanted the protective arrangements employed in his *Canopus* class battleships onto a large cruiser hull. Implementation of this was not without its difficulties. Awareness of the displacement implications of this combination of guns and armour led to discussion by the Board as to whether a secondary battery of ten rather than twelve 6-inch guns might not be preferable. White's stated preference was for the latter arrangement, as provision could still be made in wartime to supply this number of guns with sufficient ammunition. This question occupied some time and was not settled in favour of the twelve-gun arrangement until June 1897. Related questions on the subject of the guns, and particularly their mountings, would continue to preoccupy the Admiralty and affect the progress of matters such as agreed crew complements into the summer of 1898.

White initially set the design speed at 21½ knots at natural draught under trial conditions, a target which would allow for an estimated sea speed of 19¾ knots. The insistence on obtaining this speed under natural rather than forced draught was important. Unfavourable comparisons with foreign designs often rested on trials conducted with those ships running under forced draught. This resulted in a high speed, but one that could not be maintained under normal conditions because of the accelerated wear and tear it imposed on a ship's machinery. Speed estimates based on natural draught were far more realistic and represented operational realities. Bunkerage as far as possible was to conform to that of contemporary battleships, giving *Cressy* an endurance of thirty days steaming at 10 knots or five days at 19¾ knots before the coal supply was exhausted. This was achievable despite the heavier armour protection and armament, but it meant that *Cressy* possessed less endurance than the *Diadem*s. However, given the difference in function between the two classes this was regarded as acceptable. Overall, the new cruisers represented a well-balanced design, one which fitted them in White's thinking to a genuine multi-mission role. With her speed and powerful armament *Cressy* could fulfil the demands of the trade protection cruiser, and with her protection scheme could also operate with the battle fleet as a 'fast wing', if necessary engaging enemy battleships in the hope of at least disrupting them by damaging their less-protected areas and secondary armament. Explaining his concept to the Board, White stressed four key points:

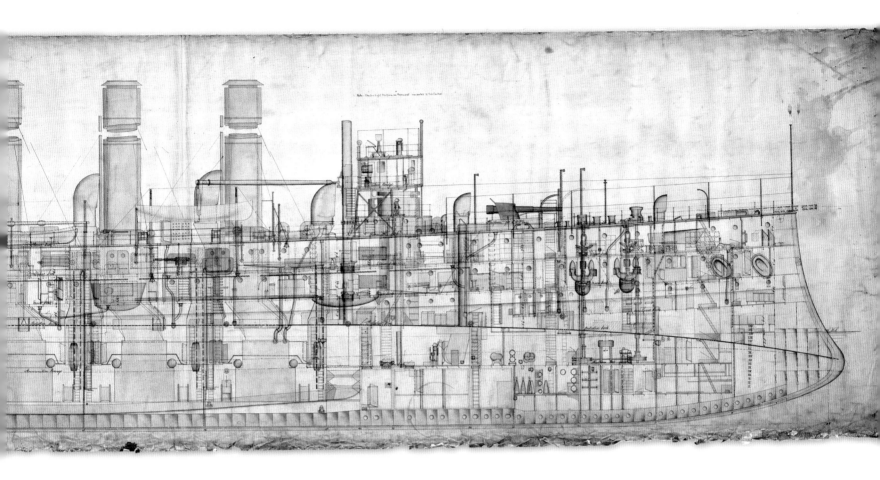

- Special adaptation for service with the Channel and Mediterranean Fleets, and the performance of all duties hitherto devolving on first-class cruisers attached to fleets.
- Capacity for close action, as adjuncts to battleships.
- Suitability for employment on detached services if required to be used for the protection of shipping, commerce and communications.
- Armament, protection, speed and coal endurance to be such that the new cruisers should be formidable rivals to the best cruisers built or building for foreign navies.

Three of the points expressed above were standard fare as far as British cruiser design had been concerned. The notable exception was the second point, wherein the new ships were expected to stand in the line of battle. Using the new Italian designs to illustrate his views, White argued that while a cruiser could never replace a battleship in the Royal Navy's force mix, there were no longer any technical reasons why a well-armed and well-protected cruiser could not participate in a fleet action. White's ideas were discussed at a further meeting of the Board on 18 June 1897. The design of the new ship was generally approved, including White's recommendation for adopting the heavier twelve-gun secondary armament. The only significant alteration imposed by the Board was that, contrary to White's opinion, the ships' hulls were to be sheathed for overseas service. The penalty imposed in speed and draught was deemed acceptable in terms of the known advantages imparted by copper

sheathing over the new anti-fouling paint that White originally wanted. Some days later the design papers were presented to the First Lord of the Admiralty, George Goschen, for approval. Impressed by the explanations of his naval colleagues, Goschen remarked that the *Cressy*s 'will undoubtedly be fine ships'.

Revolutionary as White's proposal seemed, in the most general terms the concept he was advocating was not new to the Royal Navy. Walker's large wooden screw frigates of the 1850s with their high speed and heavy armament had been designed for just such a role and these ships influenced the design of the ironclad HMS *Warrior* (1860). The early armoured cruiser HMS *Shannon* (1875) and the *Imperieuse* class (1883–4) also represented attempts to implement the idea of well-protected and heavily armed 'semi-battleship' cruisers, but these failed because the technology had not yet matured to permit an effective combination of speed, armament and protection. The small battleships of the *Centurion* and *Renown* classes which were built in the early 1890s were a step in the right direction, but although fast by battleship standards they were unable to meet the speed requirement demanded of a cruiser. *Cressy* was the first successful attempt to achieve the realisation of this idea in the era of the steel navy. White's vision of multi-role cruisers with battleship scale protection – a phrase interestingly echoed a decade later by John Arbuthnot Fisher for public consumption when describing the *Indefatigable* class – represents an important milestone on the road that led the Royal Navy to the battlecruiser in the first decade of the twentieth century.

Continued on p13

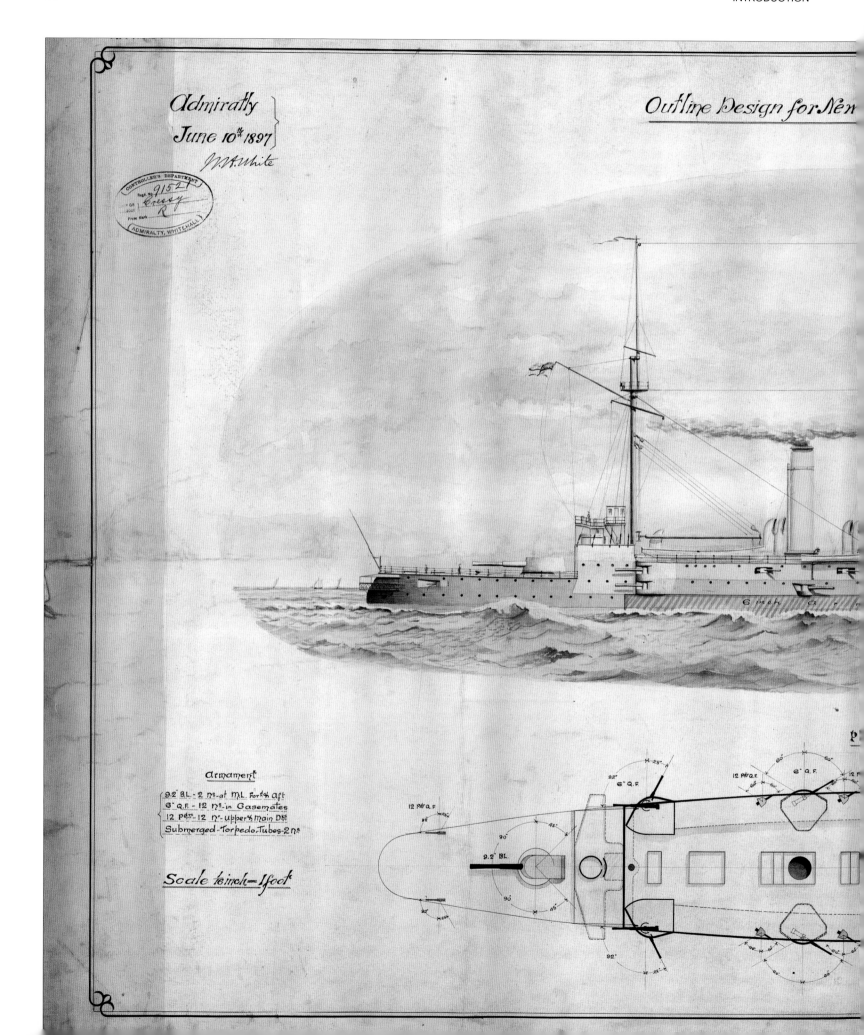

Admiralty
June 10th 1897
W. H. White

Outline Design for New

Armament

9.2" B.L. - 2 Nos. at M.L. Ford & aft
6" Q.F. - 12 Nos. in Casemates
12 Pdr. - 12 Nos. upper & Main Dks.
Submerged - Torpedo Tubes - 2 Nos.

Scale ½ inch = 1 foot

oured Cruiser

CRESSY CLASS, DESIGN PROPOSAL

The first pictorial representation of the *Cressy* class, this plan was produced to accompany the written description and design legend submitted to the Board of Admiralty in June 1897. The most important detail illustrated is the arrangement of the armour, with the area protected by Krupp plates shaded in blue and the thinner nickel steel in red. These details are complemented by the midships section which shows the interrelationship between the side armour and deck plating. Impressively, the design shown here required little alteration and very closely matched the ships as completed. (M1573)

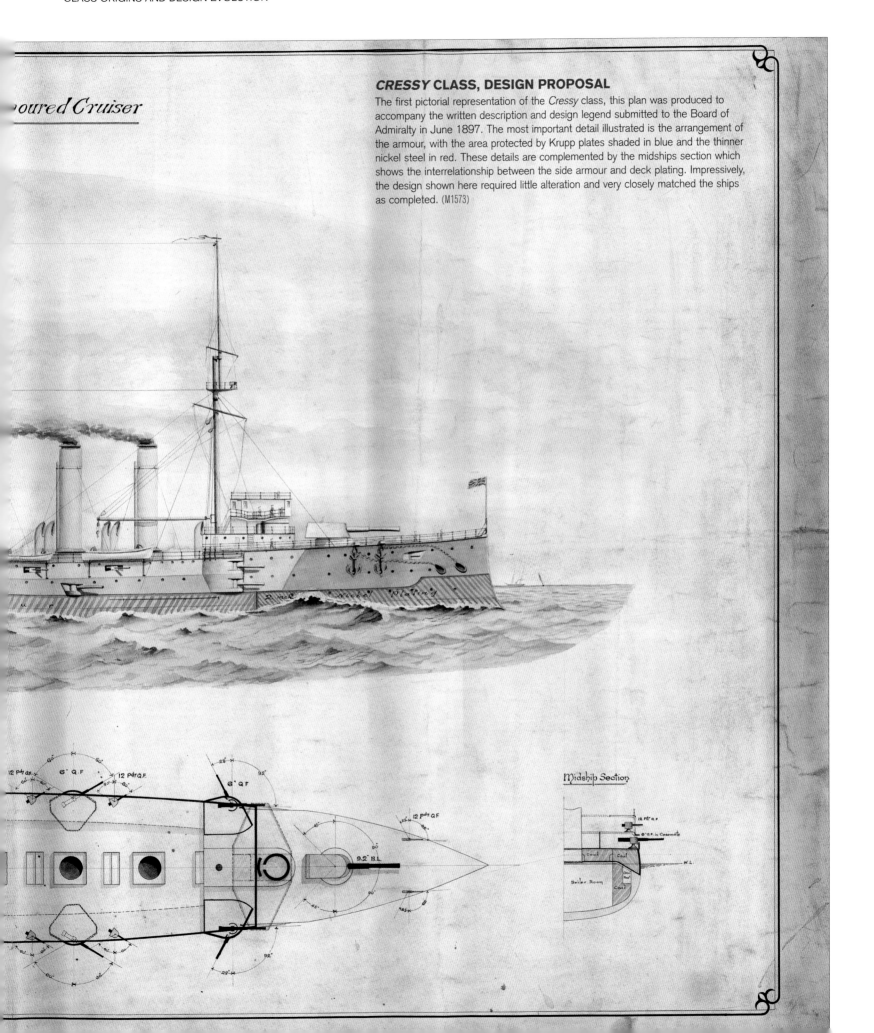

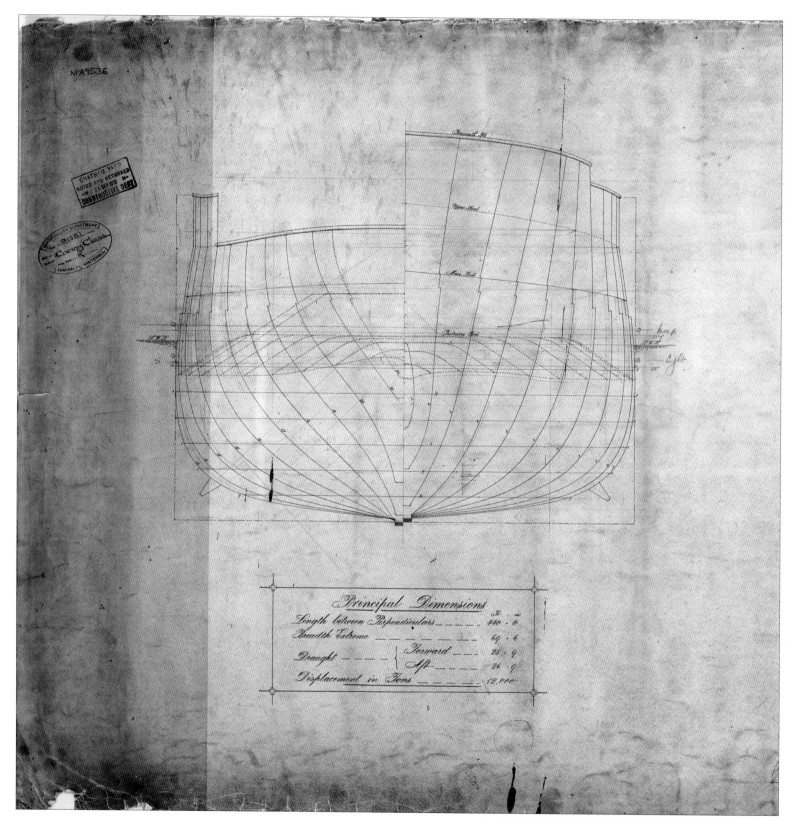

CRESSY CLASS, FORE AND AFT BODY PLAN

The drafting of a sheer drawing is the most important element in the process of translating an initial concept into a design from which a vessel can be constructed. It is based on the detailed calculations produced by the Department of Naval Construction following approval of the Board of Admiralty. The table confirms the dimensions and tonnage agreed in the summer of 1897, about five months before this plan was completed. This part shows a geometric representation of the hull form of the Cressy class, providing a split fore and aft view with the aft from midships stations depicted to the left and the forward from midships stations on the right. Also shown are the positions and curve of the decks, most notably the Protective Deck which is shown in greater detail, and the water lines which run horizontally across the hull. The stations and water lines are assigned numbers to allow cross-referencing with the other elements of the sheer drawing, those being the profile and longitudinal half-breadth. (Detail from Sheer Drawing for the Cressy class, M1761)

WEIGHT BREAKDOWN

Weights for HMS *Cressy*, comparing the design estimates with the ship's state at the time of her inclining experiment.

Item	Weight from design estimates (tons)	Weight taken from inclining experiment (tons)
Hull excluding sheathing	4800	
Hull sheathing	540	
Protective decks	980	7690
Protection to hull	900	
Protection to armament	640	
Armament	770	804
Machinery	1800	1900
General equipment	540	563
Net defence	50	Not installed
Coal	800	
Engineers' stores	80	Not recorded
Board Margin	100	
Total:	**12,000**	**11,695**

ANCHORS

Type	Number carried
110cwt close-stowing	3
40cwt close-stowing	1
14cwt Admiralty pattern	1
12cwt Admiralty pattern	1

PARTICULARS, AS COMPLETED

Builder:	Fairfield Shipbuilding & Engineering Company, Ltd, Govan	**Armour and protection:**	
Ordered:	25 March 1898	**Belt:**	6in – 2in
Laid down:	12 October 1898	**Bulkheads:**	5in
Launched:	4 December 1899	**Decks:**	3in – 1in
Commencement of trial runs:	23 November 1900	**Casemates:**	6in – 2in
Commissioned:	28 May 1901	**Turrets:**	6in
		Barbettes:	6in
Displacement:	12,000 tons loaded	**Ammunition tubes for 9.2-inch guns:**	3in
Length overall:	472ft	**Conning tower:**	12in
Length between perpendiculars:	440ft	**Armament:**	Two 9.2-inch BL guns
Beam:	69ft 6in		Twelve 6-inch QF guns
Mean draught:	26ft 3in		Fourteen 12-pounder [3-inch] QF guns (including boat/land service pieces)
Machinery:	Two four-cylinder triple expansion engines; thirty Belleville boilers		Two 3-pounder QF guns
Maximum speed:	21 knots		Eight Maxim .303 machine guns
			Two 18-inch submerged torpedo tubes
		Complement:	755 (full)

Although the question of the number and general type of armament had been agreed in the summer of 1897, the guns desired by White and by the Board were still in development. This inflicted continued uncertainties on the design process, particularly with regards weight calculations and the allocation of sufficient magazine space. Concerns were also raised about the drain imposed by the power demands of auxiliary machinery for the operation of hoists and, inevitably, there was the issue of manning which would largely depend on the required number of men for gun crews and ammunition supply parties. Weaponry ultimately accounted for 811 of *Cressy*'s total tonnage, a significant increase over the original Board estimate of 770 tons. By December 1897, the DNC acknowledged that the ship's final displacement was now expected to be 12,000 tons in loaded condition. Nonetheless, drawings were prepared and approved by the end of January 1898, the prevailing view being that docking requirements would render any increase in length and beam disadvantageous: far better to accept an increase in draught, which would bring the main deck guns 20 inches closer to the waterline and result in the armour belt being slightly more submerged than originally anticipated under conditions of maximum loading.

In February, the first invitations to tender for the construction of the hull and machinery were sent out. Meanwhile, negotiations regarding armament dragged on into April 1898. The matter of design development was further complicated by the Admiralty's desire to maintain an advantage in dealing with private firms by promoting Vickers as a viable competitor to Armstrong Whitworth for the manufacture of heavy ordnance. A compromise was ultimately reached whereby both firms supplied weapons for the class, the 9.2-inch guns and mountings for *Aboukir* and *Cressy* being of Armstrong manufacture while Vickers

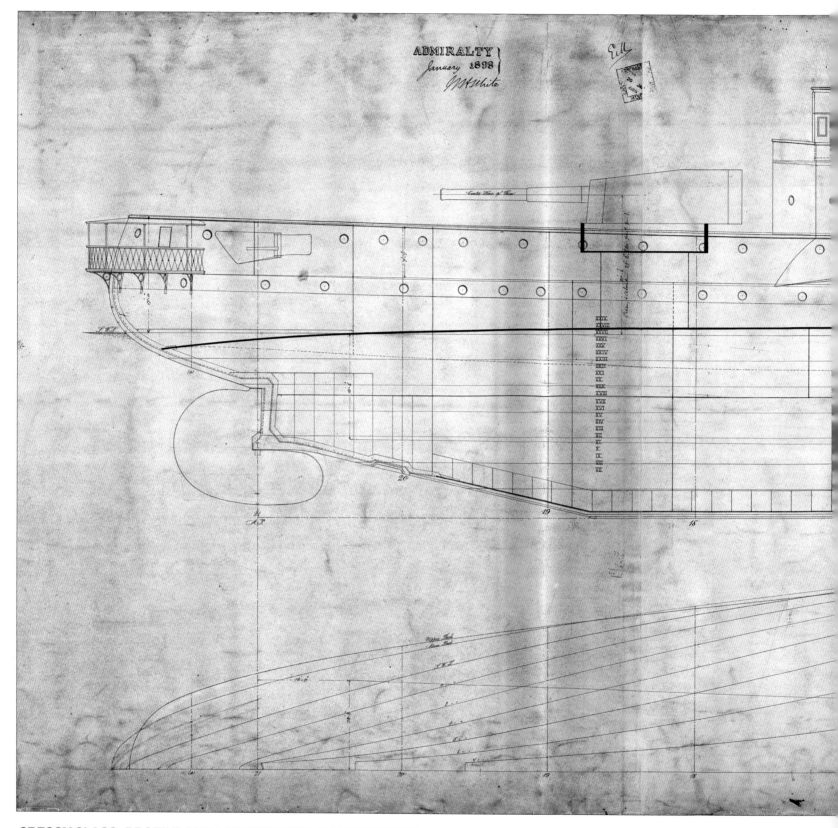

CRESSY CLASS, PROFILE AND LONGITUDINAL HALF-BREADTH

The rest of the sheer drawing shows the profile and longitudinal half-breadth. These would be developed by the draughtsmen using data derived from the body plan, and cross checked with it as the design on the plan took form. Collectively, the three perspectives would precisely illustrate the exterior form of the hull, having taken into account considerations of buoyancy, stability, seakeeping, and designed speed and power. Further detailed calculation and design analysis, up to and

including the production of the initial general arrangement plans, could not proceed until this plan had been completed and checked. Unusually, the midships section is not clearly marked, although the body plan illustrates that it lies in between Stations 11 and 12, or roughly in line with the third funnel. The most notable feature is the level of physical detail applied to the profile, something that is not strictly necessary in a sheer drawing, but which is quite common in such plans

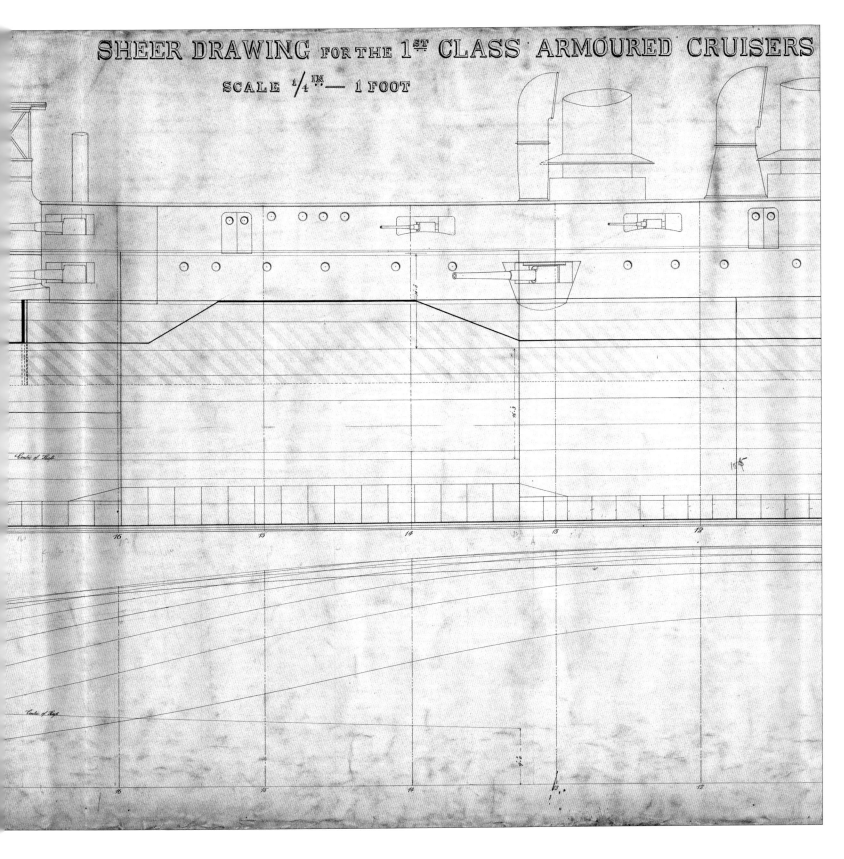

SHEER DRAWING FOR THE 1ST CLASS ARMOURED CRUISERS

SCALE ¼ IN — 1 FOOT

produced by the Admiralty in the late nineteenth century. These details include the positions and planned appearance of the fore and aft bridges, the main armament, scuttles, embarkation doors, masts, hawse holes and, rather charmingly, the ornate stern walk. Other details that are less visible but equally important are the centreline of the propeller shafts, which appear in both the profile and half-breadth, lines tracing the run of the decks (including additional lines to indicate camber) and

the positions of watertight bulkheads. The square compartments at the bottom of the hull mark the cellular double-bottom, and the wood sheathing for coppering is also marked, showing its extent from the keel to a few feet above the Protective Deck. Considerable attention is given to the armament, and markings in red ink indicate the distance between the planned load waterline and centreline of the 9.2-inch guns.

Continued overleaf

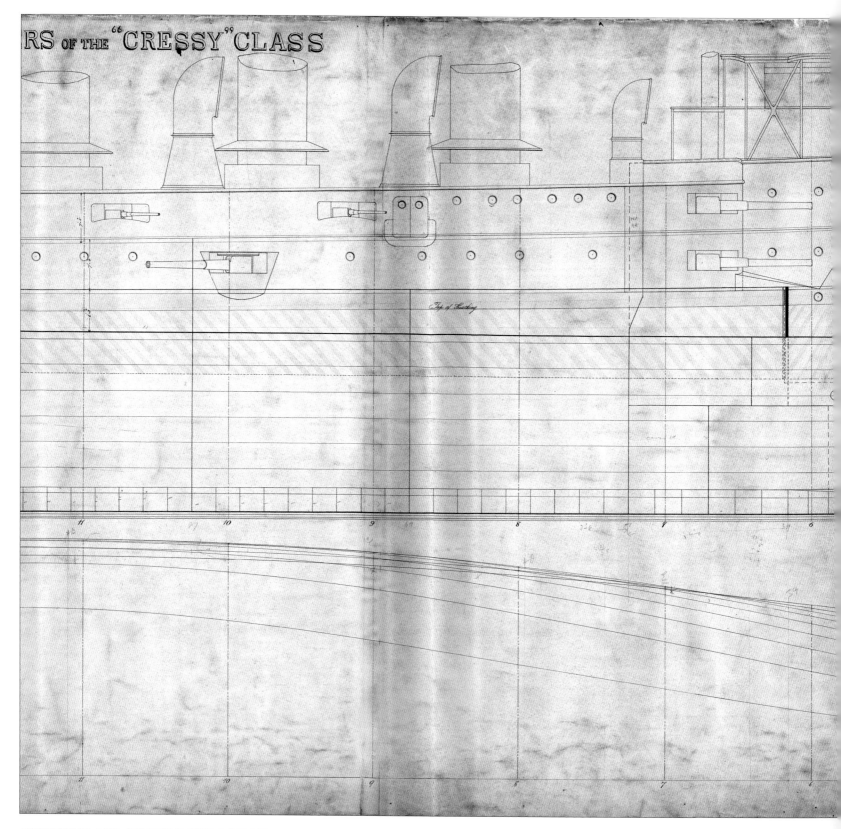

CRESSY CLASS, PROFILE AND LONGITUDINAL HALF-BREADTH (continued)

A further marking amidships indicates the command enjoyed by one of the 6-inch guns by showing the height of the Upper Deck from the waterline. The outlines of the submerged torpedo tube ports are drawn in, and can be seen in line with the forward superstructure. Embrasures in the hull to allow greater fore and aft fire for the 6-inch casemates are also clearly visible. The 9.2-inch gunhouses, 6-inch casemates, side armour of the 'citadel' and conning tower are in light grey to denote heavy armour while the thinner plating at the bow is light blue. Armour and protective plating within the ship is drawn to scale in dark blue ink, hence the varying thicknesses of the lines. This makes it easy to trace the line of the Protective Deck, the ends of the armoured citadel and the barbettes of the 9.2-inch guns. (Detail from Sheer Drawing for the _Cressy_ class, M1761)

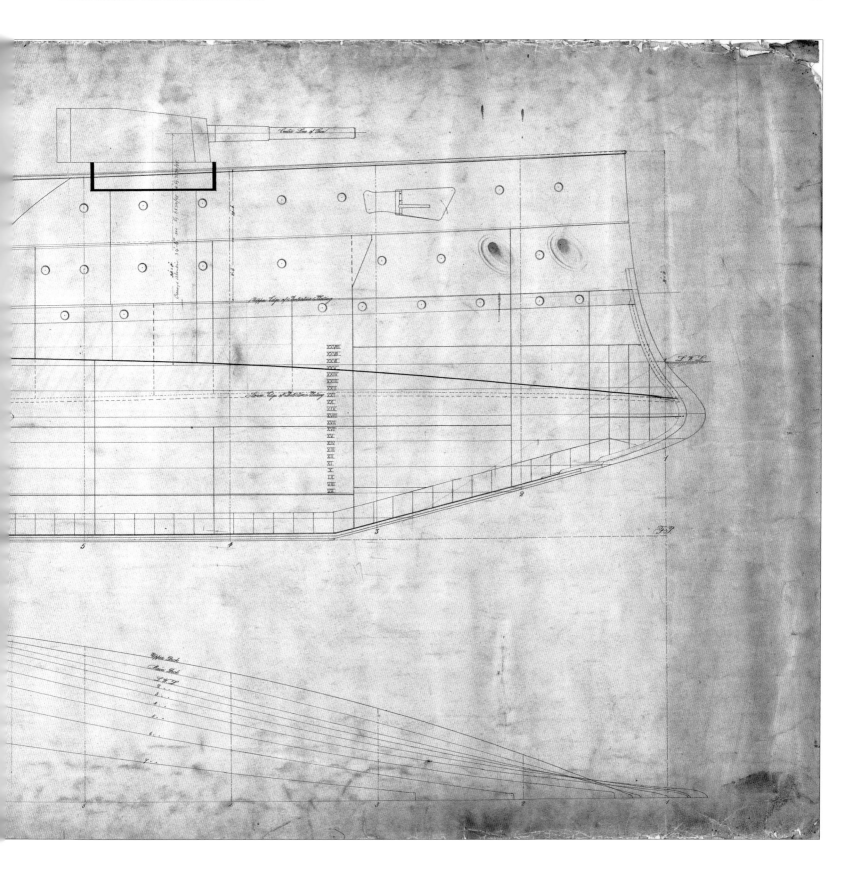

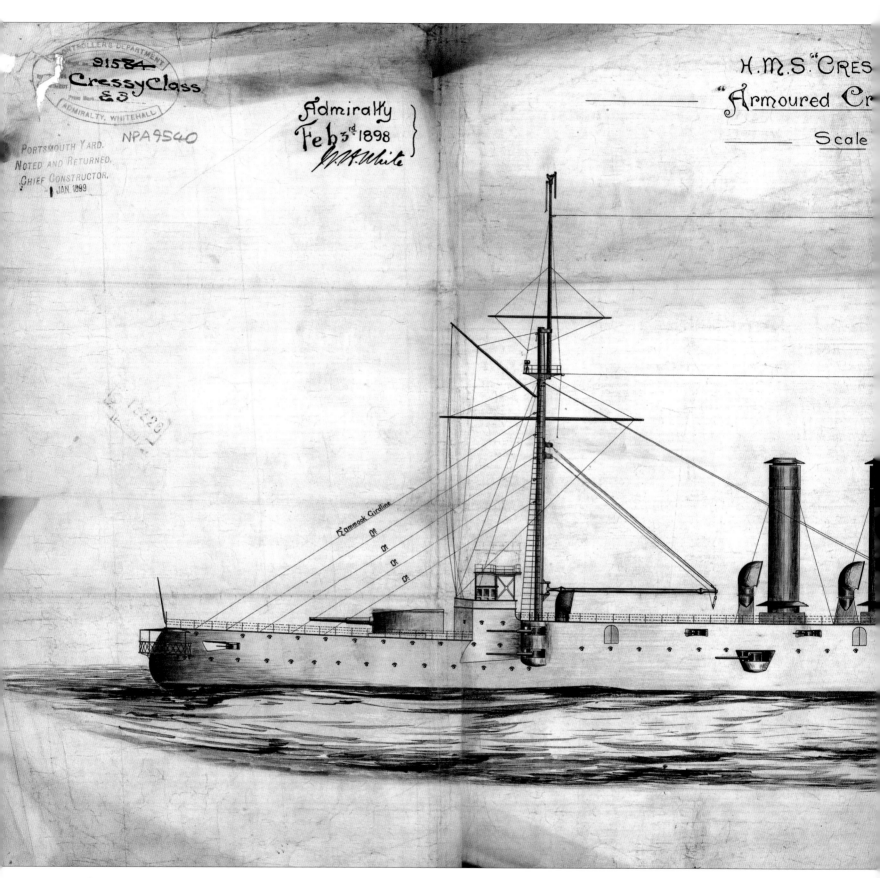

Hammock Girdline
O.
O.
O.
O.

H.M.S. "CRES

"Armoured Cr

Scale

HMS CRESSY, SKETCH OF RIG

This elaborately decorated plan, incorporating a great deal more background detail than is normally seen on a drawing of this nature, illustrates the finalised design layout of *Cressy*'s masts and rig, showing both the standing and the running rigging. Although wireless telegraphy was worked into *Cressy* prior to her completion, at this early date such equipment was not even considered. As would be expected of a cruiser of this period, signalling was the main raison d'etre for the arrangement shown, and the majority of the rigging and yards shown were dedicated to that role. The apparatus atop the mainmast is a semaphore that could

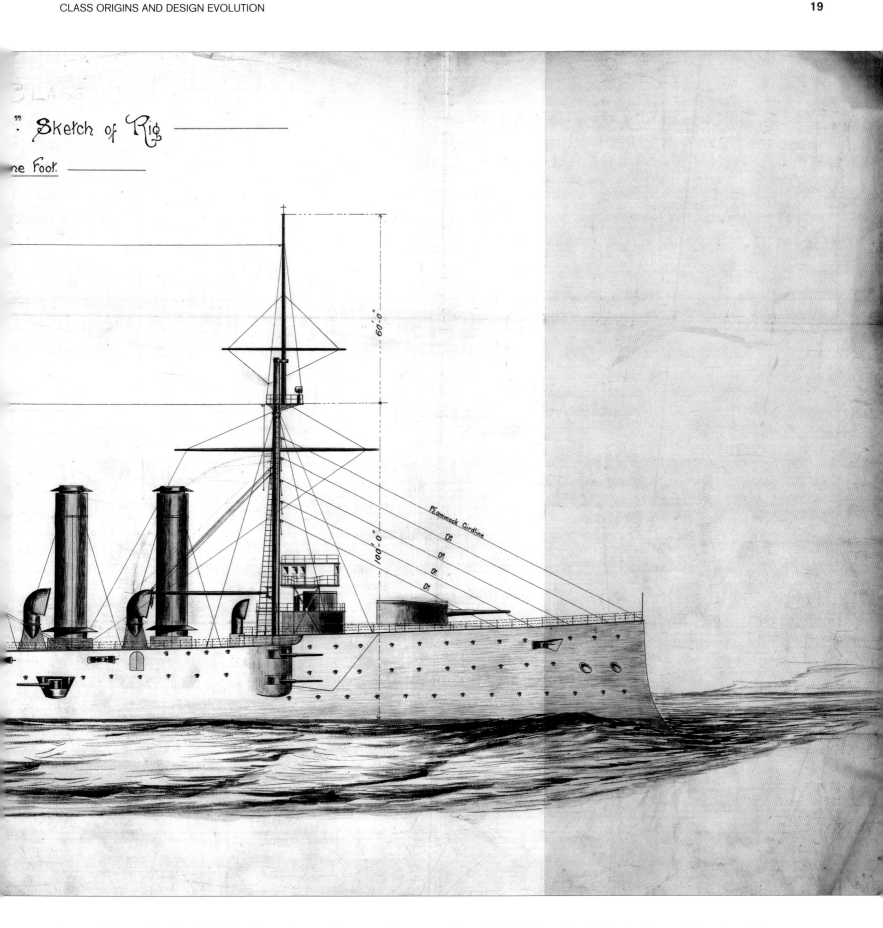

be operated by rope from the after bridge. The evenly spaced lines emanating forward and aft from the fore- and mainmasts respectively are girdlines for airing hammocks. Note the searchlights mounted at the tops of both masts. The guardrails running along the Boat and Upper Decks are also present. These are shown in their raised position, but the stanchions could be collapsed when necessary. (M1758)

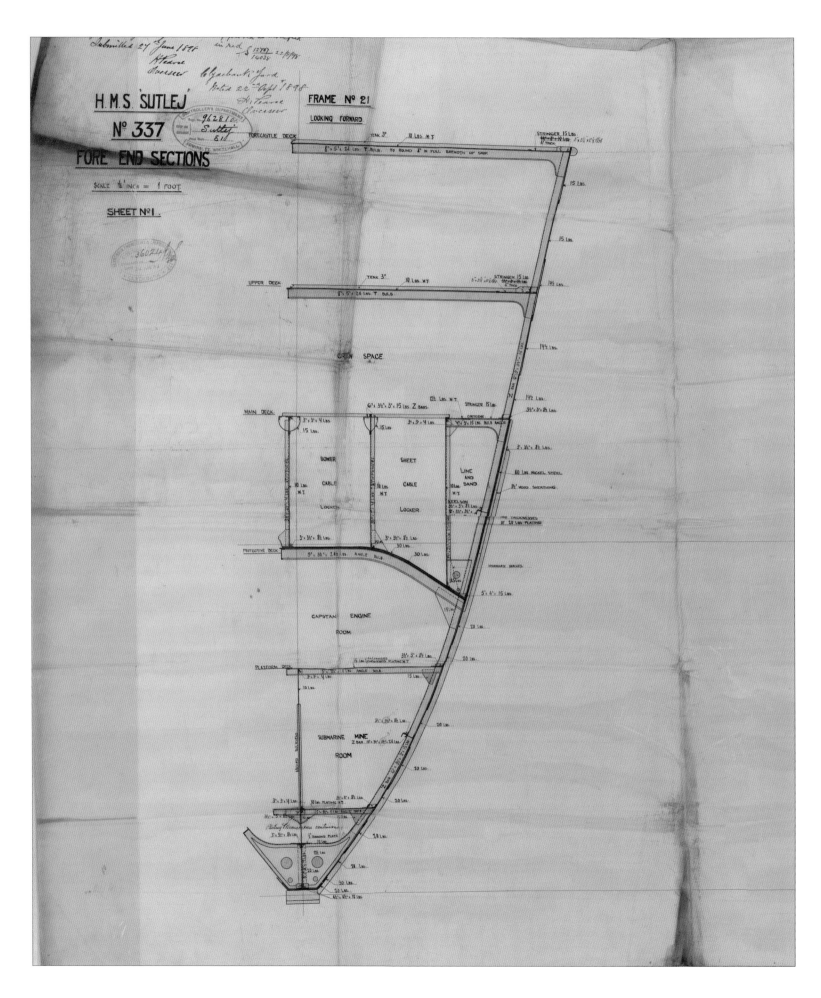

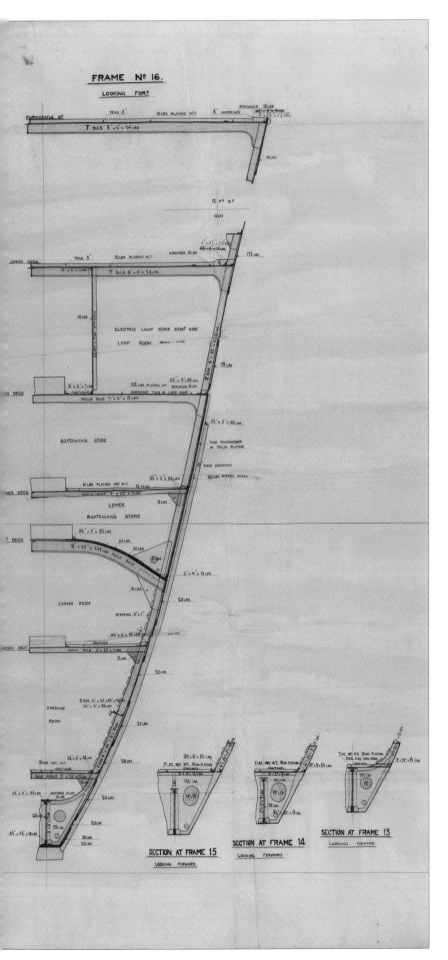

FRAME Nº 16.

LOOKING FORᴰ

SECTION AT FRAME 15
LOOKING FORWARD

SECTION AT FRAME 14
LOOKING FORWARD

SECTION AT FRAME 13
LOOKING FORWARD

LAYOUT AND STRUCTURE

Aside from the visible difference in main armament afforded by the prominent 9.2-inch gun houses, *Cressy* presented the same handsome profile as the preceding *Diadem*s with a high-sided hull for three quarters of the length of the ship and a low quarterdeck, fairly minimal superstructure and four tall funnels. This general similarity in layout was matched by dimensional similarity, with *Cressy* as designed being only ten feet longer and barely a foot beamier than the *Diadem*s. The slightly greater overall length was due to the finer hull lines forward, while the marginal increase in beam reflected a fuller hull form. This similarity was a product of the natural desire to keep costs manageable and to help ensure efficient production of components, but there was an additional tactical requirement. White's concept that the *Cressy*s operate as an adjunct to battleships meant that as a squadron they had to be able to manoeuvre in company with the battle fleet. With an eye to tactical diameter it was therefore essential that they did not greatly exceed contemporary battleships in length. The *Canopus* class battleships were 421ft 6in in overall length and the *Formidable*s 431ft 9in. At 470ft overall *Cressy* was arguably pushing the limit, although it was hoped that eliminating the deadwood aft would help improve manoeuvrability.

As important in terms of the overall design, the two cruiser classes possessed propulsion machinery that was almost identical in their space requirements. *Cressy*'s engines were more powerful, exceeding the performance of the *Diadem*s by 3000 IHP and theoretically enabling her to travel a knot faster despite being about 1000 tons heavier. *Cressy*'s heavier armour protection accounted for much of this extra weight and endurance was sacrificed to compensate. In practice this meant *Cressy* had a bunker capacity of about 300 tons less than the *Diadem*s. White's acquiescence to the Board's decision that *Cressy*'s hull be sheathed for foreign service was unfortunate. Use of the anti-fouling paint which was available at the time could have allowed a considerable saving in weight, although the *Cressy*s did benefit from it later in their careers.

Cressy had six decks. The highest was the Boat (or Forecastle) Deck, which was the only one exposed to the elements for its entire length. Beneath this in descending order were the Upper Deck, Main Deck, Protective (roughly corresponding to a Lower) Deck, the Platforms (incomplete decks and walkways about halfway up the machinery spaces, where the bulk of the engines and boilers precluded a continuous deck), and finally the Hold. The hull was subdivided by transverse bulkheads which ran from the Hold to Upper Deck level forming fifteen main watertight compartments. With the exception of the Engine Room and the wing compartments abreast the machinery spaces there was no significant longitudinal subdivision worked into the design. In keeping with established practice *Cressy* had a cellular double-bottom. (See caption overleaf)

HMS *SUTLEJ*, FORE END SECTIONS

Although the equivalent plan for *Cressy* is not as well-preserved, this one of her sister *Sutlej* is useful for representing the complexity of the forward end of the hull. The seven hull sections and associated details shown here illustrate the form of the bow from Frame 21 up to the stem, comprising the area forward of the capstans. This plan was created to guide and check the construction of this part of the ship, hence the very high level of structural detail shown, including precise dimensions and weights and physical composition (*eg* teak, nickel steel, corticene) of individual components or coverings thereof. Alterations that proved necessary once construction began are marked in red and usually concern reductions in the size and weights of metal fittings. The transverse shape of the ram bow is clearly depicted, as are details of the supporting structures behind it. These include the Protective Deck which curves down to reinforce the beak of the ram. The apparent physical strength of this sensible arrangement can be deceptive, particularly in terms of the popular perception of the utility of ramming in the late nineteenth century. Aside from the slight aberration of the *Arrogant* class cruisers, by the 1890s the notion of employing a ram as an offensive weapon had passed out of favour in the Royal Navy. The ram bows of the *Cressy* class and their contemporaries were designed primarily to secure better hydrodynamic performance. The extent and thickness of both the bow armour plating and the wood sheathing are also shown. The former was made up of 80lb plates of 2in thickness bolted onto doubled 20lb plates, while the latter generally was of 5½in thickness except over the armour, where it tapered to 3½in to preserve its form. (M1575)

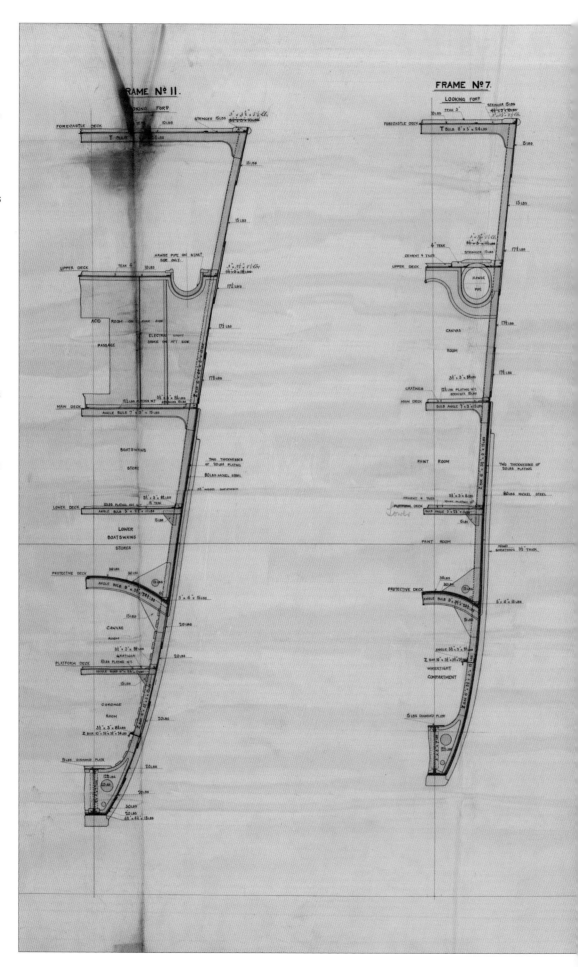

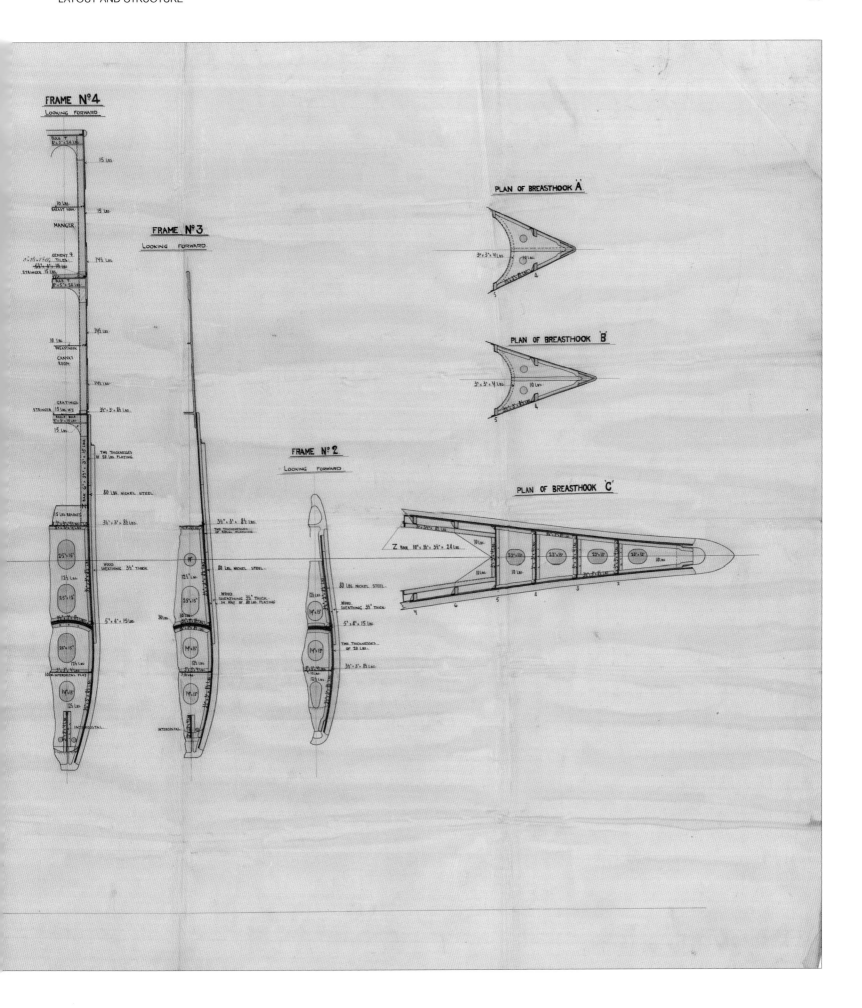

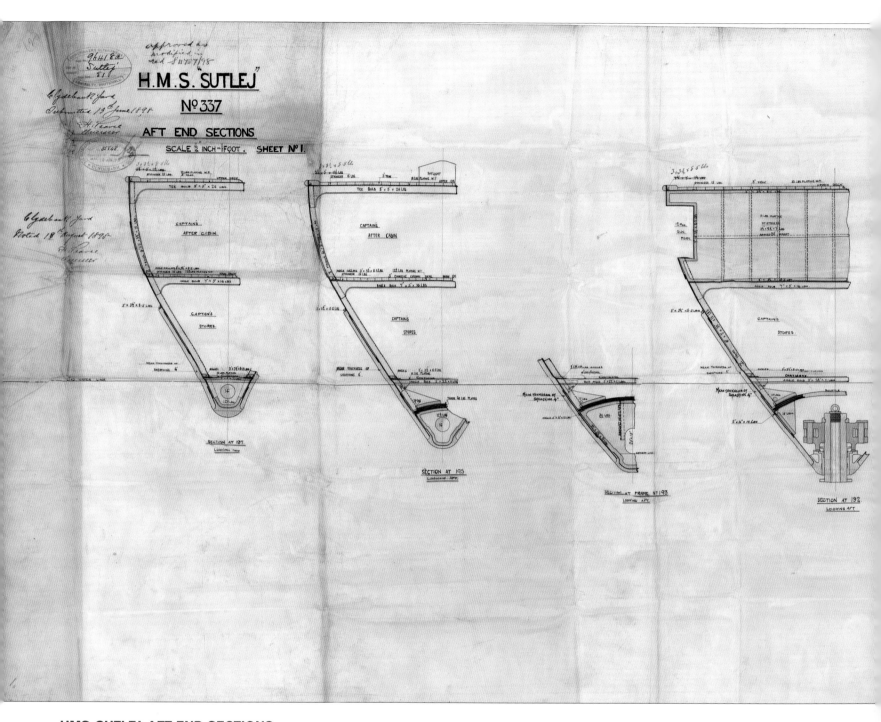

HMS *SUTLEJ*, AFT END SECTIONS

This drawing is the counterpart to the preceding plan, the eleven hull sections covering the lower hull from Frame 197 to 184. This comprises the area from the aft-most compartments (roughly midway through the captain's after cabin) to the points at which the 'A' brackets emerge from the hull. This drawing was created at the same time as the forward sections plan and for like purpose. It follows the same conventions in terms of the details shown, with alterations and corrections added in the same manner. This plan does not show the full extent to which the deadwood was reduced in the *Cressy* class when compared to the *Diadems*, as the keel begins to turn up much earlier at Frame 169. However, it is possible to trace the ascent of the line of the keel using the marked load waterline as a guide.

The rudder head mounting at Station 192 is shown in detail, and marks the point at which the keel rises sharply before resuming its gentle ascent towards the waterline. This arrangement contributed to the very impressive manoeuvrability of the *Cressy* class, and was repeated in the succeeding *Drake* class. The four sections to the right show the heavy structural support built into the design in way of the 'A' brackets, and the manner in which the Protective Deck has been worked into this scheme. Note the complete absence of side armour as the steering gear compartment is beneath the waterline and covered by the Protective Deck. In slight contrast to the arrangement at the bow, the wood sheathing has been reduced to a mean thickness of 4in. (M1576)

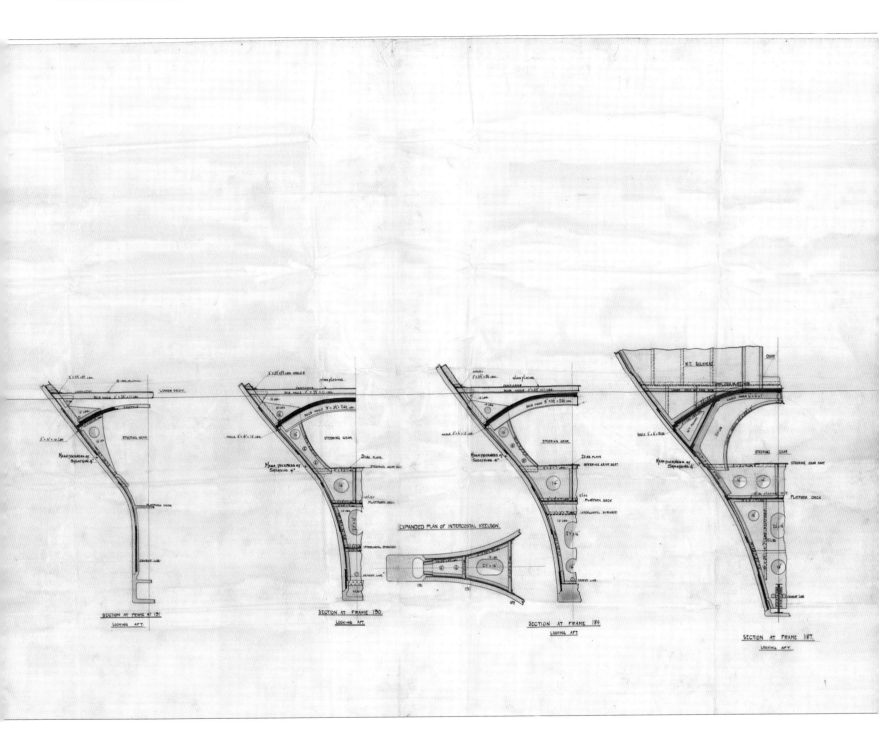

SECTION AT FRAME N° 191
LOOKING AFT.

SECTION AT FRAME 190.
LOOKING AFT.

EXPANDED PLAN OF INTERCOSTAL KEELSON.

SECTION AT FRAME 189
LOOKING AFT.

SECTION AT FRAME 187.
LOOKING AFT.

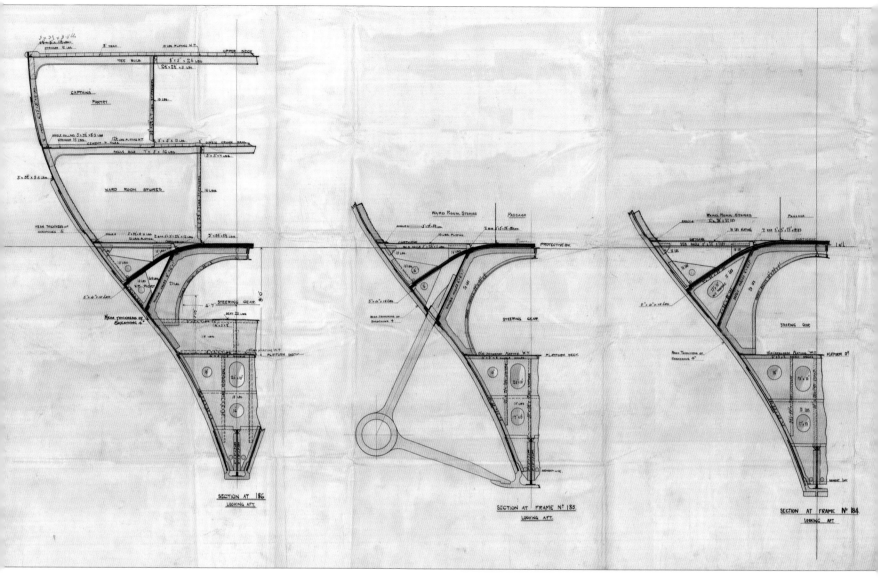

(Drawing continued from previous pages)

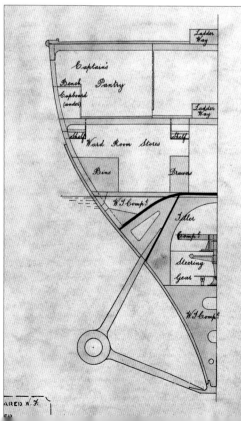

HMS *CRESSY*, FRAME 185 (left)

This hull section from *Cressy*'s as-fitted plans makes for an interesting comparison with *Euryalus*'s structural drawing above. Note the minor differences in the arrangement of the structural reinforcement around the edge of the Protective Deck at the point where the upper arm of the 'A' bracket enters the hull, as well as that of the compartments between the keel and the Platform Deck. (Detail from HMS *Cressy*, Sections as fitted, M0196).

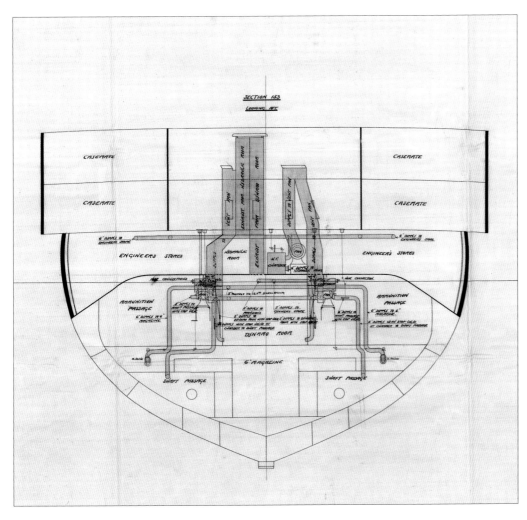

HMS *CRESSY*, VENTILATION SECTIONS

This detail from one of *Cressy*'s ventilation plans illustrates in simplified form the transverse shape of the hull in way of the after 6in casemates at Station 153, and how the latter relate to the structure of the ship. The upper view is looking aft and the lower one looking forward. The most noticeable aspect is the degree of overhang given to these casemates to permit end-on fire. The omission of the fairing at the base of the casemates makes this appear more pronounced. The inclusion of thicker lines to show the armoured parts of the hull illustrate the protection to the exterior face of the casemates and hull, the thinner splinter protection covering the inboard side of the casemates, and the protective deck. (Detail from After Sections Ventilation for *Cressy*, M1735)

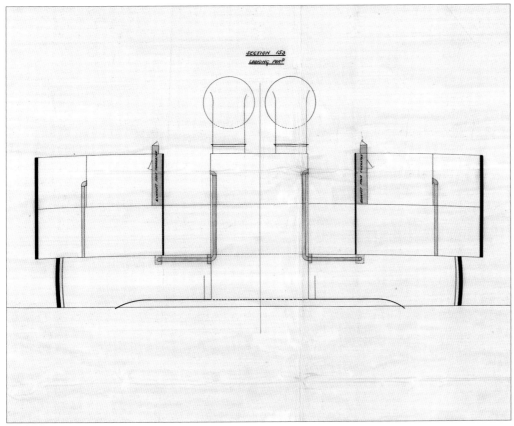

HMS *CRESSY*, WATERTIGHT ARRANGEMENTS (overleaf)

A section from a diagrammatic but nonetheless comprehensive overview of *Cressy*'s watertight compartmentalisation. Compartments which could be rendered completely watertight are crossed through in red ink, while those that did not have full watertight integrity are not. It illustrates both the elaborate systems employed to maintain the ship's buoyancy in the face of damage and flooding, but also neatly shows the great difficulties involved in doing so in a vessel of this complexity. *Cressy*'s successful operation as a fighting ship depended to a large degree on a number of open spaces and interconnected systems. An obvious example of the former is the Sick Bay at the forward end of the Upper Deck, which by its nature had to comprise a large, open and well-ventilated space. The profusion of vents, pipes and even coal scuttles made for potential flooding hazards by piercing decks and bulkheads, as did the all-important requirements of clear access between decks in certain areas for the passage of ammunition from the magazines to the guns. This part of the plan covers the watertight arrangements in profile and for the Upper and Main Decks. The profile clearly shows the extent of the watertight arrangements at Protective Deck level and below, but it is equally clear that – aside from the fore and aft ends of the Main Deck – there was little real watertight protection. The midships area of the Main Deck presents a bewildering mass of shorthand annotations, mainly detailing watertight deck hatches and scuttle covers and, interestingly, also where they all lead. For example, the annotation 'W. T. C. S. Prot. Dk 55-57' indicates that the specified feature is a watertight coaling scuttle which travels from the Main Deck to the Protective Deck between Frames 55 and 57. (Detail from Watertight Arrangements for *Cressy*, M1760)

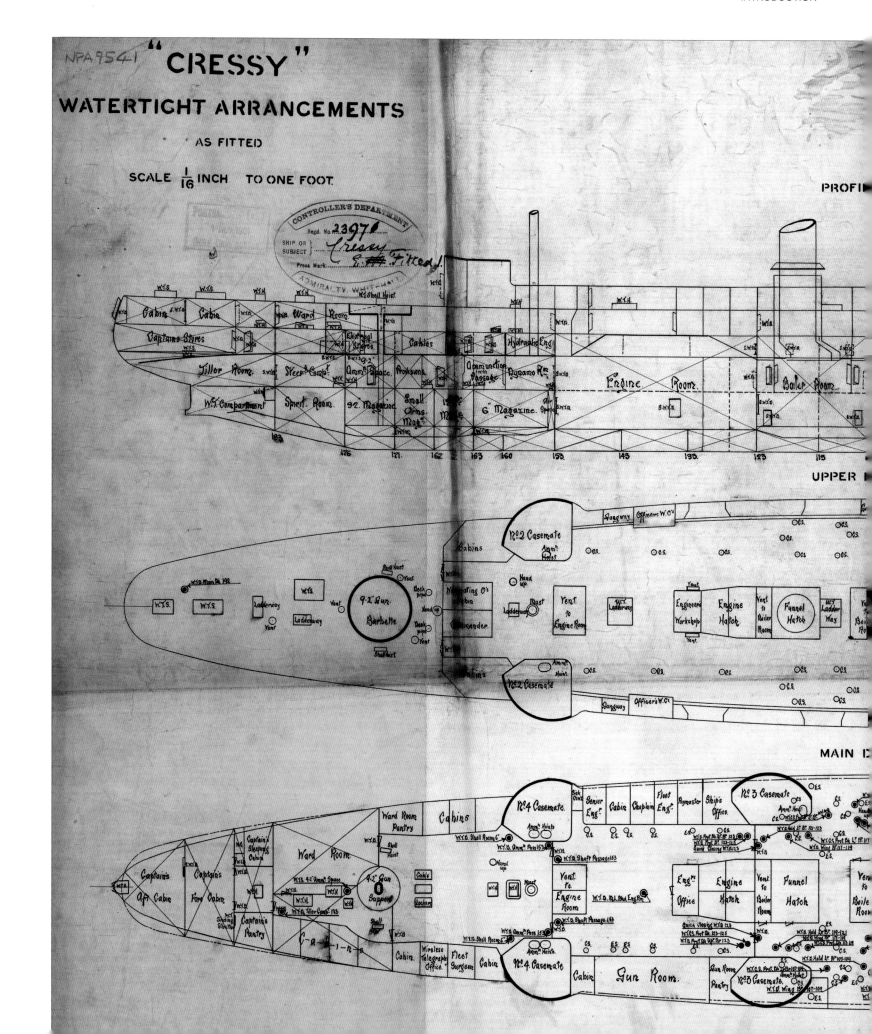

NPA 9541 "CRESSY"

WATERTIGHT ARRANGEMENTS

AS FITTED

SCALE $\frac{1}{16}$ INCH TO ONE FOOT.

PROFI

CONTROLLER'S DEPARTMENT
Regd. No. 23971
SHIP OR SUBJECT) Cressy
Press Mark.   S. Fixed
ADMIRALTY, WHITEHALL

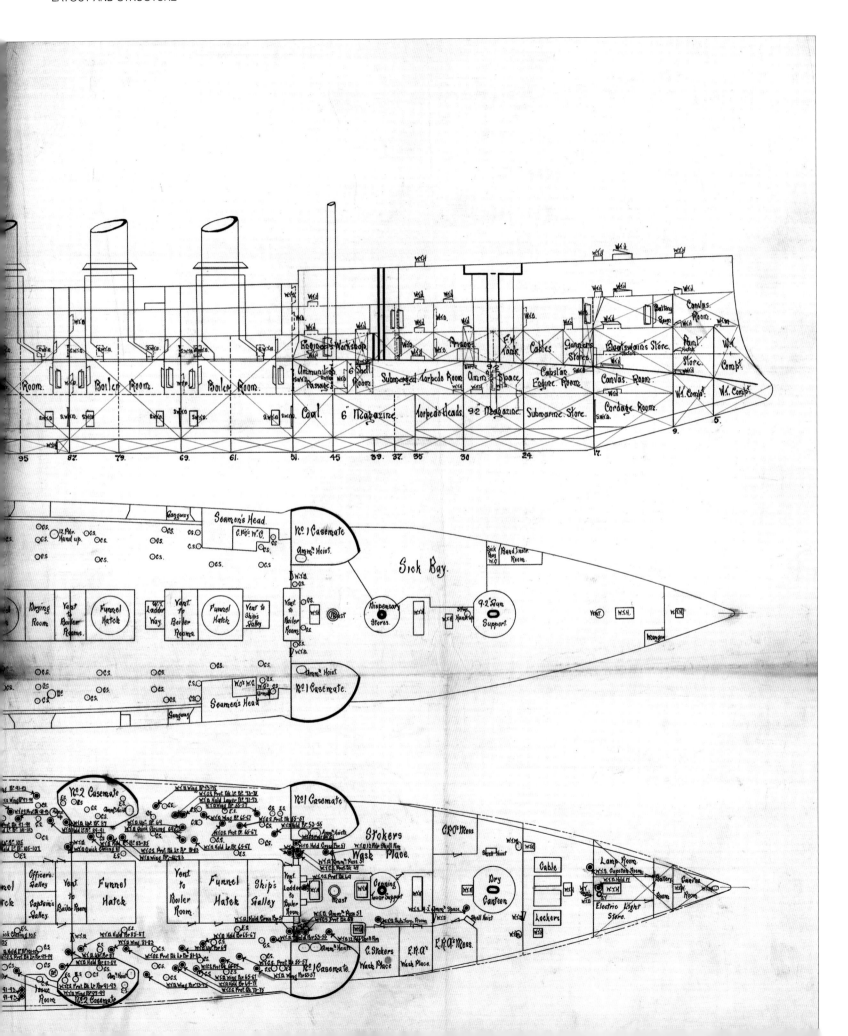

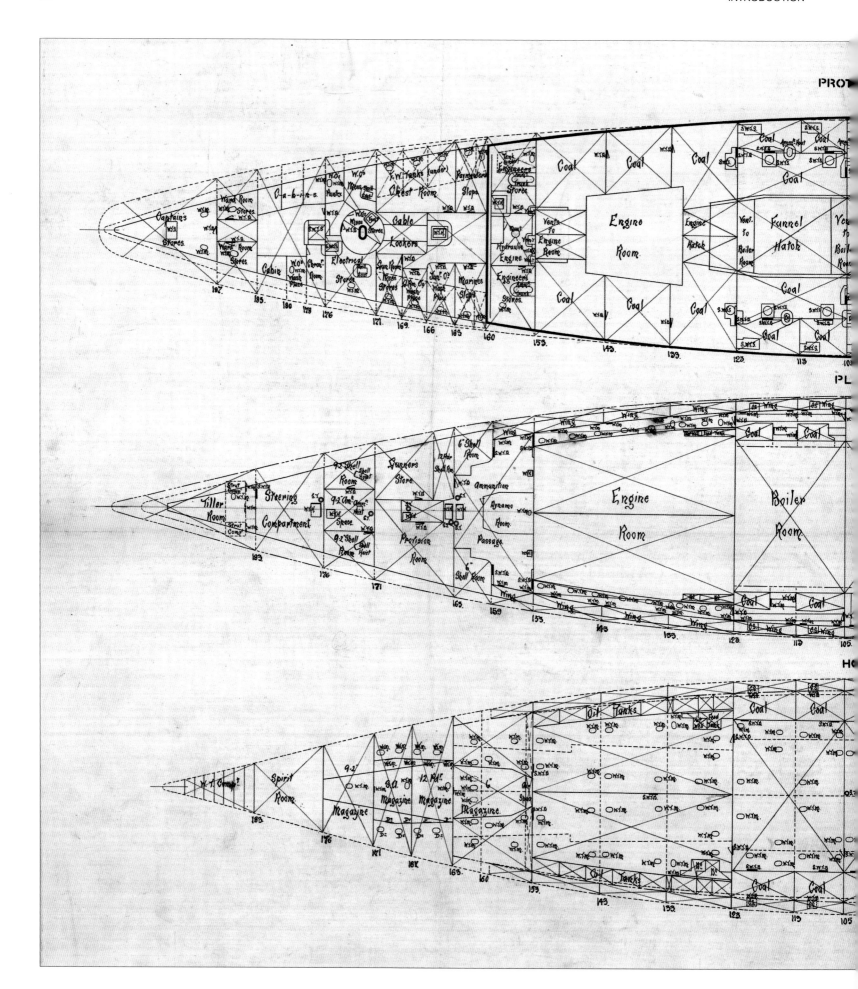

DECK

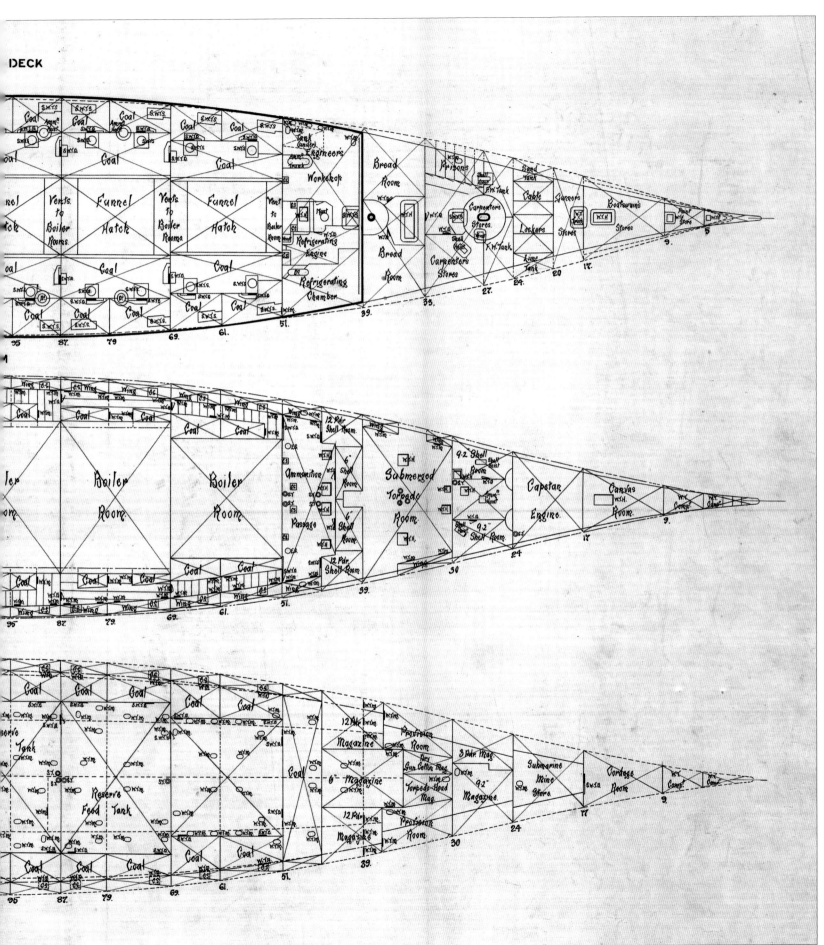

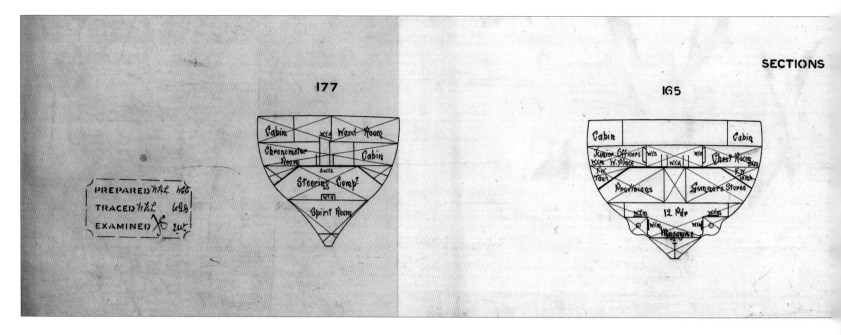

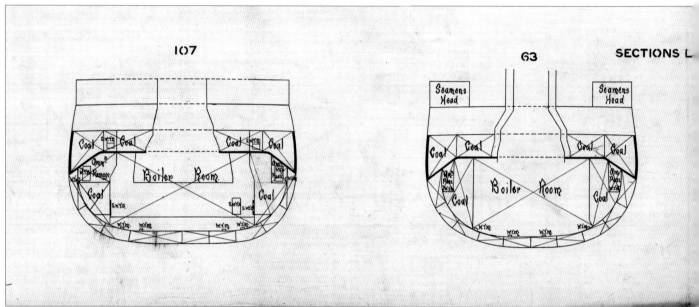

HMS *CRESSY*, WATERTIGHT ARRANGEMENTS
(previous pages)

The watertight arrangements for the Protective Deck, Platform Deck and Hold show the much more comprehensive subdivision in the lower levels of the ship, but also the great vulnerability represented by the cavernous machinery spaces. The ship's waterline in normal conditions of loading would run at about the level of the Protective Deck. The extent of the armoured citadel is clearly marked, protecting the coal bunkers, funnel hatches and vents to the machinery spaces. All of these represented significant vulnerabilities in terms of flooding, and each compartment within this space was made watertight. The Platform Deck sports similar arrangements, but while the submerged torpedo room, boiler room spaces and engine room spaces could be isolated, they were still large areas that could pose serious stability issues if subjected to flooding. The solution, in keeping with design approaches of that era, was to rely on longitudinal compartmentation in the engine room and heavily subdivided wing passages running along the side of the hull to minimise the effects of underwater damage. These closely follow the arrangement of the double bottom, the upper edge of which can be seen on the plan of the Hold. A good system in concept for the 1890s, its flaws were not appreciated until the hard lessons of the First World War. (Detail from Watertight Arrangements for *Cressy*, M1760)

HMS *CRESSY*, WATERTIGHT ARRANGEMENTS (Above)

The hull sections on this plan provide a useful perspective on the watertight scheme, again particularly in terms of the inescapable vulnerabilities posed by the necessarily large machinery spaces. These are most clear in the illustrations at Frames 63, 107 for the boiler rooms and 144 for the longitudinally subdivided engine room. Aside from this admittedly unsolvable issue, the watertight arrangements overall represented the best possible design in terms of the sort of damage the *Cressy*s were expected to endure. Torpedoes and mines were well understood threats, but in the latter half of the 1890s few could have conceived the degree to which both weapons would have advanced by 1914. When the class was designed, the greatest concern was flooding caused by cumulative shell hits and consequent loss of stability. (Detail from Watertight Arrangements for *Cressy*, M1760)

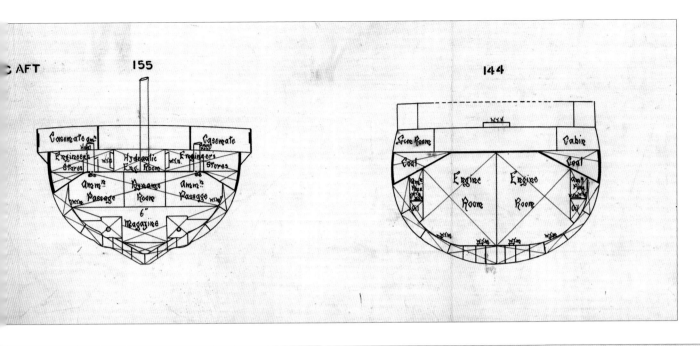

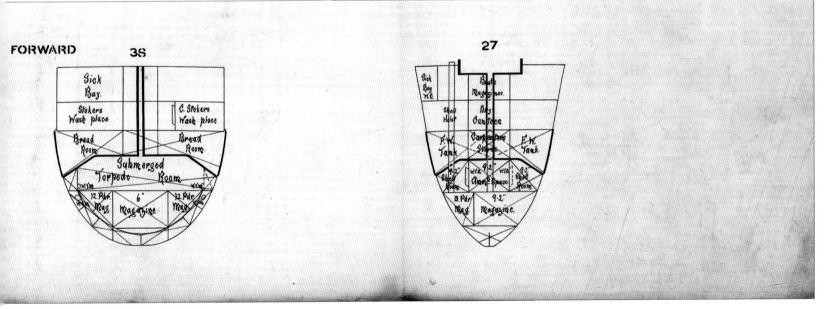

HMS *CRESSY*, WATERTIGHT ARRANGEMENTS

A table of references explaining the abbreviations and symbols used to denote different watertight fittings on the drawing. The abbreviations apply to both the openings in the deck such as coaling and escape scuttles, specifying where these benefit from deck plates, as well as watertight doors set into the bulkheads. Given the profusion of arrangements illustrated, particularly in the compartments below the Upper Deck, the table is indispensable to interpreting this plan. (Detail from Watertight Arrangements for *Cressy*, M1760).

REFERENCES

S.W.T.D	Sliding Watertight Door	W.T.S.	Watertight Scuttle	
S.W.T.S	Sliding Watertight Scuttle	S.T.	Sounding Tube	◎
W.T.C.S	Watertight Coaling Scuttle	C.S.	Coaling Scuttle	○
W.T.D	Watertight Door	E.S.	Escape Scuttle	○
W.T.H.	Watertight Hatch		Deck Plate.	◉
W.T.M.	Watertight Manhole			

PROPULSION AND MACHINERY

Propulsion for the *Cressy* class was provided by two 4-cylinder triple expansion engines, driving a pair of inward-turning screws. This arrangement was adopted because it promised an increase in speed and reduction in fuel consumption. The engines were placed abreast of each other in a large longitudinally divided compartment. Forward of this were the four Boiler Rooms which housed the thirty Belleville water-tube boilers. This system generated 21,000 IHP for a designed maximum speed of 21½ knots in calm conditions. With the increase in weight brought on by the development of the design, this was reduced in practice to 21 knots. At this speed, *Cressy* consumed 450 tons of coal per day to power her engines (464 tons if the needs of auxiliary machinery is included), limiting her to about three and a half days' steaming at best, assuming she suffered no mechanical breakdowns. At the much more economical cruising speed of 10 knots the figure was 40 tons per day (54 tons with auxiliary machinery requirements added) to generate 1700 IHP for a maximum of twenty-nine and a half days steaming. These figures assumed full bunkerage amounting to about 1600 tons of coal. *Cressy*'s engines proved well balanced and very reliable in service and reportedly produced very little vibration. However, her coal supply was considered relatively small for a ship of her size, especially given the high rate of consumption of her Bellevilles. This issue was compounded by the nature of the subdivi-

POWER OUTPUT

Figures for Indicated Horse Power (IHP) at different speeds

Speed (knots)	IHP
10	1700
12	2750
14	4350
16	6700
18	9900
20	15,400
21	19,600

ENDURANCE

Assuming a maximum coal allowance of 1600 tons embarked

Speed (knots)	Endurance (nautical miles)
20.1	1770
10	4690

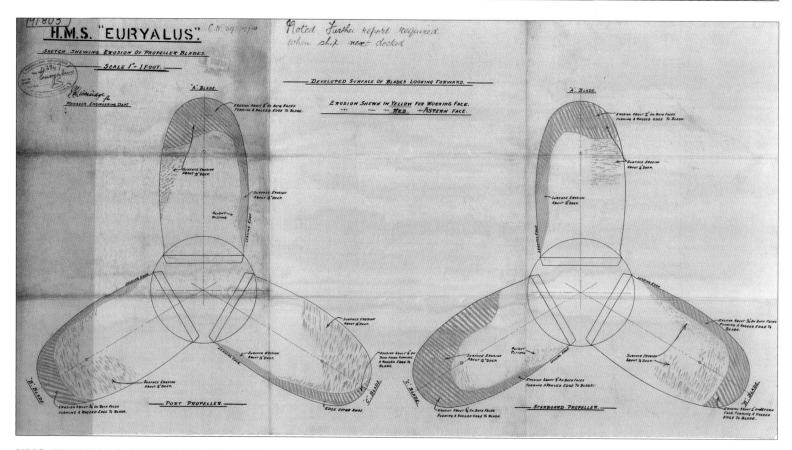

HMS *EURYALUS*, PROPELLER EROSION

No documentation survives to accompany this plan or its counterpart on the opposite page. However, both are useful for the dimensional details and general layout they offer of the two types of screws employed in the *Cressy* class. The allocation and details of these are recorded in the Ships Cover for the class, but not the reasons for the difference. Whatever that may have been, it does not appear to have been a matter of different shipbuilders following different practices, for of the two ships built by John Brown *Bacchante* had four-bladed screws and *Sutlej* the three-bladed. Both types proved very effective, with the entire class performing well in their early years of service and showing no appreciable variations between the three- and four-bladed ships. (M1579)

sion of the bunkers which made the coal supply difficult to access once a certain amount had been used.

One of the notable features of the ships of the late Victorian navy was the degree to which steam technology permitted automation. In addition to her main engines for propulsion, *Cressy* possessed dynamos and subsidiary machines for a variety of shipboard operations. The main systems were water distillation, electric lighting (including power for searchlights), steering engines, air compressors, ammunition and boat hoists, capstans, ventilation, fresh and salt water supply and refrigeration. Some specific examples of the machinery supporting these are:

■ Four evaporators and two distilling condensers with associated steam pumps.

■ Three sets of combined compound engines and dynamos for electric lighting, each capable of maintaining and generating a steady current of 600 amp.

■ Two double-cylinder direct-acting steering engines with sufficient power to turn the rudder 70° within 30 seconds when the ship was at full speed.

■ Two sets of air compressing engines and pumps to serve the torpedo tubes, each capable of filling a 30 cubic foot reservoir with air at 1700lbs per square inch within 70 minutes.

■ Two double-cylinder boat-hoisting winches with a maximum lift capacity of 18 tons.

■ Two vertical refrigerating machines, each capable of maintaining a temperature of 15° F (-9° C) in a 1900 cubic foot chamber.

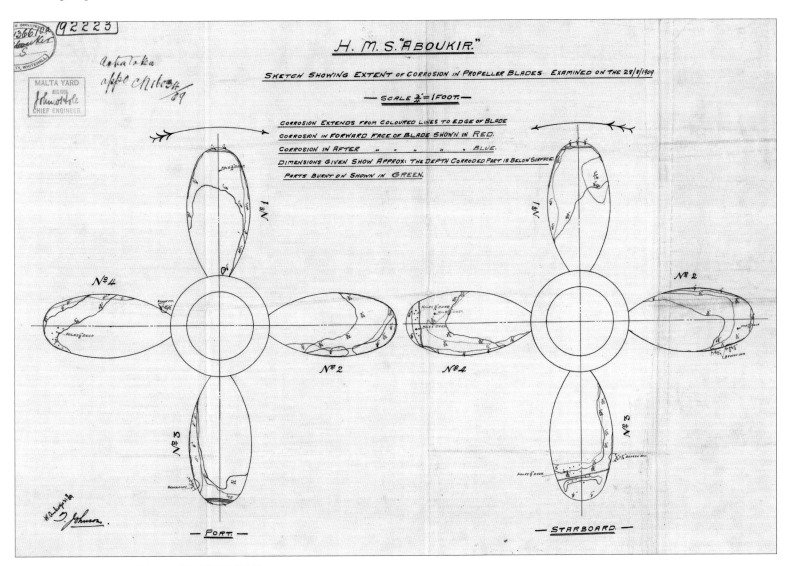

HMS *ABOUKIR*, PROPELLER EROSION

This drawing makes for an interesting comparison with its equivalent for *Euryalus*. It was drafted in Malta in 1910 during *Aboukir*'s service in the Mediterranean with the 6th Cruiser Squadron, while the latter was drawn when *Euryalus* had returned to home waters from Australia. Both clearly illustrate the surface damage sustained by the ship's screws after less than eight years' service. On the whole, the three-bladed type appears to have fared better in this instance. The surface wear is not deeper than ⅛th of an inch for either vessel, but the extent of the erosion is far greater on *Aboukir*. Her blades also appear to have suffered far greater physical deterioration in terms of holes and places where parts of the blades have broken off. While this may imply that the three-bladed screws were more resilient, there is insufficient data in terms of period of service in waters of different temperatures, salinity levels and density of sediment to make a truly meaningful comparison, especially as equivalent information for the rest of the class is lacking. (M1583)

ARMOUR

Armour plate accounted for roughly 1800 of *Cressy*'s total weight of 12,000 tons. The complete weight of her protective arrangements, including backing, came to 2560 tons, an increase of 710 tons above the total allotted to the *Diadem*s. The armour comprised a mix of Harvey nickel and Krupp nickel-chromium armour plates for her vertical and high-tensile steel plating for her horizontal (protective deck) protection. The side armour was backed by teak, and the coal

bunkers behind it provided an additional level of indirect protection.

The armour belt extended for nearly the entire length of the ship from the level of the Main Deck to the base of the Protective Deck but was thinner at the fore end. The main part of the belt comprised 6 inches of Krupp armour plates, protecting an area 231ft in length and 11ft 6in in height on each side of the hull. This was closed at its ends by 5-inch Krupp armoured bulkheads to create a citadel protecting the vitals of the ship. The hull forward of the citadel was protected by

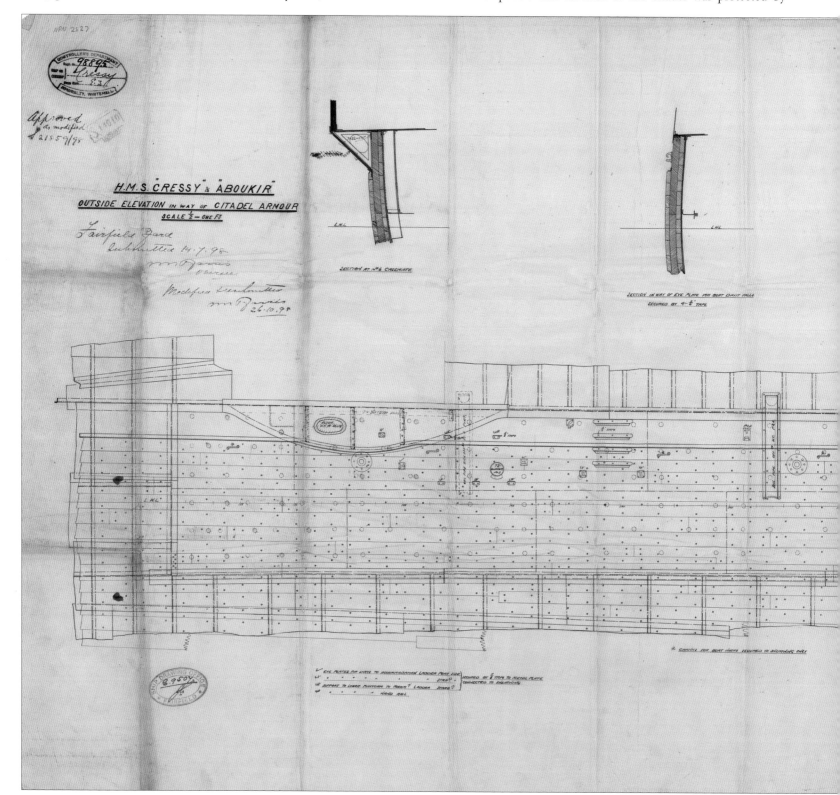

ARMOUR

Table illustrating the effectiveness of the Krupp armour as applied to *Cressy*

Thickness of Krupp plate	Equivalent thickness of wrought iron plate required to resist attack by 'capped' shells
5 inches	10 inches
6 inches	13.5 inches

HMS *CRESSY* AND HMS *ABOUKIR*, CITADEL ARMOUR

The nature of the task of fitting the side armour is clear from this plan. Drafted and approved with alterations in the summer of 1898, this plan was completed roughly a fortnight after the laying of *Cressy*'s keel and about a month prior to *Aboukir*'s. This allowed about a year for the armour plates to be produced to the required specifications, the actual fitting taking place after the hull was launched. Given the very recent exposure of British manufacturers to the Krupp process, a long lead up time was very necessary. The plan also demonstrates the interaction between the Admiralty and the shipbuilder, with annotations on the plan recording proposed changes and the necessary approvals. *Continued overleaf.*

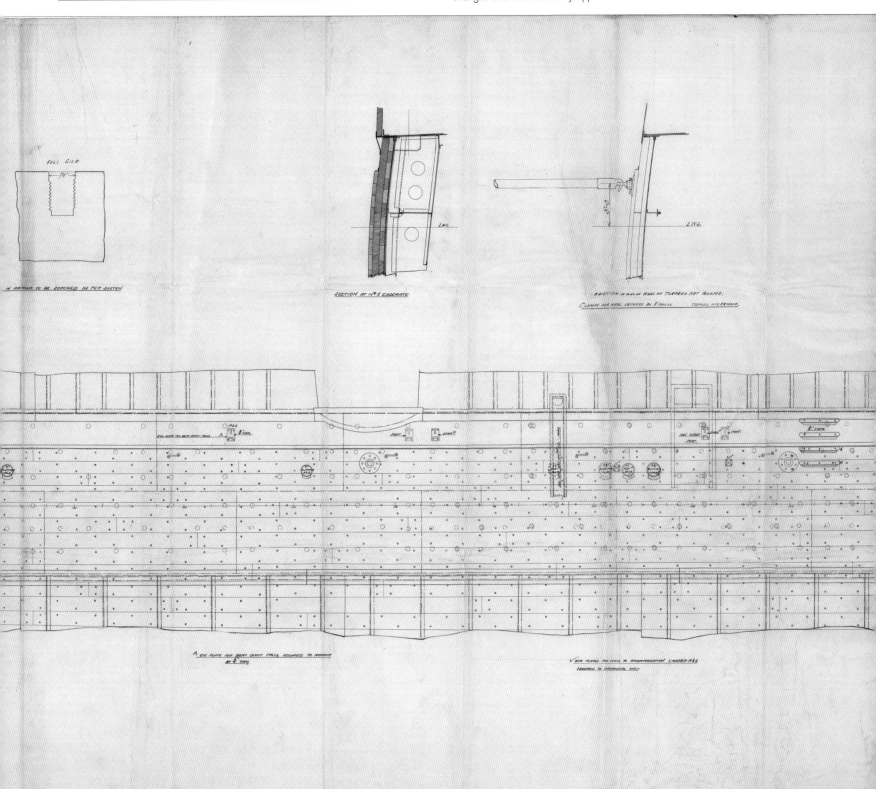

The sections along the upper row illustrate the wooden backing for the armour plates, as well as the sheathing outside it. The elevation drawing below it shows the citadel from the starboard side, with exterior details like ash shoots on the port side picked out in red. The armour plates are also indicated in red, with very small holes marking fixing points. The illustration in between the second and third section shows a generic transverse view of one of these fixing points. Most exterior fittings such as soil pipes, ash shoots and naval steps were secured to the wooden hull sheathing, while more substantial fittings such as the planned heels for torpedo net booms would have been secured directly to the armour plates. (M0197)

thinner 2-inch Harvey armour which continued to the stem post, but there was no side armour aft of the rearmost 6-inch casemates. The provision of side armour in *Cressy* allowed for thinner curved plating on the Protective Deck. This was made up of high-tensile steel plates rather than armour plating *per se*. Behind the side armour the Protective Deck was 1½ inches thick, increasing to 2½ inches aft of the citadel until it reached the stern. The area covering the steering gear was better protected with 3 inches. In keeping with well-established

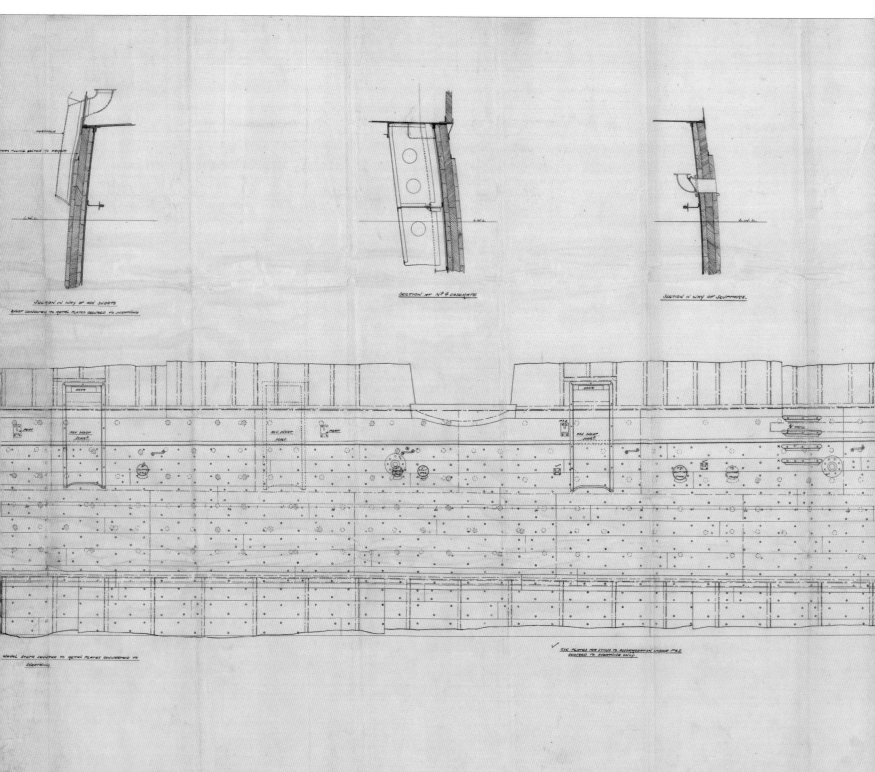

practice, armour protection was thickest at the conning tower. The sides had 12 inches of Harvey armour while the roof comprised much thinner plating. The 9.2-inch gunhouses and barbettes were given 6 inches of Krupp armour while their ammunition hoists were protected by 3-inch Harvey plates. The casemates for the 6-inch guns each had 6 inches of Krupp armour on their outboard faces and 2 inches of nickel steel plating on their sides and rear, but their ammunition passages and hoists received no dedicated protection as they were behind the side armour. *Cressy* makes for interesting comparison with HMS *Canopus*, the battleship whose protective arrangements inspired her own. The latter understandably enjoyed much greater protection to her turrets and barbettes, and the citadel bulkheads were greatly thickened in way of the turret trunks. However, in the categories of belt protection, casemates and conning tower, *Cressy* was as well protected as *Canopus* in terms of thickness of armour plate, and in some areas of the ship her Protective Deck plating was stronger.

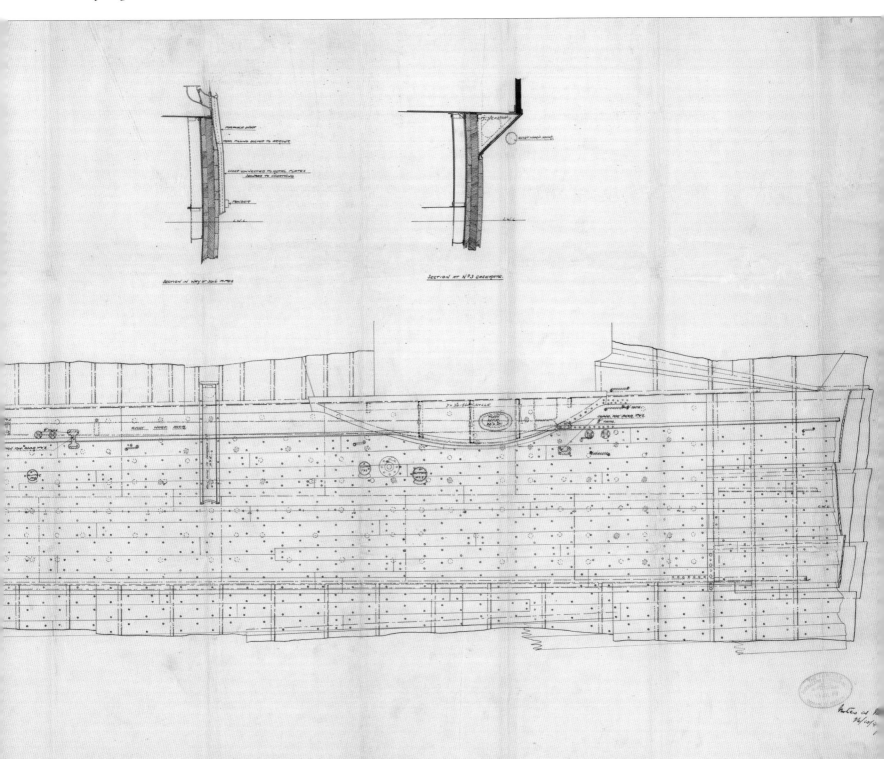

ARMAMENT

Cressy's most powerful weapons were the Elswick Ordnance Company's Mk X 9.2-inch guns. These were a new pattern introduced in 1900. Each was inside a fully enclosed Mk V hydraulic mount, also of Elswick design, one forward and one aft on the centreline. The Mk V was an improvement on the preceding versions that had equipped the protected cruisers of the *Powerful* class but it did not have split hoists for shell and powder bags. There was also no power-operated car for bringing shell and charge close to the gun breech as would have been found on contemporary battleships. Aside from this, the only other manual elements in the operation of the mount were ramming of shell and charge, and the control of elevation and depression. The omission of a car despite the weight of the 9.2-inch shell is understandable in terms of space and weight, as well as reducing the complications of additional auxiliary machinery. The mounting allowed 15 degrees elevation and 7½ degrees depression. This was reasonable in a period where battle ranges were expected to be comparatively short, 7000 yards being considered likely, although at full elevation the gun had a maximum range of roughly twice that figure. The forward gun enjoyed a commanding position on the Forecastle Deck 34ft above the waterline and good field of fire. The after gun was a full deck – 13ft 6in – lower, but this does not appear to have been a great impediment to efficient firing. At shorter ranges, these weapons were considered formidable chase guns. The rate of fire averaged three to four rounds per minute and muzzle velocity was 2100 feet per second. The maximum ammunition allowance was 105 rounds per gun. The Mk V mounting performed well in trials but was less satisfactory once installed aboard *Cressy*. On the ship's first commission, both the hydraulic hoists and turret training mechanisms reportedly gave trouble.

The secondary armament comprised twelve Vickers 6-inch Quick Firing guns, dispersed in casemates along the sides of the ship. These were another new type, the earliest examples entering service in 1901. The guns that equipped the *Cressy* were somewhat unusual, as their official designation was Breech Loader Mk VII. Taken with the fact that their ammunition was not fixed (*ie* shell and cartridge were separate) the terminology would suggest that they were not true QF guns at all. However, they were capable of an impressive rate of fire of eight rounds a minute in ideal conditions, an output which certainly justi-

fied them being classed as QF even though they were also BL! This arrangement was financially economical as shells and cloth bag charges were cheaper than brass-cased fixed ammunition. Equally importantly, separate ammunition was simpler to stow, allowing for the most efficient use of available magazine space. This was essential for the secondary armament to excel in its role of dominating close-range engagements with massed rapid fire.

The guns were mounted on the new Vickers PIV pedestal, *Cressy* being perhaps the first warship to receive them. Overall they represented an improvement on the type which had equipped the *Diadems*, but they had delayed the progress of the *Cressy* class in its design stages

Continued on p45

CRESSY CLASS, PROPOSED ARRANGEMENT OF 9.2-INCH GUN MOUNTING

The design drawing for the Vickers 9.2-inch gun mounting, which was adopted on four of the six *Cressys*. The exceptions – *Cressy* and *Aboukir* – had Elswick-manufactured mounts, although in terms of general design and operation the two types were essentially the same, differing only slightly in such features as the layout of their hydraulic machinery for the shell hoists. The mounting was hydraulically operated with the option of training by hand if necessary. The interior of the gunhouse presented a very cramped space. In addition to the gun itself with its associated mechanisms, room had to be allocated for two sighting hood positions, sufficient space for eight ready-use shells, and the necessary equipment for reloading and supplying ammunition from the magazines. A further thirty-two shells were stored in the shallow barbette beneath the gun, arranged in a circle around the hydraulic training machinery. These could be moved via a hand hoist mounted on an overhead rail. One of the more interesting space-saving features of this arrangement was the siting of the tops of the two shell hoists at Upper Deck level outside the barbette. The rear of the gun platform had to be rotated over one of them before the shells could be hoisted in. (M1584)

1. Hydraulic arms for training mechanism.
2. Platform for lookout and adjacent floor hatch for embarking shells brought up by the shell room hoists into the gunhouse.
3. Derrick for lifting shells from hoists and barbette.
4. Training machinery in barbette.
5. Plan and elevation views of hoist shell cage and hydraulic lifting cylinder.
6. Manual rammer shown at loading position. Use of this required the door at the rear of the turret to be open.
7. Shells stowed in barbette.
8. Lid for the top of the cordite hoist. Unlike the shells, cordite was from the magazine and supplied directly to the gunhouse.
9. Front elevation of depression rail.
10. Elevation view of cordite hoist.

PARTICULARS OF GUNS

Data	9.2-inch Mk X, 46.6 calibre	6-inch Mk VII, 45 calibre	12-pounder [3-inch] Mk I, 40 calibre	12-pounder [3-inch] Mk I, 28 calibre
Weight of gun (tons)	28	7.4	12cwt	8cwt
Total length of gun (inches)	442.35	269.5	123.6	87.6
Weight of shell (lbs)	380	100	12.5 (charge included in weight)	12.5 (charge included in weight)
Weight of charge (lbs)	103	20	N/A	N/A
Muzzle velocity (feet per second)	2100	2700	2210	1607
Perforation of wrought iron at 3000 yards (inches)	22	9.8	2.4	N/A
Perforation of Krupp steel at 3000 yards (inches)	9.5	4.25	N/A	N/A

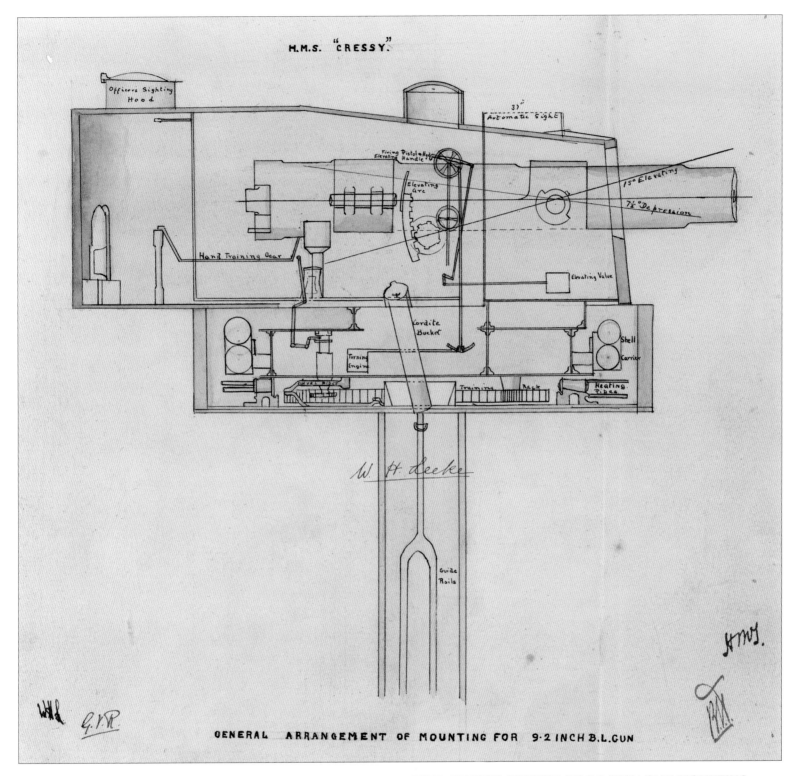

H.M.S. "CRESSY."

Officers Sighting Hood

Automatic Sight

Firing Pistol & Elevating Handle

Elevating Arc

15° Elevating

7½° Depression

Hand Training Gear

Elevating Valve

Cordite Bucket

Turning Engine

Shell Carrier

Training Rack

Heating Pipes

W. H. Leeke

Guide Rails

GENERAL ARRANGEMENT OF MOUNTING FOR 9·2 INCH B.L. GUN

CRESSY CLASS, ENLARGEMENT OF 9.2-INCH GUNHOUSE

(see previous page)

1. Ready-use shells.
2. Pump and hose for 'washing' the breech between firing. Interestingly, this detail is not shown on Leeke's drawing, although one would have been present.
3. Hand training gear. This was the larger of two sets installed in the gunhouse, the other one being mounted on the other side and slightly forward.
4. Hydraulic training gear.
5. Overhead rail for shell hoist. This is drawn in Leeke's illustration, but not labelled.

HMS *CRESSY*, SKETCH OF 9.2-INCH GUN MOUNTING

This illustration was produced by Midshipman Walter Leeke for inclusion in his Journal to satisfy his training requirements. Like his contemporaries, Leeke was required to demonstrate his understanding of his ship's equipment and weaponry. Leeke's drawing is understandably basic compared to the Vickers plan, drawn as it is from the perspective of the end user rather than the designer. However, it is detailed enough to highlight the broad similarities and at least one apparent difference in detail. The latter is the smaller space occupied by the top of the cordite hoist in the Elswick design. In terms of helping to comprehend the working of the mount, this drawing is arguably the more useful of the two as it highlights the items most pertinent to the gunhouse crew. (9.2-inch Gunhouse Sketch for *Cressy* from Midshipman's Log of W H Leeke, S5656-003)

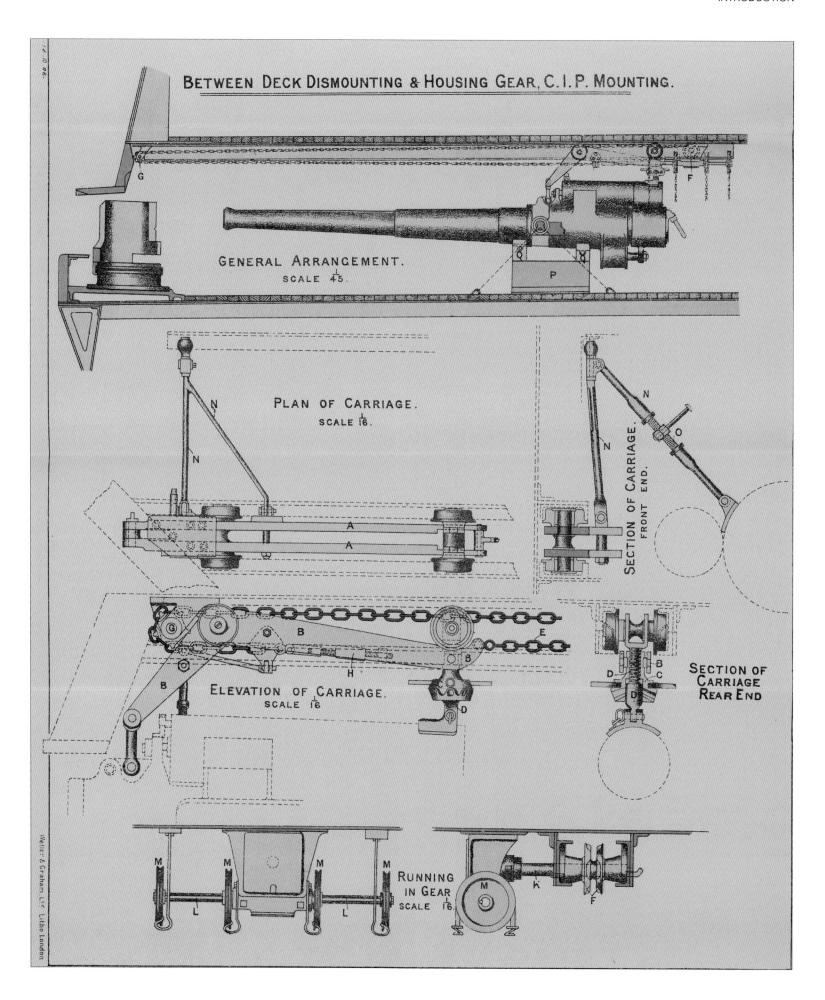

BETWEEN DECK DISMOUNTING & HOUSING GEAR, C.I.P. MOUNTING.

GENERAL ARRANGEMENT.
SCALE 1/45.

PLAN OF CARRIAGE.
SCALE 1/16.

SECTION OF CARRIAGE.
FRONT END.

ELEVATION OF CARRIAGE.
SCALE 1/16.

SECTION OF CARRIAGE REAR END

RUNNING IN GEAR
SCALE 1/16.

Weller & Graham Ltd Litho London.

by still being in development until about 1899. The mount permitted 15 degrees elevation and 7 degrees depression. In good conditions these weapons could achieve a maximum range of about 10,000 yards. Four of these guns enjoyed reasonably good positions on the Upper Deck, the forward pair sited abreast the foremast, and the aft pair abreast the mainmast. The remainder were on the Main Deck, four sited directly beneath the Upper Deck guns and the rest in between. The Upper Deck guns were about 17¾ft and the Main Deck weapons 11ft above the waterline. In anything other than calm conditions the Main Deck guns tended to suffer from water ingress, especially when the ship was moving at speed. A problem common for many warships with casemates close to the waterline, this could have an adverse effect on the ship's available firepower. Muzzle velocity was 2700 feet per second, but apparently this fell to 2400 feet per second once 235 full charges had been fired. The high muzzle velocity combined with the rapid-fire capability of the guns meant that the rifling could deteriorate fairly quickly. The maximum ammunition allowance for the 6-inch battery was 200 rounds per gun (in peacetime 100), so it was unlikely that problems would manifest themselves over the course of a single action. However, it did mean that large stocks of spare barrels would be required.

The tertiary guns comprised twelve 3-inch (12-pounder) 12cwt QF guns on SII mounts and three 3-pounder QF guns. The latter were of little use in a naval engagement but were used for ceremonial duties, training, picket boat work and, where necessary, operations ashore. Mountings were placed for them on the ship's superstructure. The 3-inch guns were the primary anti-torpedo boat armament and were evenly distributed around the ship. Ten were on the Upper Deck – eight in the vicinity of the funnels and two in embrasures at the bow. The remaining pair were sited in embrasures at the stern at Main Deck level.

The final element of the armament comprised two torpedo tubes mounted in submerged positions on the Platform Deck just aft of the forward 9.2-inch working chamber. Seven 18-inch and five 14-inch Whitehead torpedoes were allocated; the former for the torpedo tubes and the latter for the ship's picket boats. Despite the great length of *Cressy*'s hull, the arrangement of machinery, coal and magazines meant there was insufficient space to accommodate more than one submerged torpedo room in the design. The arrangement adopted for

ARRANGEMENT OF DISMOUNTING AND HOUSING GEAR FOR 6-INCH GUN

This illustration is from the 1906 edition of the Admiralty Handbook relating to these weapons. The layout shown is generic, and applies equally to guns in open 'between deck' batteries and those in individual casemates amidships. Mountings had improved in detail over the preceding decade, but most operational essentials remained unchanged. Consequently, this same picture graced all the Admiralty 6-inch gun handbooks from the mid-1890s up to the First World War. The arrangements shown here for dismounting the gun from the PI pedestal would have very closely matched those on HMS *Cressy* for the midships PIV type on the Main Deck. The system comprised overhead rails on which ran a chain-operated carriage which could be fitted over the rear portion of the gun. Once the body of the gun was unfastened from the pedestal it could be hauled inboard and rested on a pedestal, partly secured by the carriage. (Dismounting and Housing Gear for 6-inch Guns from 1906 Admiralty Handbook, S5655)

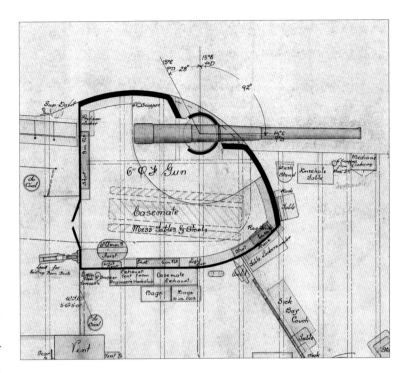

HMS *CRESSY*, 6-INCH CASEMATE

This plan shows the internal arrangement of the port forward 6-inch casemate on *Cressy*'s Upper Deck. It clearly demonstrates the cramped nature of the space, with the mess table and benches nestled close to the gun in a manner reminiscent of the age of sail. The former could be rapidly collapsed or stowed when necessary to allow the working of the gun, which in theory could train to cover a 120° arc. Shot bins and equipment racks line the rear walls of the casemate, and the aperture for the 6-inch ammunition hoist can be seen near the doors. Unlike the amidships casemates, the layout of the ship precluded the installation of long overhead dismounting rails, and guns such as this would have been moved on dedicated transporting trolleys. (Detail from Upper Deck for *Cressy*, M0191).

these weapons in *Cressy* was again very similar to the *Diadem*s, but she lacked the above water 'chase' torpedo tube mounted at the stern of the latter ships.

For use by landing parties and picket boats *Cressy* also carried two more 3-inch 8cwt guns which could be mounted on her steam launches on SI mounts or wheeled field carriages. This armament was supplemented by a complement of eight .303 Maxim machine guns, for which sets of cone mounts for shipboard or boat use or tripod mounts for land use were supplied. The final element of the ship's armament was the provision of .303 rifles, pistols and cutlasses for the use of the Royal Marine detachment and armed shore parties.

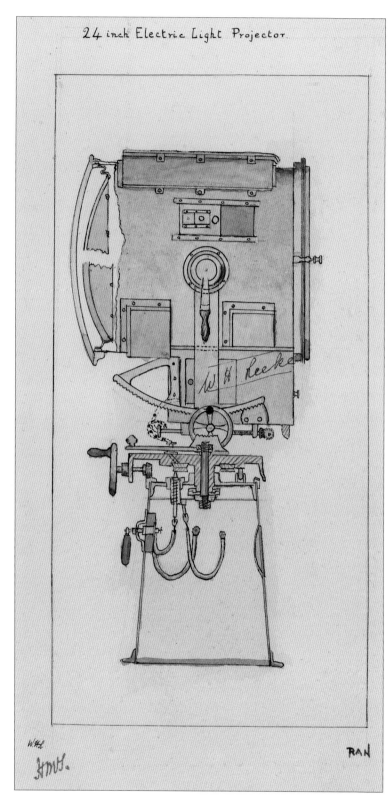

24 inch Electric Light Projector.

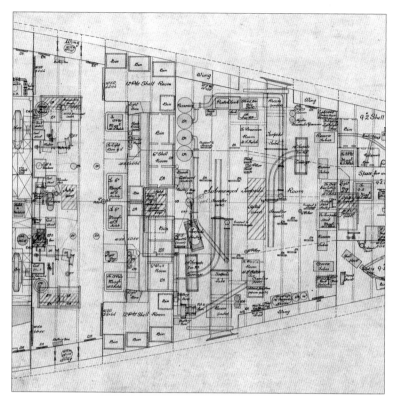

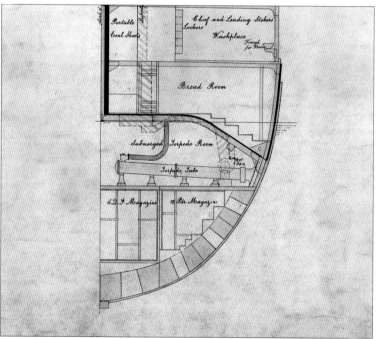

HMS *CRESSY*, SKETCH OF 24-INCH ELECTRIC LIGHT PROJECTOR

A detailed sketch showing the mechanical elements of a 24-inch electric light projector. Six of these units equipped each member of the *Cressy* class, with one each on the fore and main tops, and the remainder on the fore and aft bridge wings. The latter were mounted on rails to give them some degree of mobility. The primary purpose of these devices was illumination at night or in poor visibility. Signalling by light was a familiar concept, but searchlights of this type did not possess shutter arrangements or fine control required for this purpose. (24-inch Electric Light Projector Sketch for *Cressy* from Midshipman's Log of W H Leeke, S5656-001)

HMS *CRESSY*, ARRANGEMENT OF SUBMERGED TORPEDO ROOM

Ostensibly one of the largest compartments on the Platform Deck aside from the machinery spaces, the submerged torpedo room represented a very confined working space. The bulk of it was taken up by the torpedo tubes and air compressing machinery, which due to limited space had to be arranged en echelon to make the most of the available room. Six torpedo bodies were housed in this compartment on supports, and could be moved by a combination of overhead traveller rails, two carriages and one trolley which were supplied for this purpose. Most of the torpedo warheads were housed separately one deck below in the Torpedo Head Magazine, with four housed in ready-use overhead racks near the torpedo tubes. The tubes were fixed with no ability to train, and were loaded from the rear. (Detail from Platform Deck and Sections plans for *Cressy*, M0194 & M0196)

ACCOMMODATION AND HABITABILITY

Cressy was designed for a complement of 728 officers and men, a figure that was not expected to increase in service as she was not originally intended to serve as a flagship. However, the plans show dedicated accommodation for a Fleet Surgeon and Fleet Engineer. Some allowance was made for supernumeraries, and in many respects the accommodation was similar to that of the *Diadem*s despite the slightly higher manpower requirements dictated by the *Cressy*'s weaponry. When *Cressy* first commissioned her authorised complement had risen slightly to 755.

As conceived *Cressy* possessed thirty-two cabins for officers, later increased to thirty-four. The captain enjoyed the most space with accommodation that occupied an area roughly equivalent to five ordinary cabins. In addition to this, he had the use of a sea cabin in the forward superstructure and a deck cabin at the end of the Forecastle Deck. There were fourteen more cabins for officers on the Main Deck, with a further six on the Upper Deck and four on the Protective/Lower Deck. Even the smaller cabins afforded a reasonable degree of comfort, furnished as they were with bed places, drawers, folding tables or desks and at the very least a wash stand. Accommodation arrangements for seamen and stokers were little changed from those that had existed throughout the nineteenth century. Collapsible mess tables and stools were provided on the Upper and Main Decks, the latter being the primary accommodation and sleeping space. Men slept in hammocks slung from the beams overhead, and which were stowed when not required. In theory, each man was allowed a space of 18 inches width to rig his hammock, but in practice this often proved slightly less. The mess spaces also included racks for eating utensils and storage for seamen's bags and possessions.

The space allocated for provisions and consumables was for a minimum of four weeks' supply; the desired maximum stowage allowed for the carrying of provisions for thirteen weeks. In practice this worked out to 69 tons 15cwt and 8lbs of supplies, the amount recorded when *Cressy* sailed on her first commission. Cooking facilities comprised a crew's galley forward on the Main Deck, while the captain and officers enjoyed their own smaller galleys amidships. The cooking arrangements for the men generally conformed to naval practice in the nineteenth century as well, with each man taking turns

WEIGHT OF PROVISIONS

Victuals embarked aboard for the first commission on the China Station, 1901, as recorded 25 September 1901. This records thirteen weeks' supply for the crew.

Description of items	Weight			
	Tons	Cwt	Qt	Lbs
Beef	11	12	1	8
Pork	18	0	0	0
Oatmeal	0	14	2	16
Peas	5	12	0	8
Flour and rice	4	8	3	15
Suet	0	17	2	0
Raisins	0	15	1	8
Sugar, tea and cocoa	10	10	0	20
Vinegar and lemon juice	3	2	0	2
Bread	26	18	0	24
Preserved meats and vegetables	6	4	0	11
Spirits	6	13	1	0
Other provisions	7	18	0	4

to prepare his messmates' food at the mess table before taking it to the galley to be cooked. The officers' galleys were by comparison something of a luxury, but nonetheless proved a cause for some complaint, as expressed here by *Cressy*'s first captain: 'The Captain's and Ward Room Galleys are badly situated and small, and are so hot that cooking is carried on with difficulty and great discomfort. It is very inconvenient for dishes having to be brought so far; my galley fire being over 72 yards from my table, and a good many obstacles have to be passed en route.' Measurement of this area on the plans reveals this to have been remarkably accurate!

Cressy was equipped with a comprehensive system for ensuring the supply of seawater. Fresh water for drinking was limited in supply, but tanks were distributed evenly around the ship for use of the crew, even in the engineering spaces. Hot water was also available, albeit in even more limited quantities. This system depended in part upon a small gravity tank on the Forecastle Deck just aft of the foremast, which proved unequal to the task of producing enough pressure to supply all parts of the ship simultaneously. Men further away (usually the more senior officers) could find their hot water temporarily cut off if someone closer to the tank on the same pipe run turned on a tap! The seawater system apparently did not mate well with the new pattern of officers' water closets, which were known to occasionally overflow after flushing. Washing facilities varied considerably by rank, ranging from the captain who had a bathtub and wash places in his cabins to the seamen who made use of tubs stowed and used in their mess spaces. Stokers by nature of their jobs merited designated washing areas, with fifty-eight wash basins supplied for the use of 182 men.

Ventilation was generally regarded as satisfactory, with the decks above Main Deck level enjoying good natural airflow. Below the Main Deck the crew relied entirely upon mechanical ventilation, which did not always function efficiently. This was not helped by the profusion

COMPLEMENT

Captain	1
Wardroom Officers	22
Gunroom and Junior Officers	25
Warrant Officers	4
Chief Petty Officers	35
Seamen	460
Engine Room Artificers	16
Chief Leading Stokers	28
Stokers	164
Total:	**755**

of un-lagged steam pipes in compartments outside the machinery spaces, which raised the temperature significantly and could render the lower spaces of the ship very uncomfortable in warmer climates. They also tended to leak badly, and despite remedial efforts on *Cressy's* first commission this caused problems with damp. An unforeseen issue with the ventilation system was a tendency to contamination by coal dust when it passed through the ship's bunkers. As described in a somewhat sarcastic missive by *Cressy's* captain:

> the amount of coal dust which comes direct from the bunkers is a most irritating nuisance, it pours out of louvres and bunker manholes in a way which soon renders the ship hopelessly dirty…it is practically impossible to keep the ship clean when she is doing much steaming. I think that the Constructors might be called upon to devise some better system of ventilation for the bunkers than the present louvres, which all vomit coal dust whether they are marked 'Exhaust' or 'Supply'. Perhaps they might be arranged to exhaust into the funnels.

The obvious discomfort and nuisance factor aside, it is curious that the potential fire hazard this represented was not mentioned.

One of the more interesting – and ultimately unsuccessful – safety features worked into *Cressy* was the use of chemically fireproofed wooden fittings. The Battle of Santiago Bay in July 1898 underlined the dangers of fire and the devastated hulks of the Spanish cruisers after that action were a stark warning. Unfortunately in *Cressy's* case, the execution did not live up to the concept. The agent employed comprised a mix of sulphate of ammonia, borax, phosphate of ammonia, tungstate of soda and Epsom salts, and while this combination was found to be effective in protecting wood, tests showed that it gave off toxic fumes when exposed to fire. There were further concerns that its use might not prove healthy for the crew; the compound was potent enough to cause discolouration in the brass buttons of a coat that had been hung up facing the treated wooden panelling.

BOATS

Type	Number carried
56ft steam pinnace	1
40ft steam pinnace	1
42ft sailing launch	1
36ft sailing pinnace	1
30ft sailing cutter	1
32ft sailing cutter	2
26ft sailing cutter	1
27ft whaler	1
30ft gig	2
13ft 6in balsa raft	1
16ft skiff dinghy	1

DETAILS OF SICK BAY FITTINGS AND EQUIPMENT

Description	Number
Swinging cots	8
Billets [space allocated for hammocks]	19
Mess & amputation table	1
Locker seats (4 lockers each)	2
Rack for twelve 40oz bottles	1
Hat hooks	4
Cooking stove	1
Cook's cupboard	1
Linen cupboard	1
Bath with portable frame for wash basins	1
Mess rack	1
Filter tank (25-gallon capacity)	1
Dispensaries	2
Medicine chest	1
Wash basin	1
Towel rail	1
Secretaire	1
Dressing table	1
Medical history cupboard	1
Ledger rack	1
Book shelf	1
Surgical instrument cupboard	1
Cushioned seat	1
Portable operating table	1
Curtain rods	To be fitted as necessary to doors and scuttles

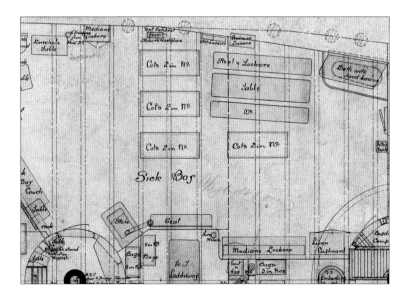

HMS *CRESSY*, DETAIL OF SICK BAY
(Detail from Upper Deck plan for *Cressy*, M0191)

CAREER SUMMARY

Cressy's keel was laid down by the Fairfield Shipbuilding & Engineering Co yard at Govan on 12 October 1898. Her construction progressed smoothly and she was launched on 4 December 1899. She ran her eight-hour full power trials almost a year later, achieving an average speed of 20.7 knots despite slightly adverse weather conditions. In terms of her design expectations this was disappointing, but her engines had performed reliably and her coal consumption (1.93 tons per unit of power per hour) was considered efficient. As it turned out, she was the only member of the class not to meet or exceed her design speed on trials. In April 1901 she successfully underwent her turning trials, the mean tactical diameter being 632½ yards. This compared very favourably with the *Diadem*s, which at best required 900 yards, and was a result of the reduced deadwood aft in *Cressy* compared with the earlier cruisers.

The ship commissioned on 28 May 1901 at Portsmouth for the China Station under Captain Henry Tudor. However, she did not depart until October due to a structural failure in her steering quadrant which necessitated lengthy repairs. The voyage east was uneventful, proving a useful test of the new ship, and – barring some issues – overall impressions of her as a sea boat were positive. Writing from Hong Kong in December 1901 Tudor reported

[*Cressy*] is a good fighting ship, and requires far less preparations for war than older ships. When she has way on she answers her helm well, and turns in a remarkably small circle. When way is off the ship, or her speed is very slow she is almost unmanageable, and to such an extent as in a small harbour to be almost dangerous: the inward turning screws undoubtedly contribute to this, and I doubt whether their advantages outweigh their deficiency in twisting power.

Tudor also reported her to be a wet ship, although this did not appear to greatly impede her fighting power despite issues with the lower 6-inch casemates. He wrote that even in the stormy conditions of the north eastern monsoon *Cressy* was 'very steady, even when I put her broadside on [she was] a good gun platform.' However, 'the waves in a very slight seaway, dash against the projections [on the hull] – casemates, shoots etc – and squirt up the sides coming down in sheets of spray over the boat deck…We took in a fair amount of water by the Lower [sic] deck foremost casemates, and special care is requisite for

the housing of those guns.' It was noted that when the coal bunkers were fully loaded the ship appeared to be 9 inches down by the head. This was not ideal under any circumstances, although it may have helped ameliorate the tendency of the stern anchor to catch water on account of its siting outside the hull on the starboard side at Protective Deck level. The trimming phenomenon was not limited to *Cressy*, as *Hogue* reported similar trouble while with the Mediterranean Fleet in 1903. This was an acknowledged defect in the design, but the problem only occurred when the bunkers were filled to maximum capacity and the issue could be corrected as coal was used up.

An almost absurdly minor issue which concerned Tudor was one which affected the ship's ability to function in a diplomatic role. In an amusing passage he described what he regarded as the poor siting of the starboard quarter accommodation ladder, and its consequent hazards, thus:

It is very inconvenient especially in the case of receiving foreign officers: an admiral for instance arrives at the top of the ladder and having to get in through the hole in the ship's side, usually bangs his head against the top; after profuse apologies on my part his attention is distracted by the efforts of the marine guard to present arms without perforating the boom boats overhead; and he is just recovering his equanimity when he falls over the boats derricks topping lift which when the derrick is in use, leads across the entry port at a height of 2 or 3 feet.

Cressy's service on the China Station came to an end in January 1905. As with her sisters operating elsewhere this period had proven useful for ironing out defects, but the ship was never seriously put to the test as a combat vessel despite the increased tension and proximity of the fighting with the outbreak of the Russo-Japanese War in February 1904. Her first commission would prove to be the high point of her active career. Such was the ongoing pace of cruiser development that she was soon superseded by the *Drake* class armoured cruisers, the first of which had come into service in 1903. In February 1905 *Cressy* recommissioned at Portsmouth with a nucleus crew. Various alterations were proposed for her, but most came to nothing as they were deemed unnecessary or in some cases not practicable. Her greatest shortcoming was limited endurance compared to other cruisers, although this had been accepted as a necessary compromise when she was designed. Increasing the bunkerage was considered, but ultimately

MANOEUVRABILITY

Mean tactical manoeuvrability at different engine and helm settings, compared with *Diadem* and *Monmouth* class cruisers; turning circles expressed in yards

Ship	Both Engines Ahead, All Helm		One Engine Ahead, One Engine Astern, Full Power, All Helm	One Engine Only, Full Power		
	10 knots	Full Power		Propeller Against Rudder	Helm Amidships	All Helm
HMS *Diadem* (1896)	839	913	549	994	1958	735
HMS *Cressy* (1899)	632	652	487	695	1565	532
HMS *Monmouth* (1901)	751	775	595	922	1913	649

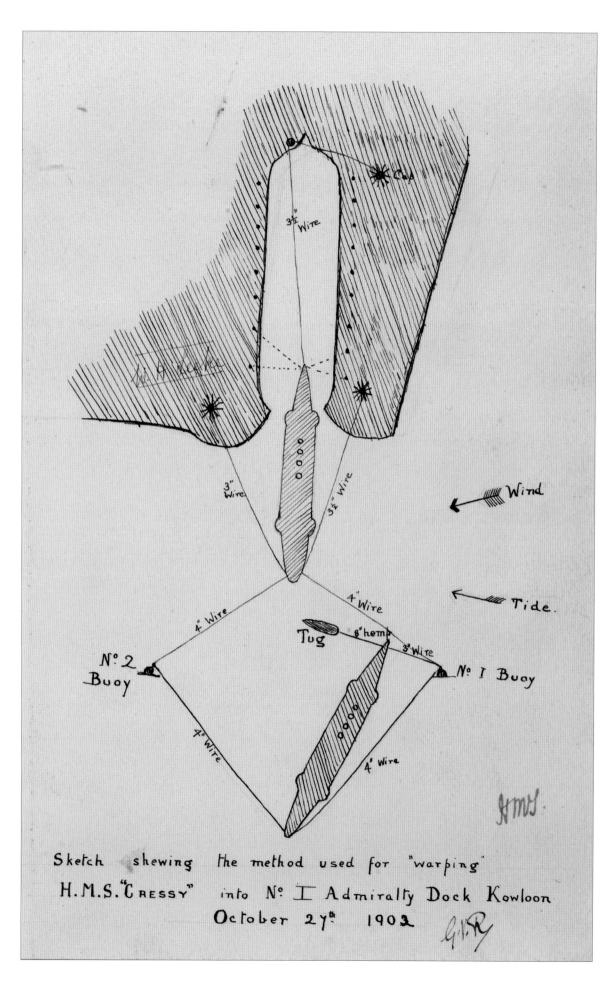

Sketch shewing the method used for "warping" H.M.S. "Cressy" into Nº I Admiralty Dock Kowloon October 27th 1902

HMS *CRESSY*, SKETCH SHOWING WARPING INTO DOCK

A remarkable sketch illustrating the involved method of warping *Cressy* into dock at Kowloon during her first commission. The provision of inward turning screws meant that the ship was very difficult to handle at low speeds, adding to the difficulty of what was a complex but otherwise routine manoeuvre. Here *Cressy* is shown in her starting position (black ink) and the point at which she can be brought into the dock (red ink). In the latter position, it can be seen that the ship is still secured to the two buoys, but has also run wires out to the three capstans around the dock. Further lines have been put out from the bow to four of the bollards to help steady the ship as she is hauled in by the capstans. (Warping Diagram for *Cressy* from Midshipman's Log of W H Leeke, S5656-002)

rejected on the grounds of cost and reduction of the ship's fighting efficiency. Two notable alterations were carried out in 1907: one was the addition of fire control positions on her masts and the other, the addition of flying topmasts for improved wireless communication. In September that year *Cressy* recommissioned to serve as a boys' training ship with the 4th Cruiser Squadron on the North America & West Indies Station, the new role allowing for a much-reduced complement of 464. She remained there until October 1909 before returning to reserve status at Chatham. When *Cressy* recommissioned for the Home Fleet two years later her complement had been further reduced to 367, and she would not be brought up to full strength until the test mobilisation of July 1914. Had the various crises of that year not intervened, *Cressy* and her sisters might have been disposed of or reduced to training ships and perhaps escaped the fate that has so coloured their reputation since.

With Britain's entry into war with Germany in August 1914, *Cressy* and four of her sisters were based at Harwich to provide heavy support to Commodore Reginald Tyrwhitt's force of light cruisers and destroyers. The latter were tasked with preventing German warships from interfering with the transfer of troops and supplies to the continent. The *Cressys*' role was to patrol the Broad Fourteens off the Dutch coast in company with Tyrwhitt's flotillas, but the heavy seas encountered in this area often precluded close cooperation and by September the cruisers were commonly left on station without the smaller ships. This situation was a cause of considerable concern to the commanders of the Harwich forces who recognised the vulnerability of the cruiser squadron. Churchill, then First Lord of the Admiralty, shared these concerns, writing to his colleague Prince Louis of Battenberg that the 'risk to such ships is not justified by the services they render'. Although Prince Louis agreed, there were as yet no suitable modern light cruisers available to replace the *Cressys* and until that changed it was decided that the older ships should maintain their patrols.

In the early morning of 22 September 1914 *Aboukir*, *Hogue* and *Cressy* were on their assigned station. Weather conditions were calm and visibility good but rough seas on the previous day had forced the detachment of their usual escorting destroyers. Aboard the cruisers some of the 6in guns were manned and lookouts were posted, but the ships were not steering evasive courses and were travelling at an economical cruising speed of about 10 knots. At 6:30am, a torpedo from the German submarine *U9* struck *Aboukir* on the starboard side. Unaware that his ship had been hit by a torpedo, Captain Drummond hoisted a mine warning signal. However, Captain Nicholson aboard *Hogue* recognised the true nature of the attack and signalled Captain Robert Johnson on *Cressy* accordingly. Despite their precautions, *Hogue* was hit by two torpedoes as she slowed to aid the survivors of the stricken *Aboukir*. *Hogue*'s alert gunners had in fact spotted the bow of *U9*, which briefly broke the surface just after she discharged her latest salvo. Even before these weapons reached their ship, they took *U9* under immediate fire, continuing to shoot even after the torpedoes struck. This spirited defence proved of little avail, for *U9* was able to dive undamaged, and within five minutes of being hit *Hogue*'s increasing list effectively precluded further firing.

Cressy had meanwhile increased to full speed, hoping to attack the submarine by either ramming or gunfire. However, finding no target and conscious of the large number of survivors in the water Johnson fatefully slowed his ship to render aid. *Hogue*'s hull had only just disappeared from view at about 7:20am when *Cressy* was herself struck by a torpedo on her starboard side forward. Lookouts had spotted *U9*'s periscope and the track of the incoming weapon, but at a range of 500 yards it was impossible for *Cressy* to build up sufficient speed to take evasive action. This first hit appeared to make little impression, but fifteen minutes later a second torpedo hit her amidships on the port side. This additional damage proved fatal and *Cressy* rolled to starboard onto her beam ends. Over the next twenty minutes she continued to slowly capsize before disappearing at about 8:00am.

This one-sided action cost the Royal Navy 1459 men killed, of whom 560 came from *Cressy*. Little wonder that Admiral Fisher, condemning the deployments that had contributed to the disaster, described the fiasco as 'pure murder'. The disaster was a profound shock for the British, and while it marked the end of any lingering official complacency about the threat posed by German submarines, it would take several more painful losses before the lessons were truly learned. Thereafter, the destruction of the 'live bait' squadron became virtually synonymous with popular perceptions of the Admiralty's unpreparedness for the realities of modern naval warfare. For the fine cruisers of the *Cressy* class, it was a sad legacy.

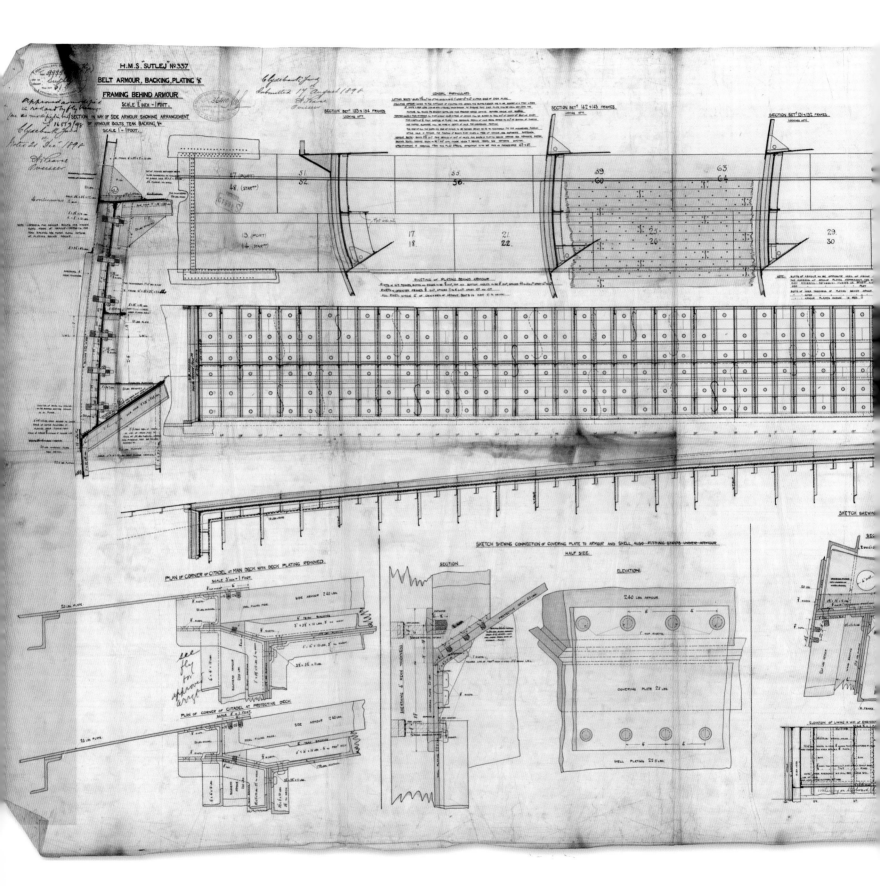

HMS *SUTLEJ*, ARRANGEMENT OF BELT ARMOUR, BACKING AND FRAMING

A very comprehensive illustration of the arrangement of the armoured belt at the citadel, showing the arrangement of the Krupp armour plates, the arrangement of the teak backing behind it, and the framing and regular hull plating supporting these. The more general elevation, section and plan views are supported by a number of detail drawings towards the bottom of the plan which elaborate on the more complex elements of the structure. Like other plans pertaining to *Sutlej*, this was a working drawing, and reflects alterations authorised over the summer of 1898. (M1574)

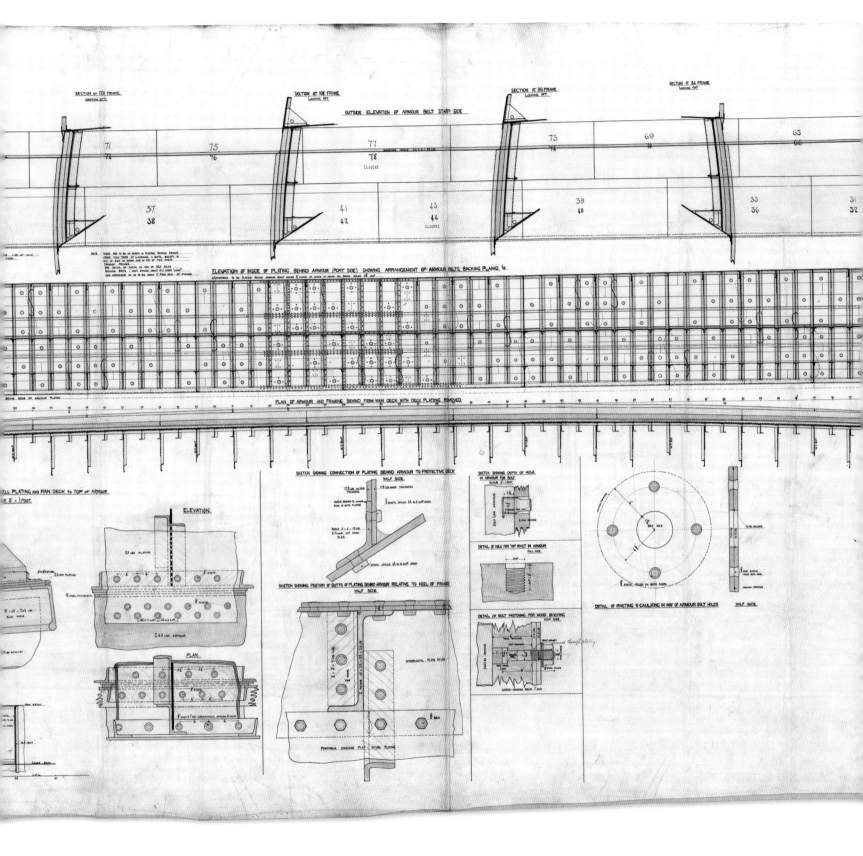

SECTION AT 120 FRAME.
LOOKING AFT.

SECTION AT 108 FRAME
LOOKING AFT.

SECTION AT 96 FRAME
LOOKING AFT.

SECTION AT 84 FRAME
LOOKING FWD.

OUTSIDE ELEVATION OF ARMOUR BELT STAR'D SIDE

71   75   77   73   69   65
72   76   78   74   70   66
              CLOSERS

37   41   43   39   35   31
38   42   44   40   36   32
        CLOSERS

ELEVATION OF INSIDE OF PLATING BEHIND ARMOUR (PORT SIDE) SHOWING ARRANGEMENT OF ARMOUR BOLTS, BACKING PLANKS, &c.

PLAN OF ARMOUR AND FRAMING BEHIND FROM MAIN DECK WITH DECK PLATING REMOVED

SKETCH SHOWING CONNECTION OF PLATING BEHIND ARMOUR TO PROTECTIVE DECK
HALF SIZE.

SKETCH SHOWING DEPTH OF HOLE
IN ARMOUR FOR BOLT
SCALE 3 = 1 FOOT

SHELL PLATING AND MAIN DECK TO TOP OF ARMOUR.
SCALE 3' = 1 FOOT

ELEVATION.

PLAN.

SKETCH SHOWING POSITION OF BUTTS OF PLATING BEHIND ARMOUR RELATIVE TO HEEL OF FRAMES
HALF SIZE

DETAIL OF HOLE FOR TAP RIVET IN ARMOUR
FULL SIZE

DETAIL OF BOLT FASTENING FOR WOOD BACKING
HALF SIZE

DETAIL OF RIVETING & CAULKING IN WAY OF ARMOUR BOLT HOLES   HALF SIZE.

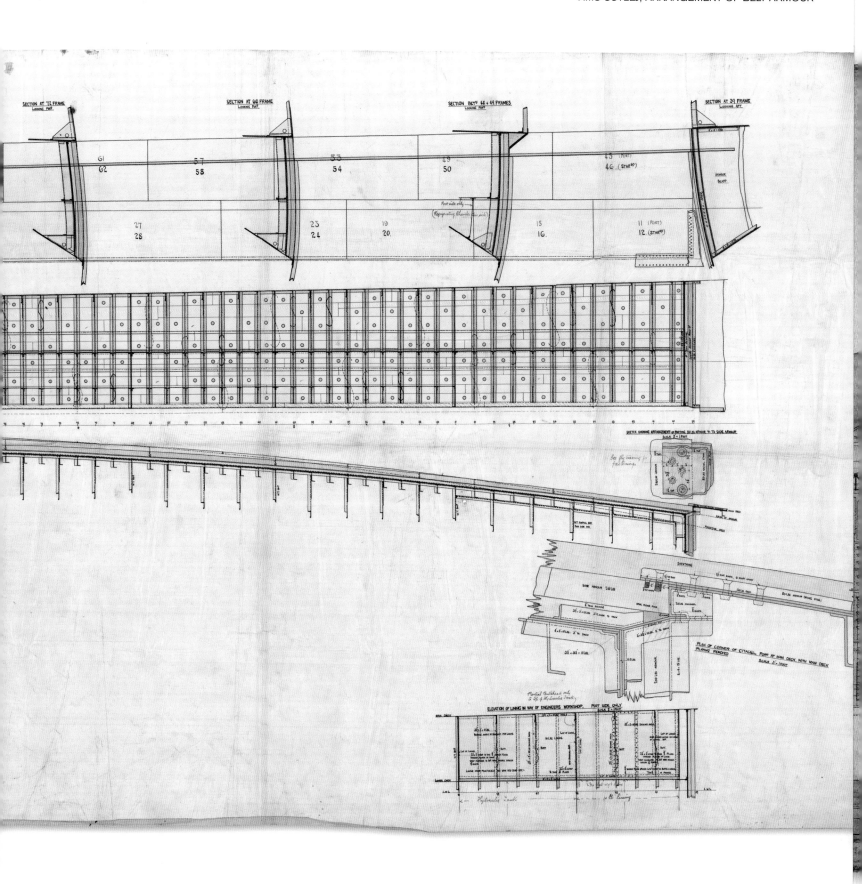

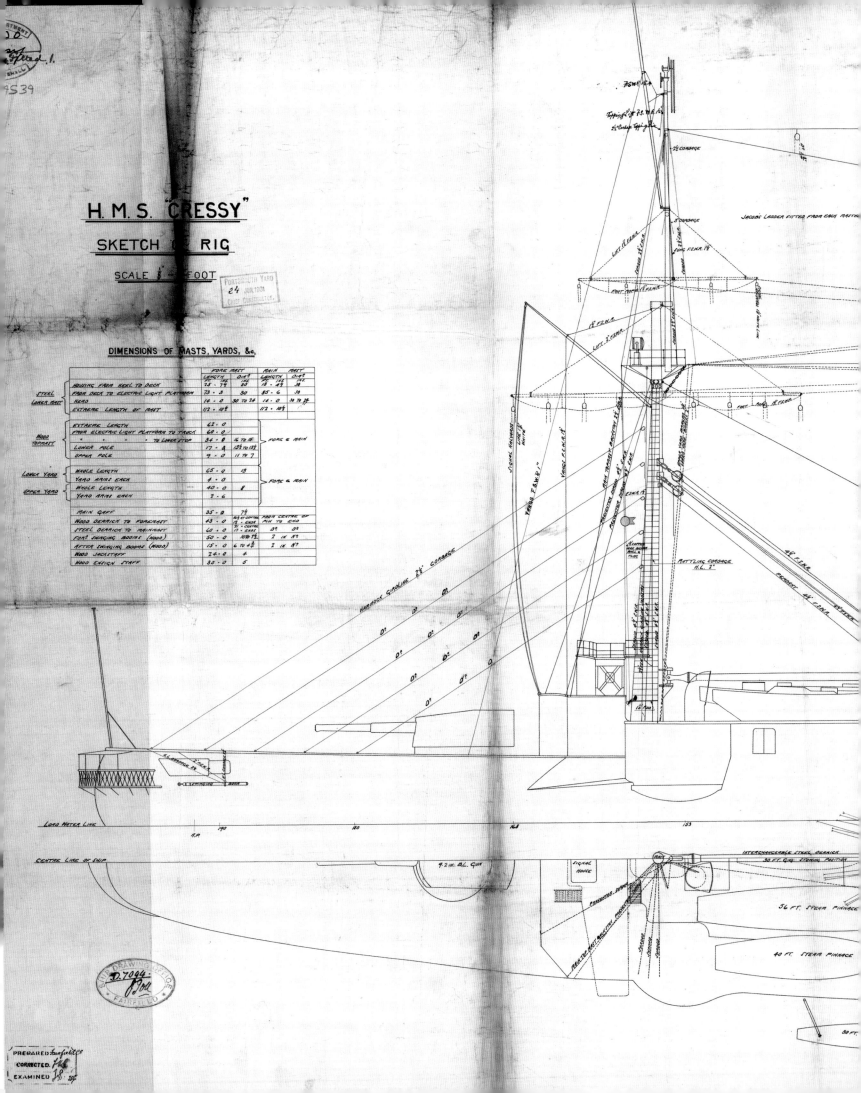

H. M. S. "CRESSY"

SKETCH OF RIG

SCALE ⅛ = FOOT

DIMENSIONS OF MASTS, YARDS, &c.

		FORE MAST		MAIN MAST	
		LENGTH	DIAR	LENGTH	DIAR
STEEL LOWER MAST	HOUSING FROM KEEL TO DECK	25 - 7½	30	18 - 4½	30
	FROM DECK TO ELECTRIC LIGHT PLATFORM	73 - 3	30	85 - 6	30
	HEAD	14 - 0	30 TO 24	14 - 0	30 TO 24
	EXTREME LENGTH OF MAST	112 - 10½		112 - 10½	
WOOD TOPMAST	EXTREME LENGTH	62 - 0		FORE & MAIN	
	FROM ELECTRIC LIGHT PLATFORM TO TRUCK	60 - 0			
	" " " TO LOWER STOP	34 - 0	16 TO 15		
	LOWER POLE	17 - 4	13¾ TO 12¾		
	UPPER POLE	9 - 0	11 TO 7		
LOWER YARD	WHOLE LENGTH	65 - 0	13	FORE & MAIN	
	YARD ARMS EACH	4 - 0			
UPPER YARD	WHOLE LENGTH	40 - 0	8		
	YARD ARMS EACH	2 - 6			
	MAIN GAFF	35 - 0	7½		
	WOOD DERRICK TO FOREMAST	43 - 0			
	STEEL DERRICK TO MAINMAST	60 - 0			
	FORD SWINGING BOOMS (WOOD)	50 - 0		2 IN No	
	AFTER SWINGING BOOMS (WOOD)	15 - 0	6 TO 4½	2 IN No	
	WOOD JACKSTAFF	24 - 0	4		
	WOOD ENSIGN STAFF	30 - 0	5		

LOAD WATER LINE

CENTRE LINE OF SHIP

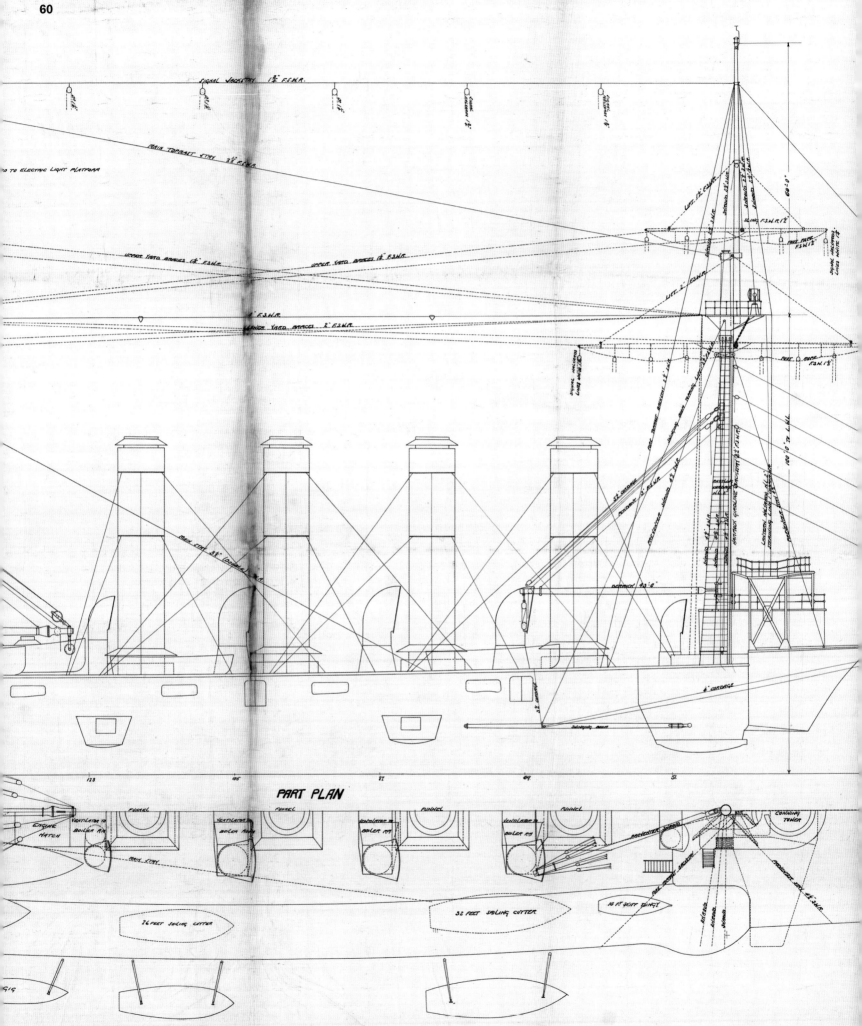

PART PLAN

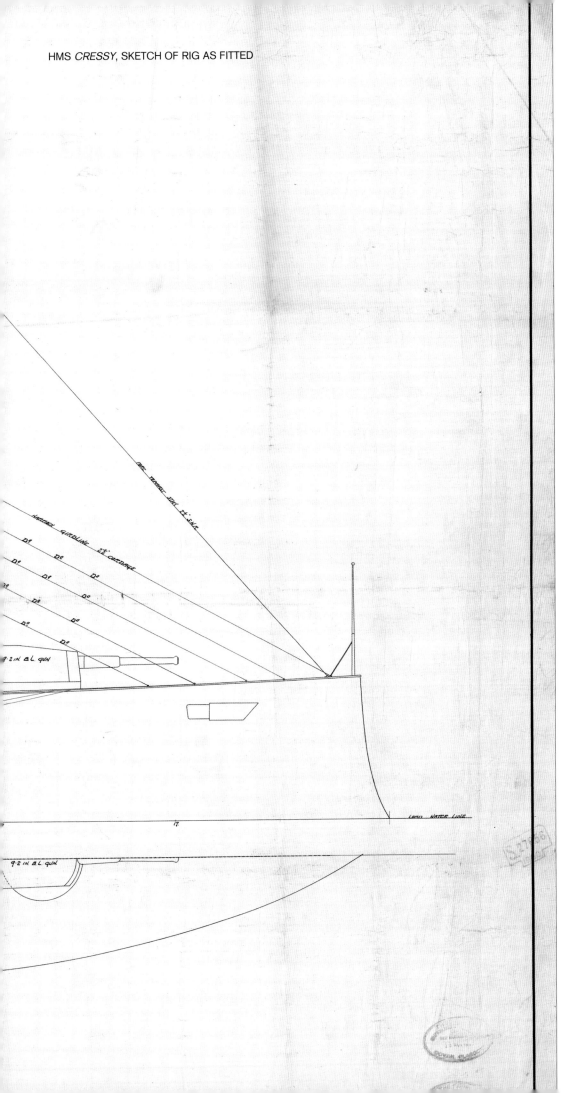

HMS *CRESSY*, SKETCH OF RIG AS FITTED

Cressy is shown here in her completed state as of June 1901 with all of her standing and running rigging drawn in. The blue lines denote various grades of steel wire rope, while the rest are various forms of cordage, lines and in at least one instance copper wire. The working rig illustrated on this plan is devoted primarily, albeit not exclusively, to signalling and boat handling. A notable absence from this ensemble is that of wireless telegraphy fittings. This omission may be due to the fact that W/T arrangements were sometimes drawn on a separate plan (if so, this has not survived), but could also be related to the very recent appearance of this technology in British warships. Interestingly, the general arrangements, which were completed five months later, show *Cressy* fitted with a wireless telegraphy office. (M1759)

DETAIL OF STORES REQUIRED FOR THE FITTING OF THE STANDING AND RUNNING RIGGING

Description	Quantity
Canvas, new, narrow	100 yards
Canvas, worn, broad, 2nd quality	500 yards
Cordage, nettlestuff, tarred, 40-thread, 2-yarn	28lbs
Cordage, nettlestuff, tarred, 40-thread, 3-yarn	42lbs
Cordage, spunyarn, tarred, 40-thread, 2-yarn	3cwt
Cordage, spunyarn, tarred, 40-thread, 3-yarn	6cwt
Cordage, spunyarn, tarred, 25-thread, 4-yarn	3cwt
Cordage, spunyarn, tarred, 25-thread, 5-yarn	3cwt
Cordage, spunyarn, tarred, 25-thread, 6-yarn	3cwt
Tanned hide	23lbs
Yellow tallow	84lbs
Mineral tar	14 gallons
Vegetable tar	27 gallons
Spirits of turpentine	8 gallons
Seaming twine	4 gallons

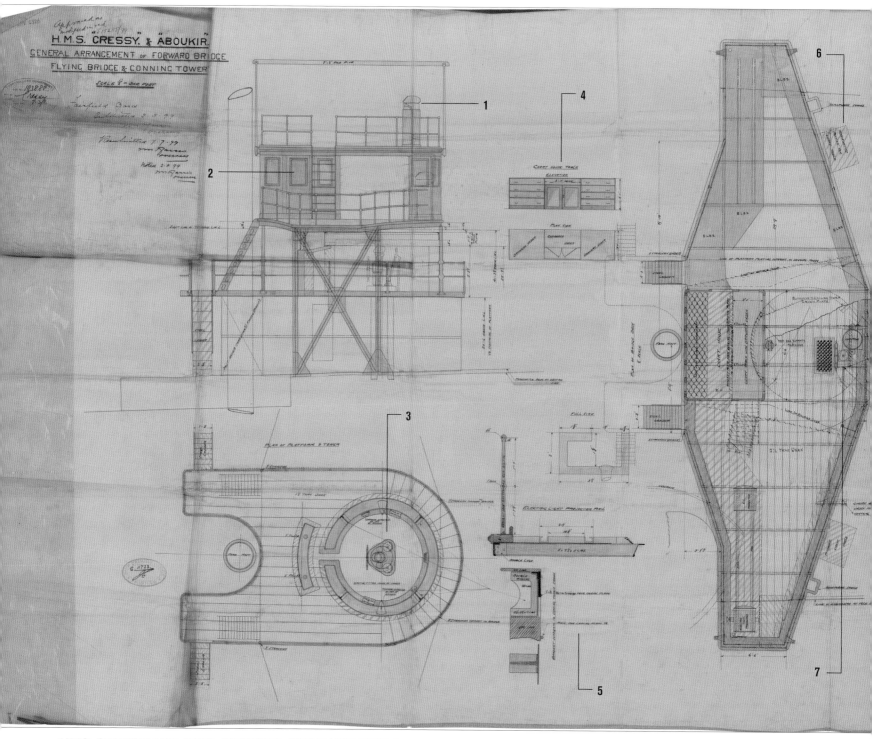

HMS *CRESSY* AND HMS *ABOUKIR*, ARRANGEMENT OF FORE AND AFT BRIDGES

This plan and its counterpart overleaf were both drawn up in the spring of 1899, and reflect alterations of varying degrees of significance as the construction of the fore and aft bridges progressed. Although the reasons for these alterations have not been recorded in the Admiralty material, the plans make for an interesting and very detailed record of how the *Cressy*'s command and control spaces evolved as she neared completion. On a cautionary note, these plans do not represent the final iteration of the bridges and comparison with the main general arrangements show some notable differences alongside the elements which were retained. An example of the former are the projections from the forward bridge wings marked as stands for semaphore apparatus. When *Cressy* was completed these platforms were used as mounting positions for Maxim guns, with the semaphores moved to new positions inboard of these. (M0198 and M0199).

1. The compass platform with standard compass shown. This space was also intended to accommodate the forward rangefinder.
2. Exterior starboard elevation of the chart house and bridge. Beneath these is the outline of the armoured conning tower. The camber of the bridge wing deck can be seen in this and the aft elevation view opposite.
3. Plan view of the interior of the armoured conning tower, showing the arrangement of the telemotor steering position, compass and engine room telegraph. A rudder indicator is shown mounted at the forward end, and torpedo control positions on the port and starboard side. The armour plate is shaded in pink.
4. Dimensions and physical details of the chart house table.
5. Details of the searchlight rails, showing their construction and arrangement on the bridge wings.

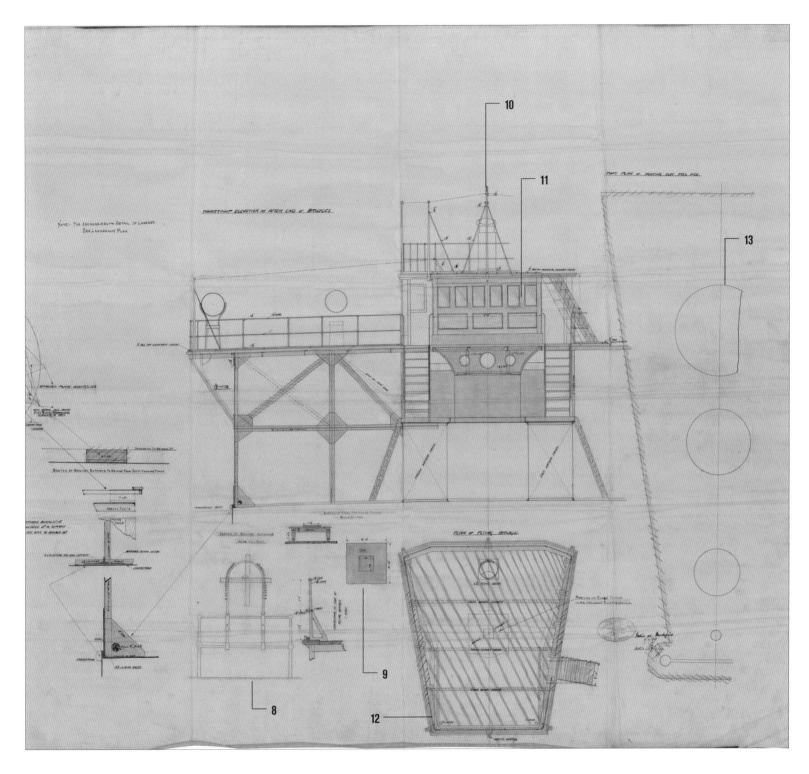

6. Semaphore stand and proposed position for the portable chart table. The former were re-purposed in the final design as mounting points for Maxim machine guns. This area shows the arrangement of the steel plating beneath the decking of the bridge wing and highlights the structural support required to bear the weight of the searchlights.

7. Plan view of the chart house and bridge, showing the arrangement of the table, couch and lockers in the former and the position of the wheel, compass and rudder indicator in the latter. The wooden platform grating for the helmsman is shown, although there is no sign of the engine room telegraphs which were fitted. As completed, the arrangement of wheel and compass shown here was swapped, with the wheel offset to the left and the compass to the right.

8. Details of the roll indicator (clinometer), showing it fitted to the guardrail stanchions.

9. Dimensions and physical details of the rangefinder mounting stool.

10. Awning stanchions.

11. Elevation view of the bridge structure, seen from astern and showing the elaborate wood panelling on the exterior of the chart house. Alterations to the structural supports are marked in red.

12. Plan view of the compass platform, showing the position of compass and rangefinder. The alterations in red show the final, narrowed arrangement of this area.

13. Full size plan view of a sighting slot, an arrangement which was subsequently cancelled. Presumably it would have been used in conjunction with the compass on the compass platform.

Continued overleaf

1. Starboard exterior elevation of the after bridge, a much more basic structure than its counterpart in the omission of a built-up bridge and compass platform.

2. Half plan view of the shelter deck beneath the after bridge. This was a raised platform at the aft end of the Boat Deck, and was the level on which the signal house was situated. The alterations in red at the forward end of the shelter deck indicate additional signal flag lockers.

3. Interior plan view of the signal house, showing the arrangement of the flag lockers in considerable detail.

4. Table showing the number and distribution of pigeon holes for signal flags and ensigns. Space was allocated in this area for 192 of the former and 6 of the latter.

5. The portside bridge wing, showing the arrangement of the teak decking, searchlight mounting and rails and projections for a Maxim machine gun mounting aft and a semaphore stand and portable chart table on the forward side. The Maxim position was suppressed in the completed ship.

6. Aft steering position with compass and wooden platform grating for the helmsman. As with the fore bridge the engine room telegraphs which were fitted are not shown. The original design arrangement of wheel offset to the right and compass to the left is also shown. This was reversed when the wheel and compass were actually installed. Alterations in red show where the structure was reduced near its junction with the mainmast.

7. This area shows the arrangement of the steel plating beneath the decking of the bridge wing and highlights the structural support required to bear the weight of the searchlights, essentially repeating the arrangement of the forward bridge wings.

8. Section through one of the signal lockers on the after bridge, showing details of its construction and materials used to compensate for exposure to the elements. The top and bottom were of teak and the inner shelves of pine. The 'seaward' side was made of thin galvanised steel and the inboard side protected by a canvas cover.

9. Details of the searchlight rails, showing their construction and arrangement on the bridge wings.

10. Elevation view of the after bridge, seen from astern. The empty pedestal next to the searchlight is the planned Maxim machine gun mounting. The signal house can be seen below the tripod awning stanchion.

11. Elevation view of the after bridge, seen from ahead. Note the heavy alterations in red which show a great reduction in the weight and density of the supporting structure.

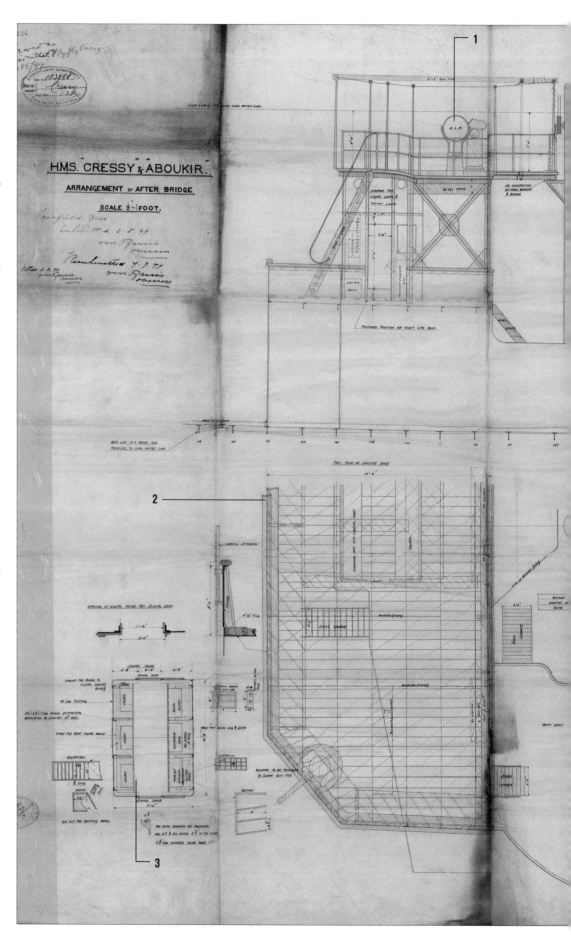

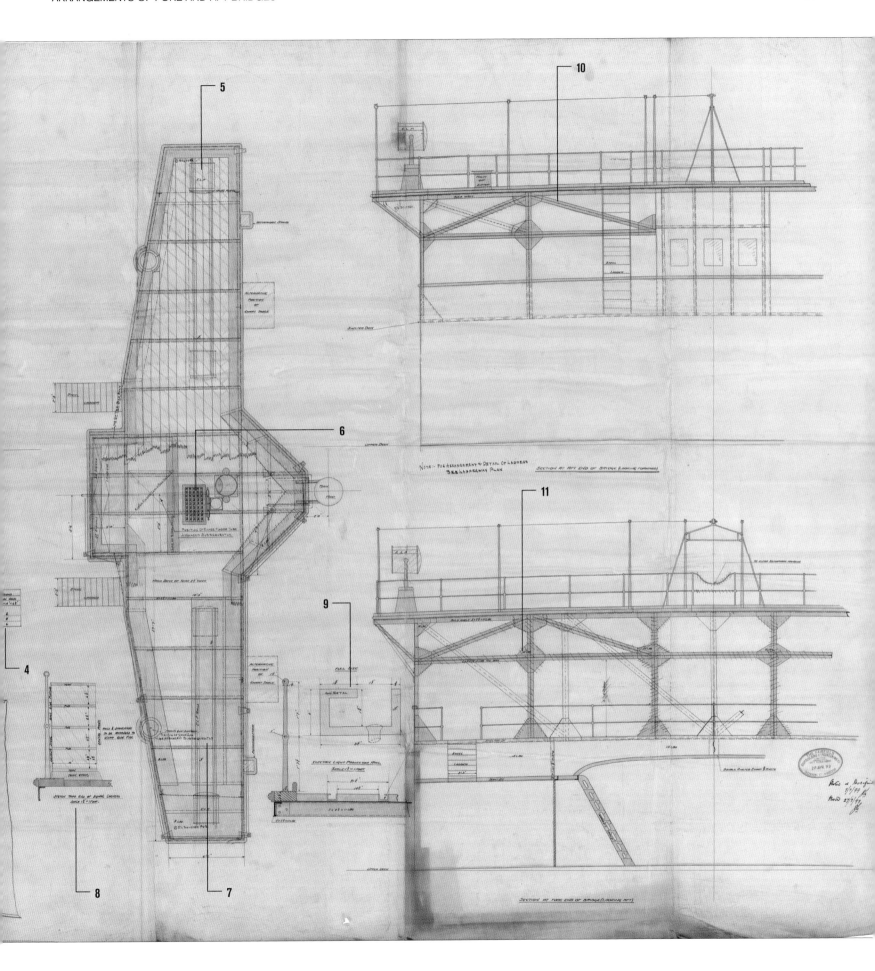

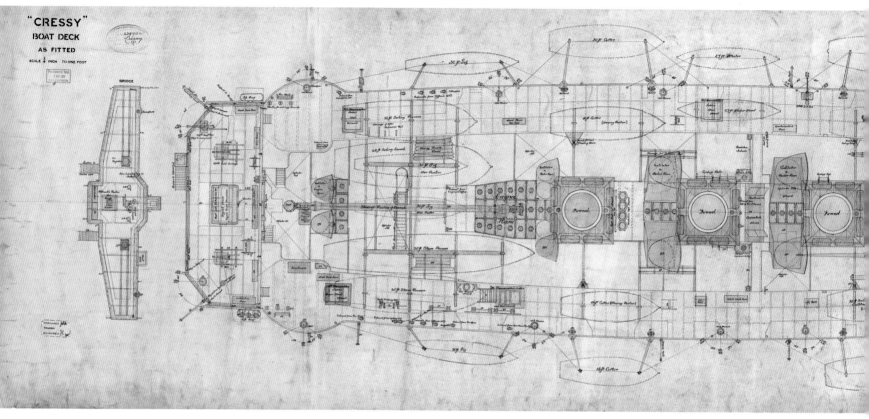

HMS CRESSY, BOAT DECK AS FITTED AND ARRANGEMENT OF WOOD AND CORTICENE DECKS

The top plan shows the arrangement of Cressy's Boat Deck as completed and is the first of the six Portsmouth Dockyard deck plans which collectively illustrate the ship in this condition. For clarity, the fore and aft bridges and the compass platform have been 'un-stacked' and drawn to the left and right of the deck. On this and the succeeding pages the 'as fitted' plans have been paired up with their counterparts from a series of plans detailing the deck covering material. Unless

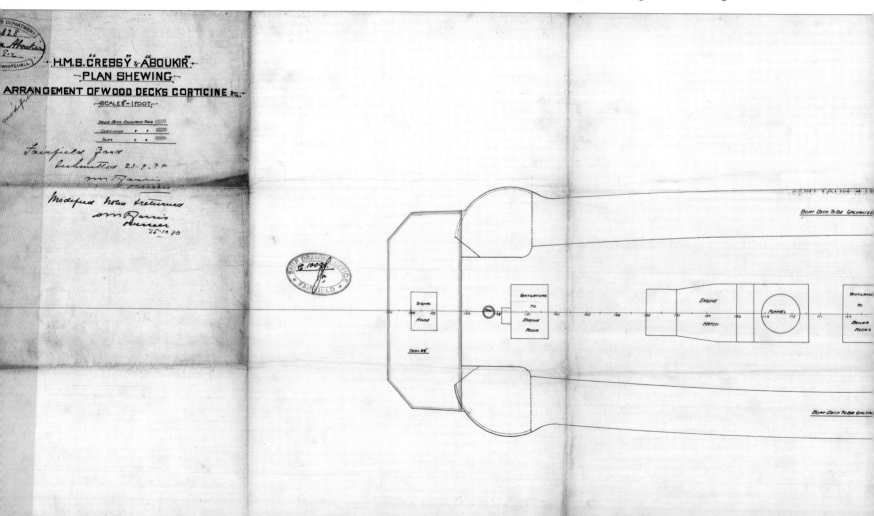

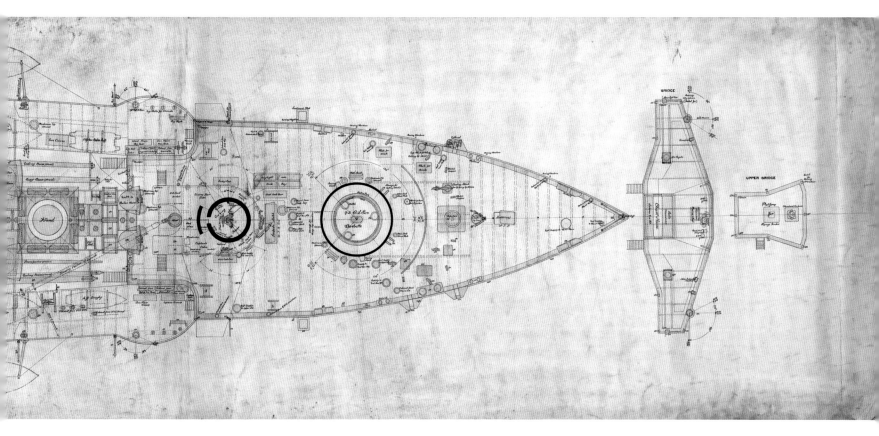

otherwise stated these are colour-coded brown for wood (generally teak), grey for corticene and red for tiles. Note that enlarged versions of the 'as fitted' deck plans can be found on pages 104–127. (M0190 and detail from Arrangement of Wood and Corticene Decks for *Cressy* and *Aboukir* M1580)

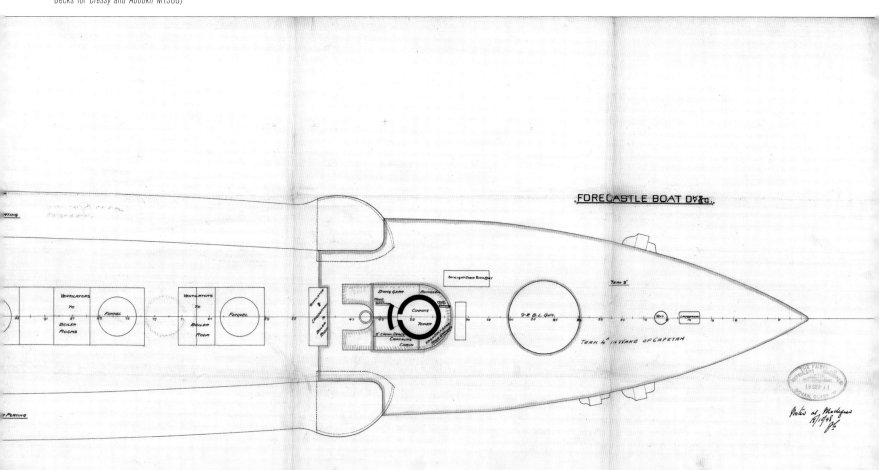

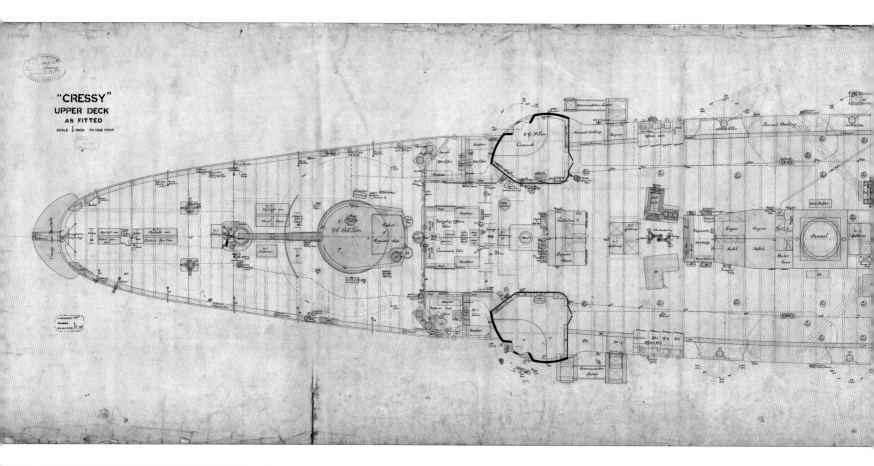

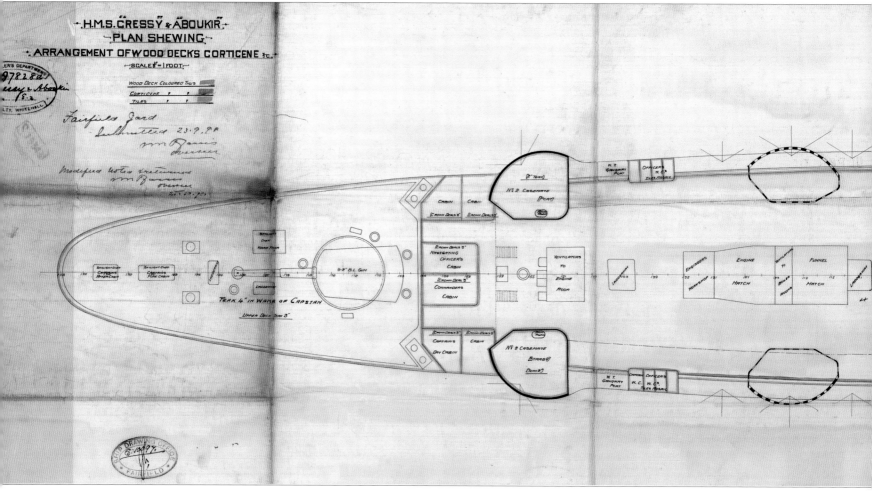

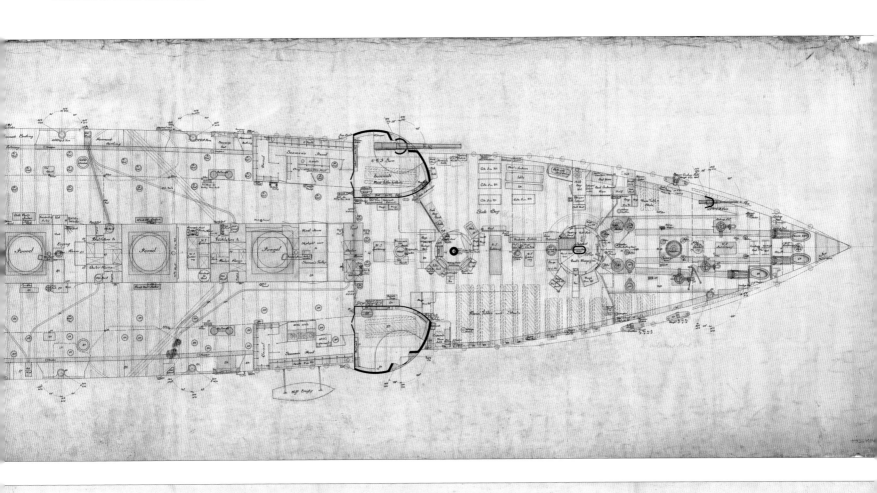

HMS *CRESSY*, UPPER DECK AS FITTED AND ARRANGEMENT OF WOOD AND CORTICENE DECKS

This plan shows the arrangement of the Upper Deck which was the highest continuous deck in the ship. The central area around the funnels between the Upper Deck 6-inch casemates and the after end of this deck were exposed to the elements. The four middle 6-inch casemates shown in dotted lines on the decking plan are the part of the group one level below. The foremost compartment on the latter drawing is quaintly labelled the 'Manger', although it had not been used for housing livestock since the days of the sailing navy. (M0191 and detail from Arrangement of Wood and Corticene Decks for *Cressy* and *Aboukir* M1581)

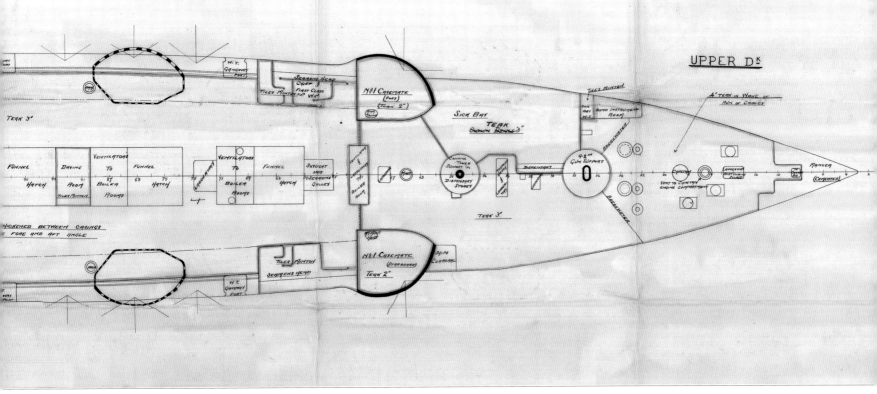

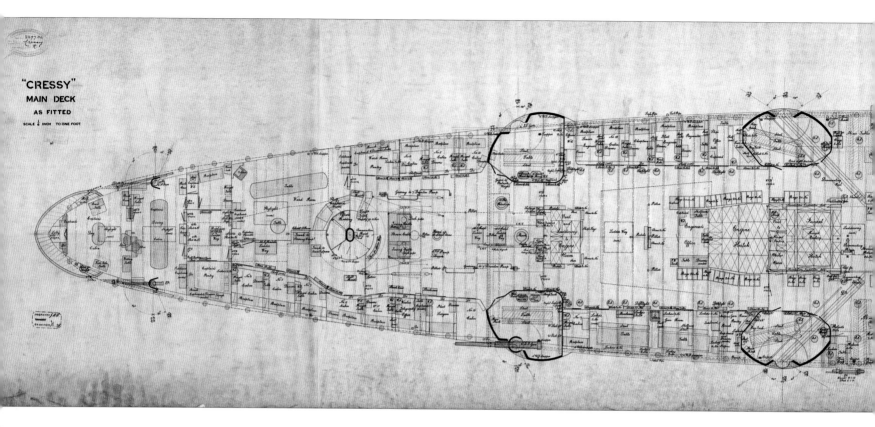

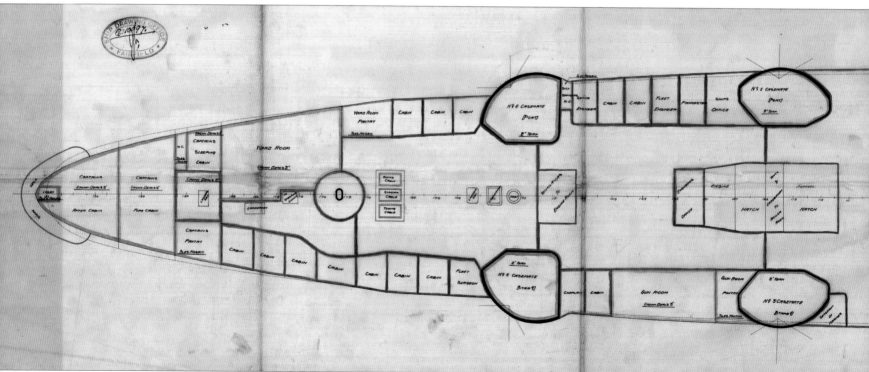

HMS *CRESSY*, MAIN DECK AS FITTED AND ARRANGEMENT OF WOOD AND CORTICENE DECKS

The Main Deck was the highest of the completely enclosed decks on the *Cressy*, and the balance it offered between shelter and good natural ventilation meant that the majority of the officer and crew accommodation was located here. Unlike the decks above where teak decking predominated, the vast majority of the deck space was covered in corticene. The exceptions were the senior officers' cabins aft, which had deal decking. The tiling arrangements also reflect the difference in rank, with officers' water closets mosaic tiled and those of other ranks Minton tiled.
(MO192 and detail from Arrangement of Wood and Corticene Decks for *Cressy* and *Aboukir* M1581)

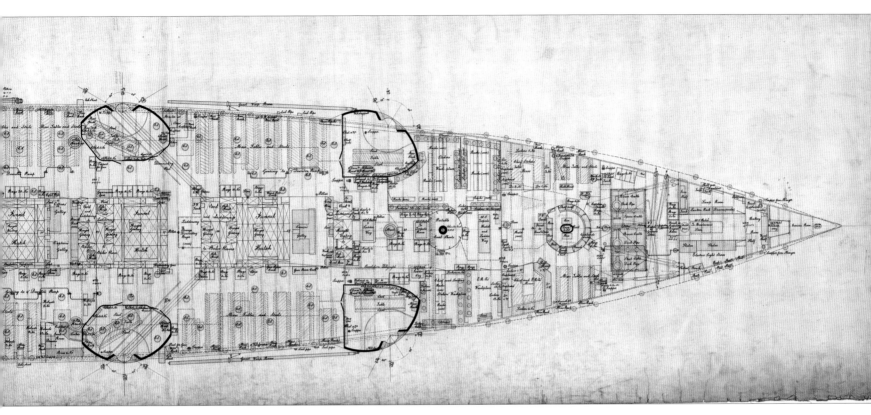

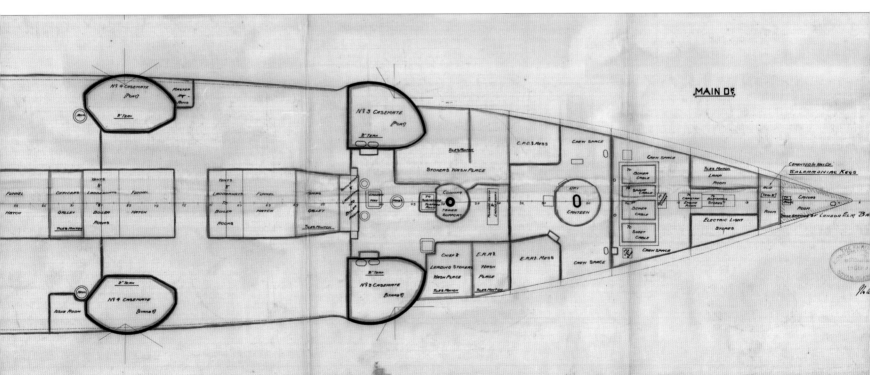

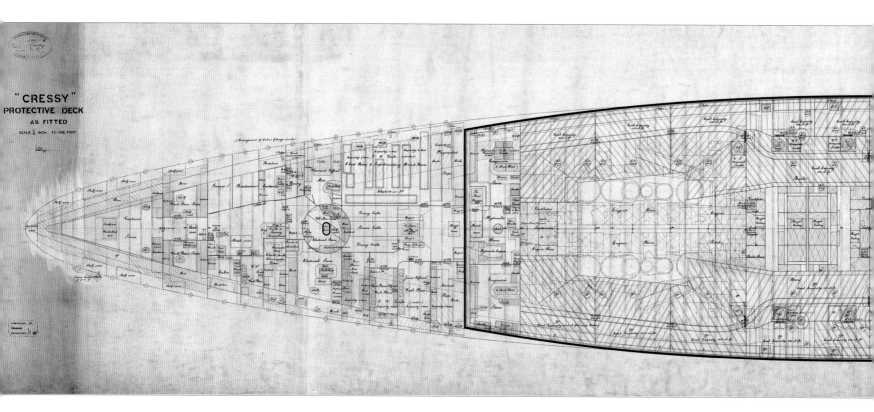

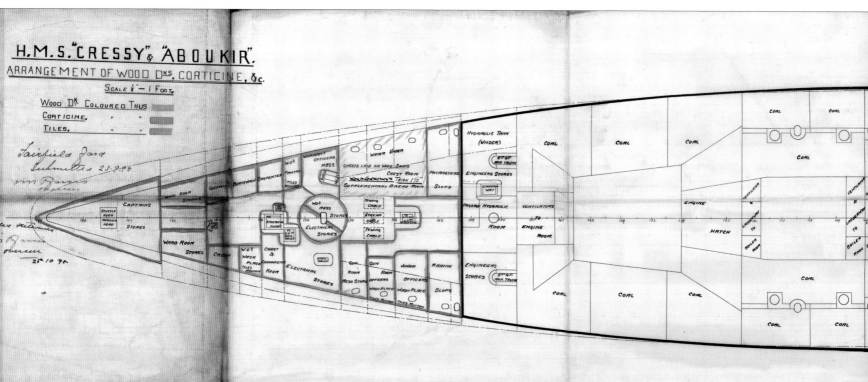

HMS *CRESSY*, PROTECTIVE/LOWER DECK AS FITTED AND ARRANGEMENT OF WOOD AND CORTICENE DECKS

The complex curve of the Protective Deck is difficult to discern in the plan view of this deck, but the space created by its steeper downward angle at the bow was utilised to insert a Lower Deck Flat, or 'mezzanine' partial deck. This is not shown in the simpler arrangement of the accompanying decking plan, presumably because the same arrangements applied to both levels. (M0193 and detail from Arrangement of Wood and Corticene Decks for *Cressy* and *Aboukir* M1582)

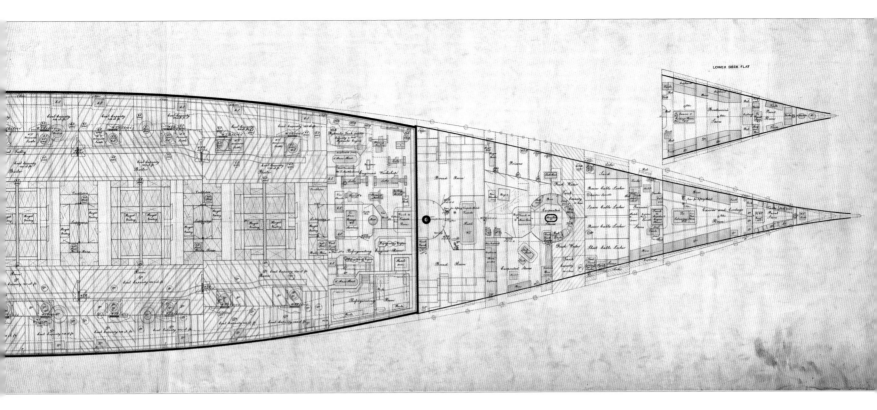

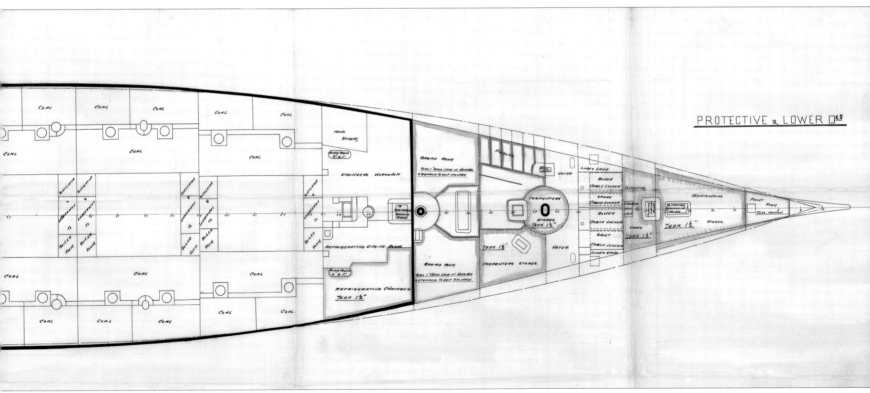

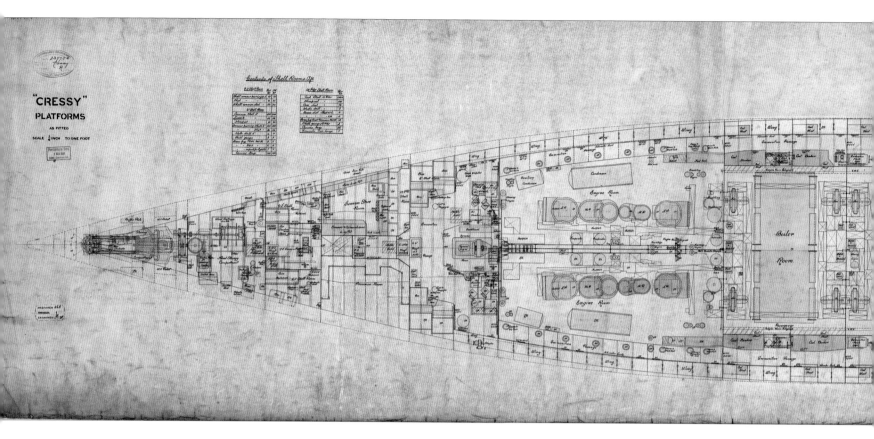

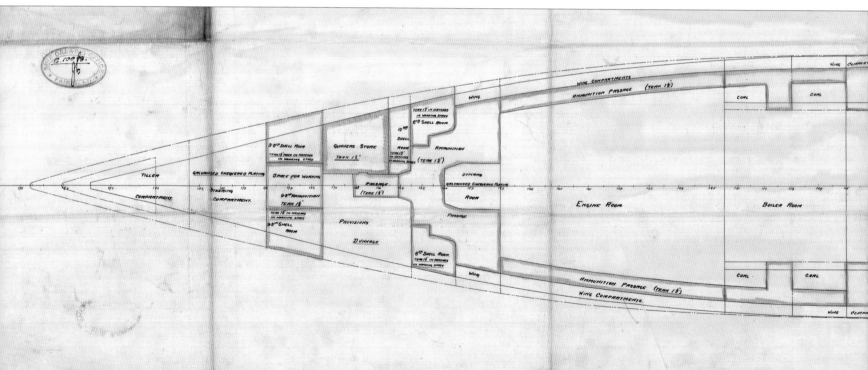

HMS *CRESSY*, PLATFORMS AS FITTED AND ARRANGEMENT OF WOOD AND CORTICENE DECKS

The Platforms were not a single continuous deck as such, but as the name suggests they were connected levels built around and roughly halfway up the boiler and machinery spaces. Communication between the fore and aft parts of this level was possible via the ammunition passages which ran along the sides. The

Platforms were below the waterline, and were the ideal place for the submerged torpedo room. (M0194 and detail from Arrangement of Wood and Corticene Decks for *Cressy* and *Aboukir* M1582)

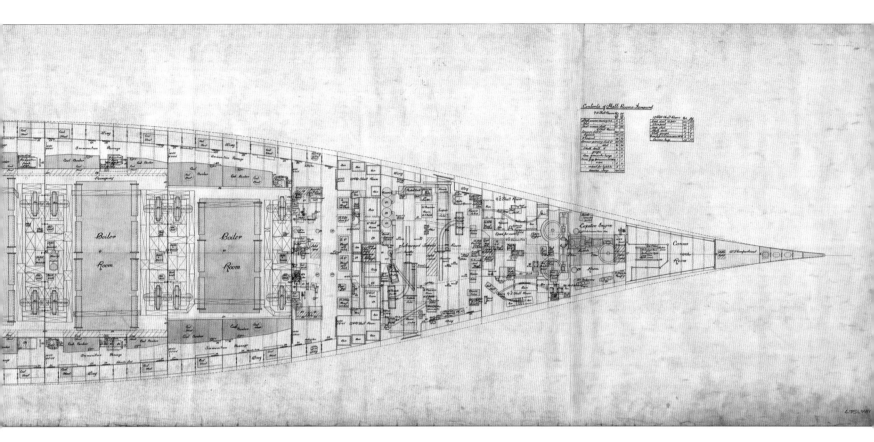

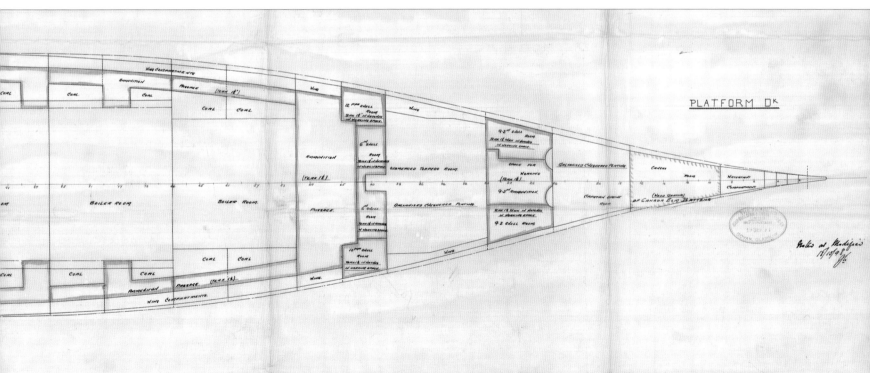

PLATFORM D^k

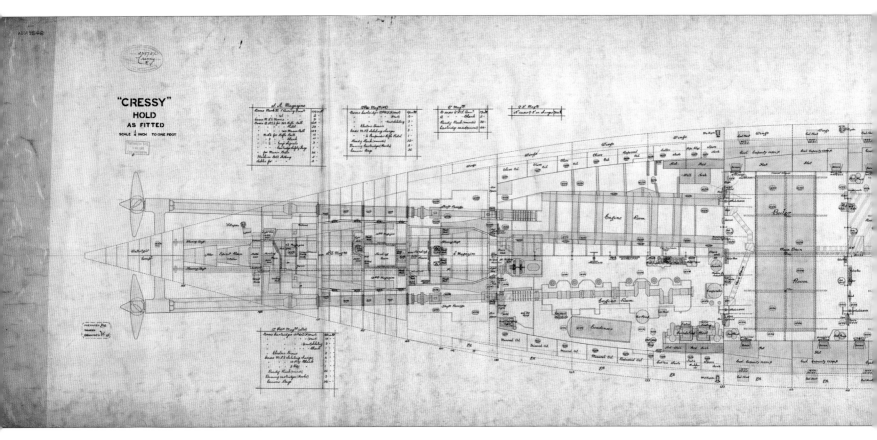

HMS *CRESSY*, HOLD AS FITTED

The Hold was the lowest deck in the ship and housed the boilers, propulsion machinery, propeller shafts, fore and aft magazines, the lower parts of the coal bunkers and in keeping with naval tradition the spirit room right aft. Portions of the cellular double bottom beneath this level were used for the stowage of reserve feed tank water for the boilers. There is no equivalent plan for deck coverings. (M0195)

HMS *CRESSY*, ARRANGEMENT OF VENTILATION

See overleaf.

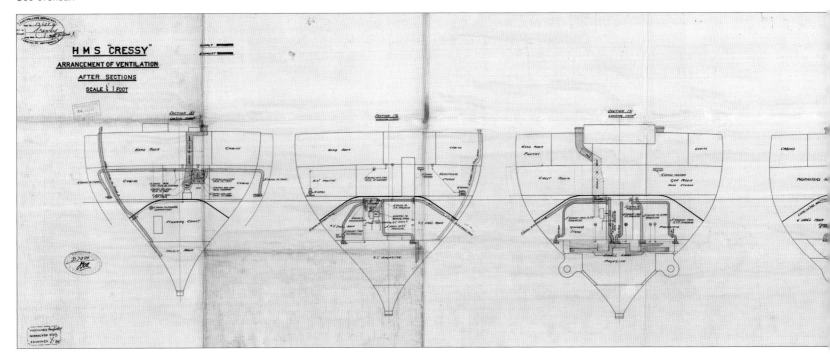

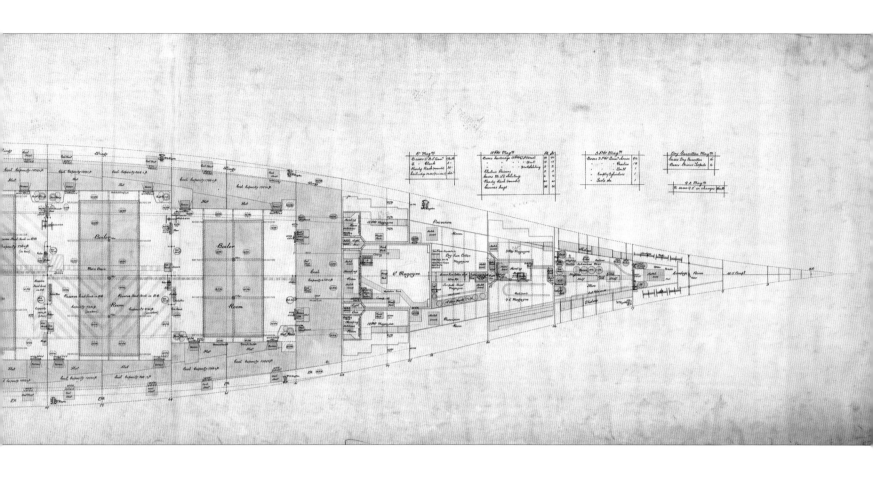

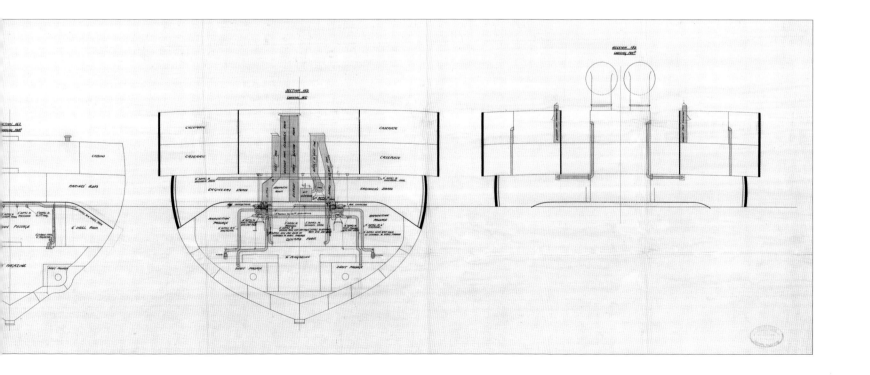

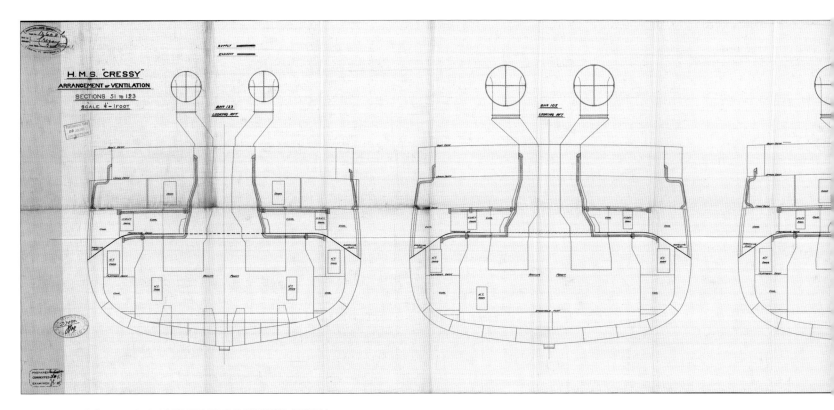

HMS *CRESSY*, ARRANGEMENT OF VENTILATION

Good ventilation systems were essential for the efficient operation of the ship's machinery as well as the comfort of the crew. Natural ventilation could serve these purposes to a degree, but had to be supplemented by mechanical means. For the men working in the lowest three decks of the ship, artificial ventilation was their most important source of fresh air. This need for ventilation and the necessity to generate 'forced draught' for the boilers was the reason for the installation of large

fans over the stokehold. This series of plans illustrates the complexity of the ventilation arrangements in *Cressy*, with the pipes colour coded blue for air supply and red for exhaust. The first (on pages 76–77) shows the area aft of the armoured citadel, the second the area which comprised the boiler rooms, and the last the area from the forward 6-inch casemates up to the bow. The greater density of pipework below the Protective Deck is evident in all three plans, as are

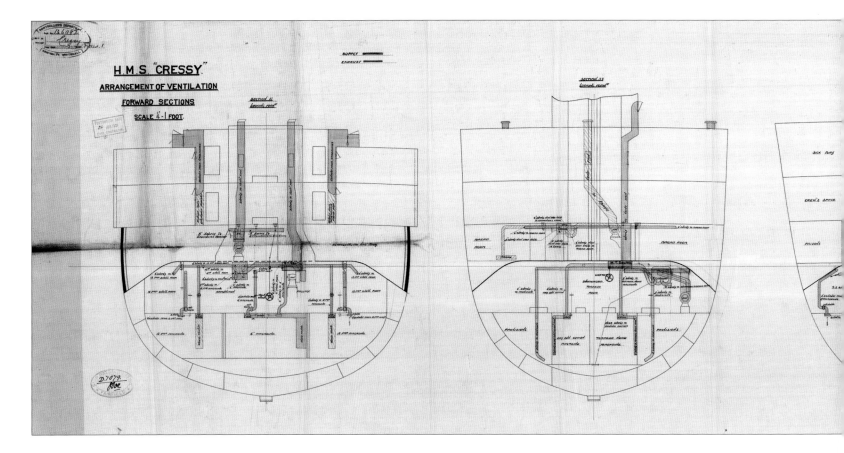

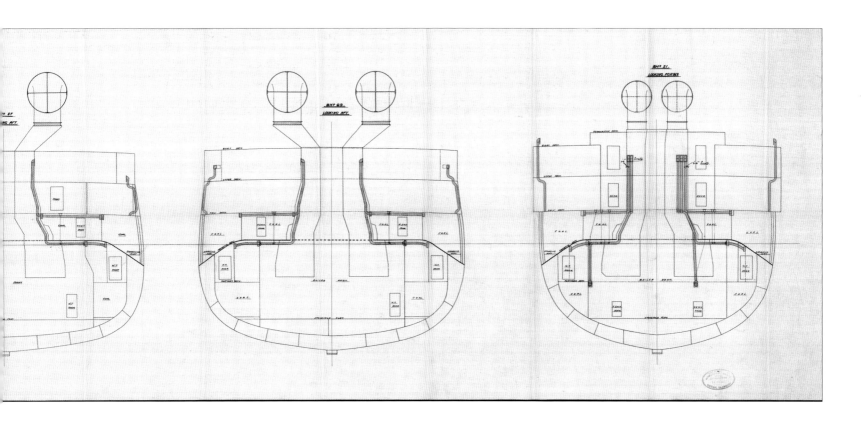

some of the systems serving the area behind the Main Deck side armour where
natural ventilation was necessarily limited. The majority of the pipes serving the
boiler spaces carry both blue and red colour-coding. These represent single-
purpose pipes arranged side by side rather than dual purpose. An interesting
feature is the outline of the windsails that could be fitted at the bow to supply
ventilation to the paint and cordage rooms below. (M1735, M1736 and M1737)

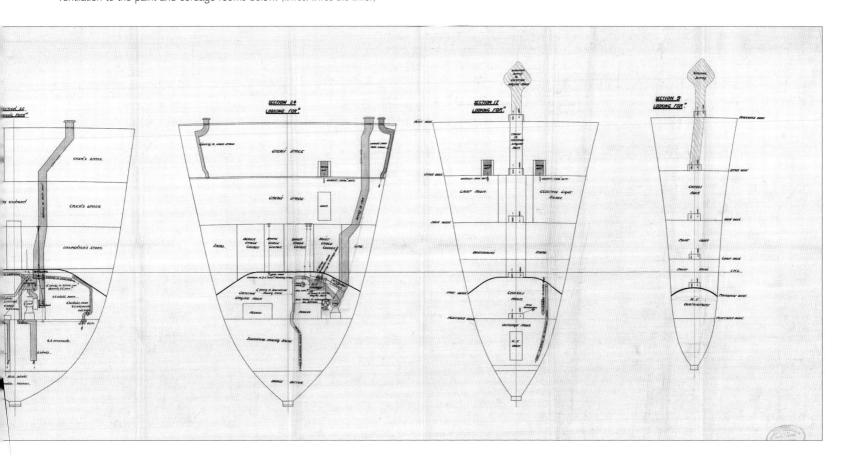

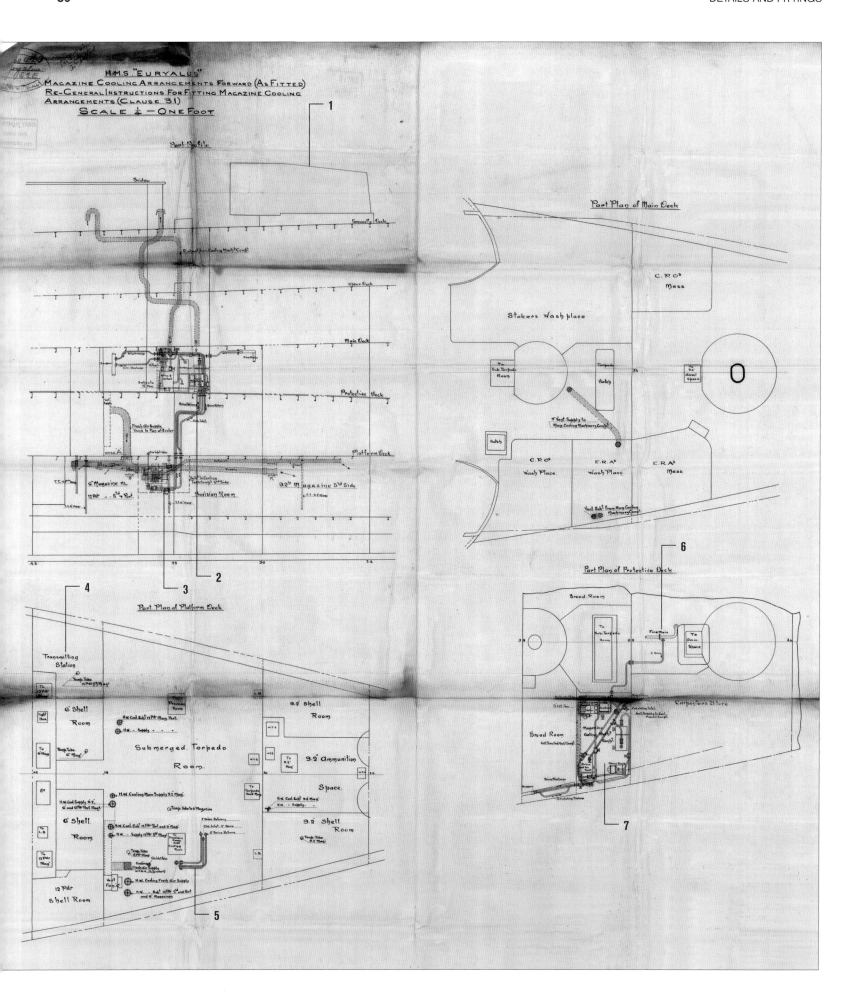

H.M.S. "EURYALUS"
MAGAZINE COOLING ARRANGEMENTS FORWARD (AS FITTED)
RE-GENERAL INSTRUCTIONS FOR FITTING MAGAZINE COOLING
ARRANGEMENTS (CLAUSE 31)
SCALE ¼ = ONE FOOT

HMS *EURYALUS*, MAGAZINE COOLING ARRANGEMENTS

This plan and its counterpart on the following pages illustrate the cooling arrangements for the fore and aft magazines of one of *Cressy*'s sister ships as these stood in 1910. Maintenance of safe temperatures in magazines had long been a concern in the Royal Navy, and despite a general perception at the turn of the twentieth century that cordite was a stable and safe propellant, strenuous efforts were made to keep magazines as cool as possible. No drawings of this nature appear to have survived for *Cressy*, but it is very likely that she would have possessed at least similar fittings. The drawings show elevation and plan views of the air cooling machinery (offset to starboard both fore and aft) and the manner in which it was integrated into the ventilation system, utilising the same colour coding of blue for air supply and red for air exhaust. They also include tables of operators' instructions for using the systems at different settings, and how they can be adjusted for different magazines. In addition to their primary purpose, these drawings are also interesting for some of the peripheral details they show. The most notable of these is the provision of a gunnery transmitting station on the port side of the Platform Deck just aft of the submerged torpedo room. When *Cressy* and her sisters were commissioned this space was a magazine for the 12-pounder armament, and its re-purposing as shown here is an important example of the adaptation of these ships to accommodate advances in naval gunnery techniques. (M1577 and M1578)

1. Forward 9.2-inch gun gunhouse.
2. Elevation view of magazine cooling machinery showing the brine and ice tank, condenser and pump.
3. Elevation view of cooling tank compartment.
4. The transmitting station which replaced the 12-pounder magazine in this space.
5. Brine delivery and return pipes linking the magazine cooling machinery on the Protective Deck with the cooling tank in the Hold.
6. Fire main.
7. Plan view of the magazine cooling machinery compartment, showing the arrangement of the pumps, condenser, evaporator and brine and ice tank.
8. Plan view of the ventilation and cooling pipe runs in the magazines.
9. Plan view of the cooling tank compartment and the adjacent exhaust fan.
10. Instructions for operation of the cooling system, table of colour-coding for ventilation/cooling and water pipes and notes on lagging.

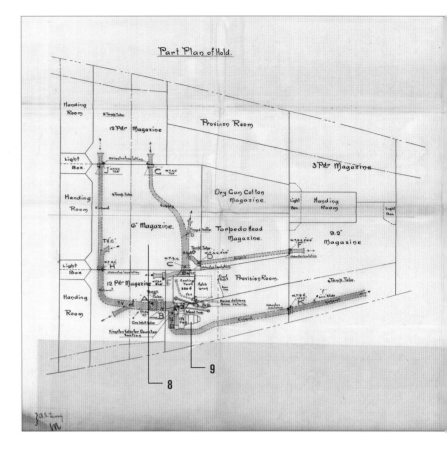

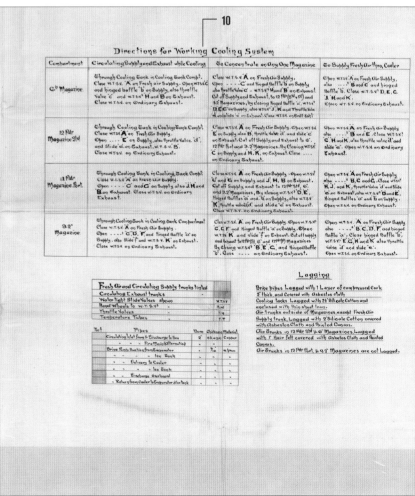

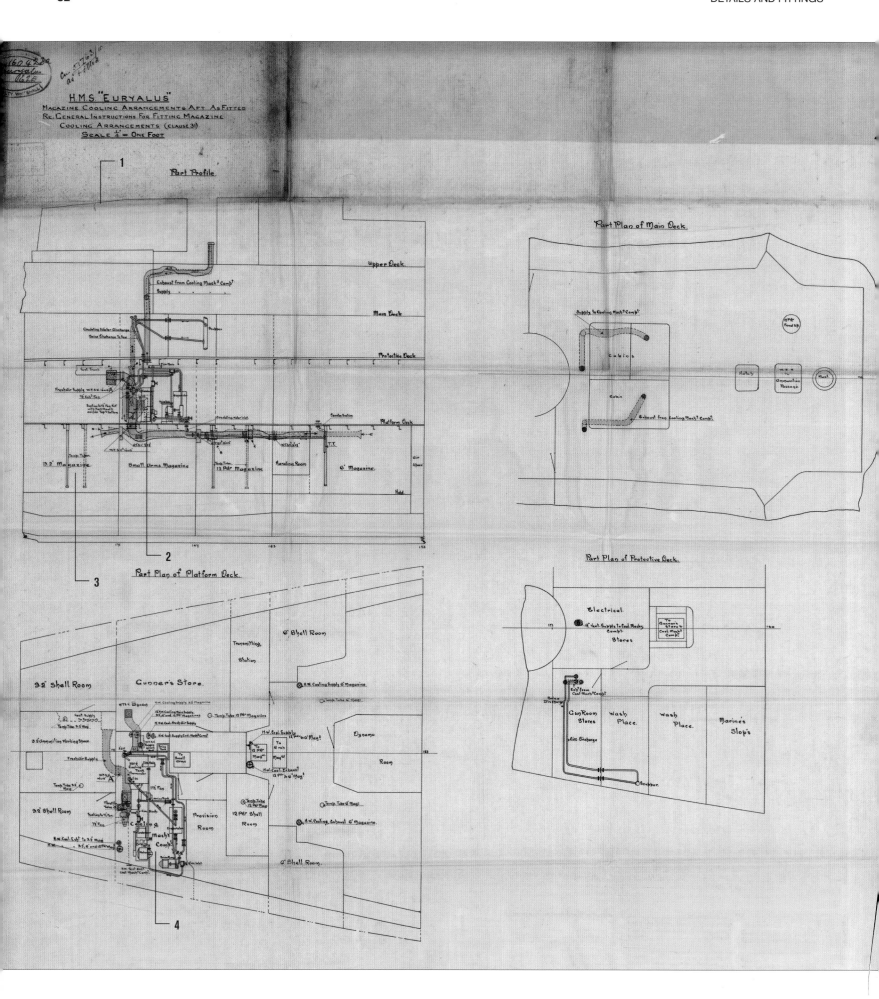

H.M.S. "EURYALUS"
MAGAZINE COOLING ARRANGEMENTS AFT AS FITTED
Re. GENERAL INSTRUCTIONS FOR FITTING MAGAZINE
COOLING ARRANGEMENTS (CLAUSE 31)
SCALE ¼" = ONE FOOT

Part Profile.

Part Plan of Main Deck.

Part Plan of Platform Deck.

Part Plan of Protective Deck.

FRAME 185 (LOOKING AFT)

The half-section at this frame shows the arrangement of the starboard side of the hull, showing the structural arrangement of the shaft 'A' bracket in reasonable detail for this scale. The narrowness of the hull and very cramped arrangement of the tiller compartment is clearer in this view than in the profile, as is the heavy structural reinforcement required to support the protective plating and the 'A' bracket. Note the additional line of heavy plating which runs from the crown of the Protective Deck to join the top of the upper strut of the 'A' bracket.

The Captain's Pantry, showing the sliding door and bench with built-in cupboard. This was situated opposite the Captain's Sleeping Cabin.

Lobby separating the Captain's Pantry and Sleeping Cabin. A ladderway ran through this space down to Protective Deck level, as indicated by the coamings on the plan. Although not shown here, this area had racks for rifles and ready-use ammunition for the 12-pounder guns in the Captain's Dining Room, and also the safe for the Shell Room keys.

One of two Wardroom Stores in this area, the other being on the port side, showing the various storage units.

Watertight compartment occupying the space formed by the curve of the protective plating and a 'platform' constructed over it to form the deck of the Wardroom Store.

Starboard 'A' bracket for the propeller shaft. Frame brackets such as this are more suitable for fast ships and despite the slender appearance of the struts represent a very strong structure.

Tiller Compartment showing the steering gear. This shows the space following the steering gear failure and subsequent repairs which delayed *Cressy*'s departure for the China Station.

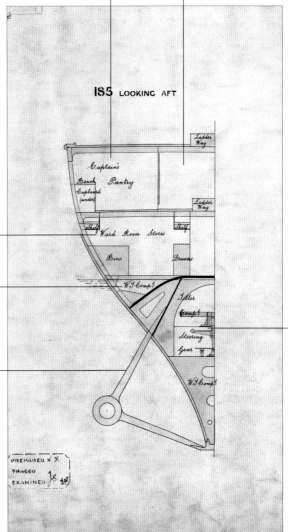

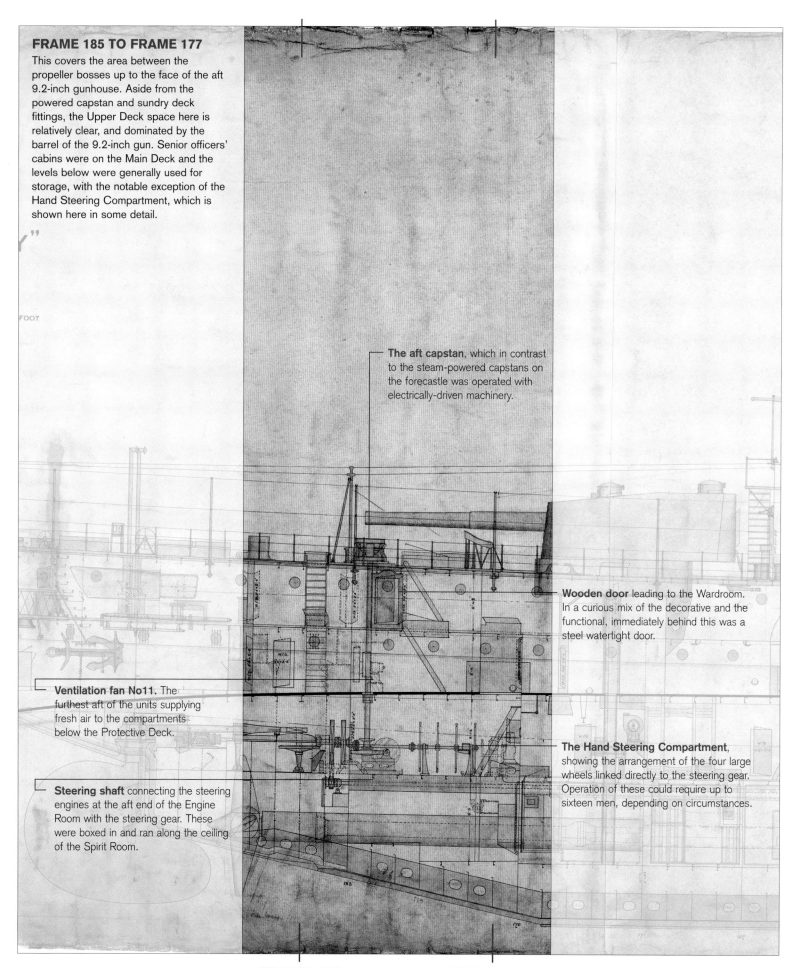

FRAME 185 TO FRAME 177

This covers the area between the propeller bosses up to the face of the aft 9.2-inch gunhouse. Aside from the powered capstan and sundry deck fittings, the Upper Deck space here is relatively clear, and dominated by the barrel of the 9.2-inch gun. Senior officers' cabins were on the Main Deck and the levels below were generally used for storage, with the notable exception of the Hand Steering Compartment, which is shown here in some detail.

The aft capstan, which in contrast to the steam-powered capstans on the forecastle was operated with electrically-driven machinery.

Wooden door leading to the Wardroom. In a curious mix of the decorative and the functional, immediately behind this was a steel watertight door.

Ventilation fan No11. The furthest aft of the units supplying fresh air to the compartments below the Protective Deck.

The Hand Steering Compartment, showing the arrangement of the four large wheels linked directly to the steering gear. Operation of these could require up to sixteen men, depending on circumstances.

Steering shaft connecting the steering engines at the aft end of the Engine Room with the steering gear. These were boxed in and ran along the ceiling of the Spirit Room.

FRAME 185   **FRAME 177**

FRAME 177 (LOOKING AFT)

This section shows the arrangement of the hull at almost the forward end of the Hand Steering Compartment. The Main Deck in this area is still primarily devoted to accommodation for senior officers and the Protective Deck to storage, with the more vital compartments below the Protective Deck continuing to comprise steering mechanisms and stores of a more sensitive nature (in this case the Spirit Room).

The depression rail for the 9.2-inch gun. As the name implies the purpose of this structure was to limit the depression of the gun at certain angles of train to minimise blast damage to the ship. These rails were not permanent structures and stowage space was allocated for them in their dismantled state on the Boat Deck. Note the difference between this and the smaller rail shown in the Vickers design (page 41).

A senior officer's cabin, and one reasonably representative of its type in size and amenities. The metal shelf shown on the drawing was one of two in each room, the other running longitudinally at the same height. On the left is a cross-section of the bed place, showing the storage space underneath. The table in the centre was hinged to provide more space when it was not in use, and to the right of it is a wash stand. In addition to these, the cabins on this deck were furnished with an additional chest of drawers. The space outside where the rifle rack is mounted is the lobby between the cabins and the Wardroom.

The Chronometer Room, showing some of the shelves, cupboards and the chronometer chest. The purpose of the cofferdam formed by the dwarf bulkhead adjacent to the chest was to help limit water ingress in the event of flooding.

The propeller shaft. Given the distance between it and the hull, and the close proximity of the Chronometer and Spirit Rooms, it is perhaps just as well that vibration from *Cressy*'s engines and shafts was reportedly very low.

Trunked ladderway leading to the Hand Steering Compartment. This provided both access to the compartment as well as a means of escape in an emergency. The presence of this trunk compromised the Protective Deck, and a hinged armoured grating was fitted to cover the gap.

The Hand Steering Compartment showing a detailed forward elevation view of the compass and telemotor steering wheel. This was the fifth such steering position in the ship, and its presence indicates the huge importance placed on redundancy in steering capacity to offset the impact of battle damage. The large hand steering wheels are not shown in this half-section because they were offset to port.

The Spirit Room, although none of the casks or racks are shown. The cupboards close to deck level were for the use of the engineering personnel, and occupied the forward end of this compartment. The tanks to the side and slightly above the cupboards were used for storing varnish.

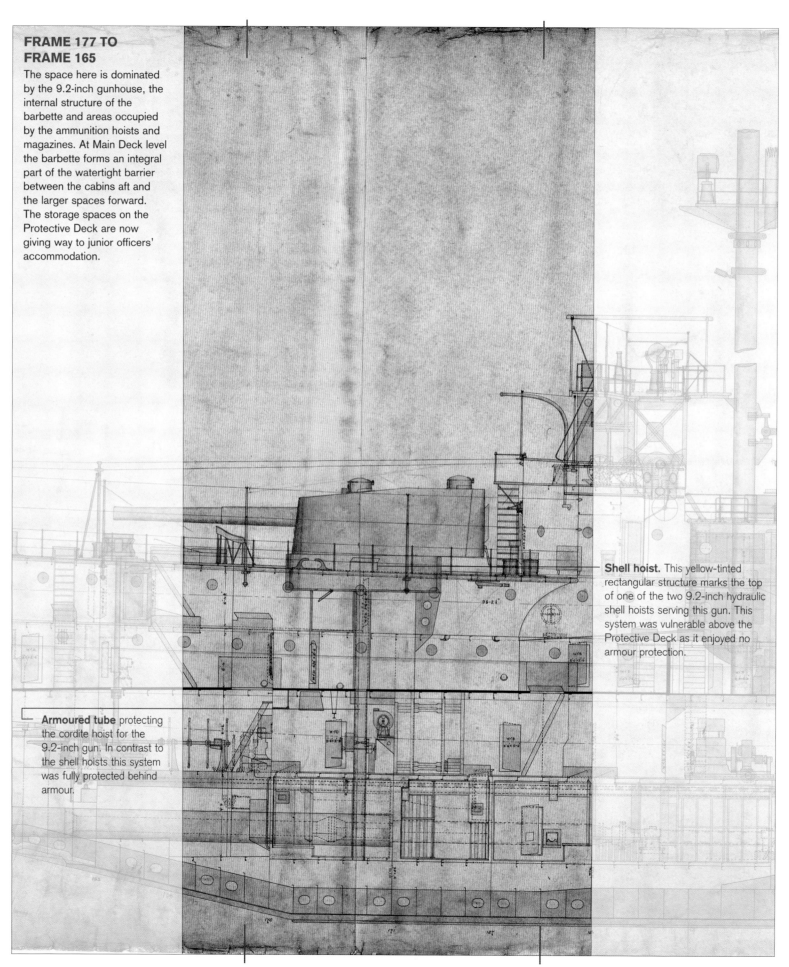

FRAME 177 TO FRAME 165

The space here is dominated by the 9.2-inch gunhouse, the internal structure of the barbette and areas occupied by the ammunition hoists and magazines. At Main Deck level the barbette forms an integral part of the watertight barrier between the cabins aft and the larger spaces forward. The storage spaces on the Protective Deck are now giving way to junior officers' accommodation.

Shell hoist. This yellow-tinted rectangular structure marks the top of one of the two 9.2-inch hydraulic shell hoists serving this gun. This system was vulnerable above the Protective Deck as it enjoyed no armour protection.

Armoured tube protecting the cordite hoist for the 9.2-inch gun. In contrast to the shell hoists this system was fully protected behind armour.

FRAME 177   **FRAME 165**

FRAME 165 (LOOKING AFT)

The illustration here shows the point at which the propeller shafts emerge from the hull. The narrowness of the shelter deck (the aft end of the Boat/Forecastle Deck) and supporting superstructure is due to the latter being angled inboard to allow a greater field of fire for the 9.2-inch gun on forward bearings. This arrangement permitted an additional 15° of firing arc forward of the beam. In most other respects, the pattern of the previous sections is continued with accommodation spaces occupying the spaces above the Protective Deck and storage below – in this particular instance one of the Provision Rooms and part of the 12-pounder magazine and Handing Room.

The Captain's and Commander's Deck Cabins on the Upper Deck and Fleet Surgeon's Cabin below make for an interesting comparison. The apparent lack of space in the first is again due to the narrowing of the superstructure. The Commander's Cabin shows some of the superior furnishing, most notably the kneehole desk and book rack, but even this does not do full justice to these spaces. Not shown here is the stove which was installed in the Captain's Deck Cabin, a feature not enjoyed by any others in the vicinity of the after superstructure. The accommodation and amenities details for this area are completed by the communal Junior Officers' Wash Place on the Protective Deck. The fresh water tank beneath this was an unrelated system, as the limited supply onboard was needed for crew consumption and the boilers.

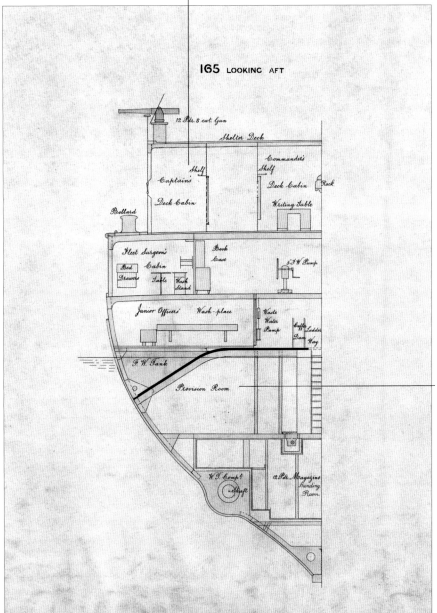

The Provision Rooms were intended for storage of consumables that did not require special treatment (*eg* bread) and that did not have to be refrigerated. It was not mirrored on the opposite side of the ship, the equivalent compartments there being the Gunner's Store and a 12-pounder Shell Room. Below these were the 12-pounder magazines, the latter arranged on each side of the hull near the propeller shafts separated by the Handing Room in the middle.

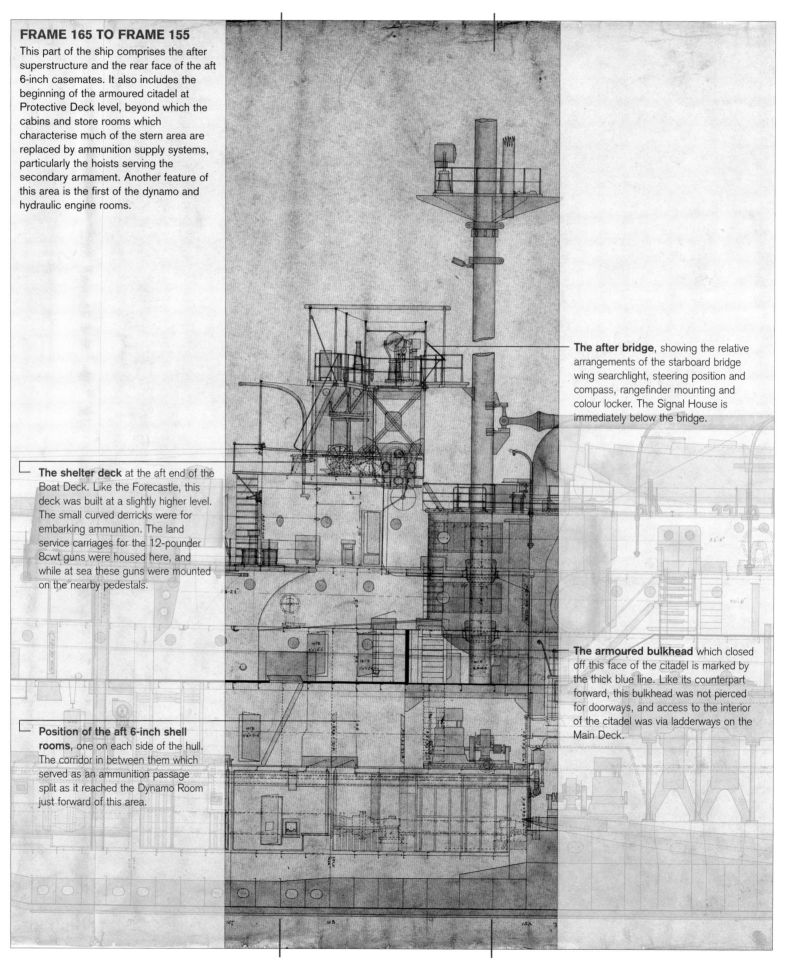

FRAME 165 TO FRAME 155
This part of the ship comprises the after superstructure and the rear face of the aft 6-inch casemates. It also includes the beginning of the armoured citadel at Protective Deck level, beyond which the cabins and store rooms which characterise much of the stern area are replaced by ammunition supply systems, particularly the hoists serving the secondary armament. Another feature of this area is the first of the dynamo and hydraulic engine rooms.

The after bridge, showing the relative arrangements of the starboard bridge wing searchlight, steering position and compass, rangefinder mounting and colour locker. The Signal House is immediately below the bridge.

The shelter deck at the aft end of the Boat Deck. Like the Forecastle, this deck was built at a slightly higher level. The small curved derricks were for embarking ammunition. The land service carriages for the 12-pounder 8cwt guns were housed here, and while at sea these guns were mounted on the nearby pedestals.

The armoured bulkhead which closed off this face of the citadel is marked by the thick blue line. Like its counterpart forward, this bulkhead was not pierced for doorways, and access to the interior of the citadel was via ladderways on the Main Deck.

Position of the aft 6-inch shell rooms, one on each side of the hull. The corridor in between them which served as an ammunition passage split as it reached the Dynamo Room just forward of this area.

FRAME 165   **FRAME 155**

FRAME 155 (LOOKING AFT)

This section shows the arrangement of the 6-inch casemates and the extent to which they project from the hull. It also illustrates the structural challenges they represent in terms of building in sufficient strength to support the weight of the guns and armour in a two-storey arrangement, in addition to the side armour beneath the casemates. The relatively open areas inboard of the casemates up to the mainmast are also clearly shown, contrasting with the much busier arrangements below the Main Deck.

Interior of the 6-inch casemates, showing a reasonable amount of detail in terms of the position of the guns and shell racks. The plan shows how the ammunition supply system served the guns, with the trunk of the ammunition hoist for the lower casemate passing through the Engineer's Store from the ammunition passage below. A second, separate hoist immediately forward of this one served the upper casemate. These hoists brought up both shells and cordite charges which were brought to the ammunition passage from shell rooms and magazines.

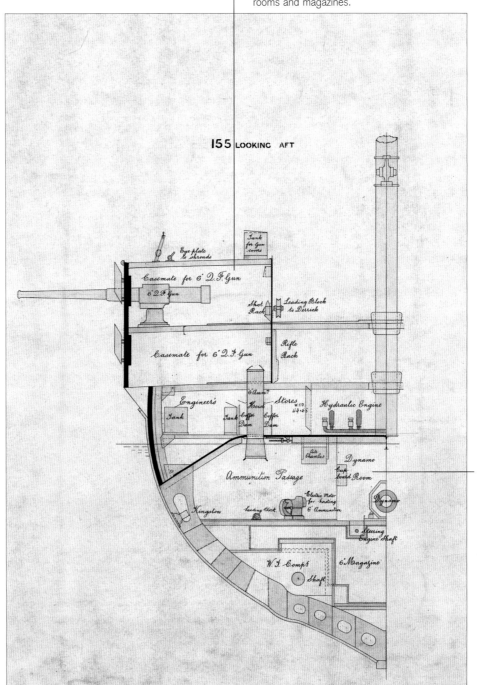

The Dynamo Room, housing one of the ship's three dynamos. In addition to the primary task of supplying electricity for lighting, these also provided power for a variety of other shipboard devices such as the aft capstan engines and the smaller ammunition hoists. The placement of all three in very close proximity to each other (the other two were in the Engine Room) made design sense in the 1890s, but was a very vulnerable arrangement.

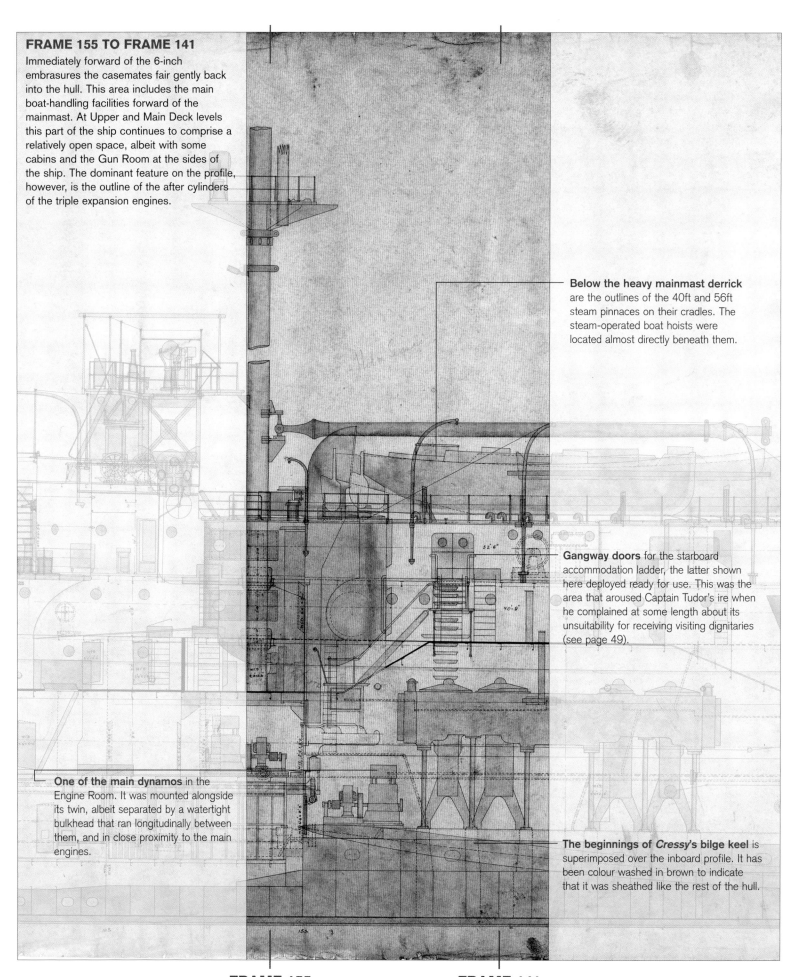

FRAME 155 TO FRAME 141
Immediately forward of the 6-inch
embrasures the casemates fair gently back
into the hull. This area includes the main
boat-handling facilities forward of the
mainmast. At Upper and Main Deck levels
this part of the ship continues to comprise a
relatively open space, albeit with some
cabins and the Gun Room at the sides of
the ship. The dominant feature on the profile,
however, is the outline of the after cylinders
of the triple expansion engines.

Below the heavy mainmast derrick
are the outlines of the 40ft and 56ft
steam pinnaces on their cradles. The
steam-operated boat hoists were
located almost directly beneath them.

Gangway doors for the starboard
accommodation ladder, the latter shown
here deployed ready for use. This was the
area that aroused Captain Tudor's ire when
he complained at some length about its
unsuitability for receiving visiting dignitaries
(see page 49).

One of the main dynamos in the
Engine Room. It was mounted alongside
its twin, albeit separated by a watertight
bulkhead that ran longitudinally between
them, and in close proximity to the main
engines.

The beginnings of *Cressy*'s **bilge keel** is
superimposed over the inboard profile. It has
been colour washed in brown to indicate
that it was sheathed like the rest of the hull.

FRAME 155   **FRAME 141**

FRAME 141 (LOOKING AFT)

The contrast between the upper decks and the much more comprehensively protected lower decks is very evident in this section. The crown of the Protective Deck has been raised to Main Deck level to ensure adequate protection for the triple expansion engines. The arrangement of the coal bunkers demonstrates the part that the ship's fuel played in the overall protection scheme, supplementing the protection of the side armour by potentially dispersing the force of a penetrating hit before the Protective Deck is affected.

The Captain's Water Closet on the Upper Deck was part of a quartet of such facilities for senior officers, although naturally his was somewhat larger than the other three. Beneath these was the large and well-furnished Gun Room, which among its creature comforts included a stove. These arrangements were mirrored on the port side, although in the case of the WCs they were for the use of junior officers, while the compartments opposite the Gun Room were cabins.

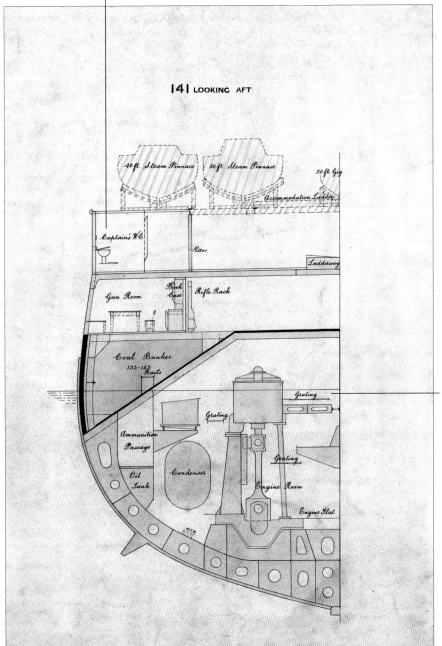

The Engine Room. This elevation view illustrates the cramped nature of this space, despite it being the largest compartment in the ship. The gratings running between and around the engines give some impression of their size, as well as the scale of the seatings which housed them.

FRAME 107 (LOOKING FORWARD)

The viewpoint shifts from aft to forward in this section, although the perspective is still from the starboard side. The ventilation cowl is one of the pair just aft of the third funnel, placing this section roughly in between the previous Frame 141 and the next illustration at Frame 63. The reason for this is the relative uniformity of the hull form along the boiler and machinery spaces.

Ventilation to the Boiler Rooms. The main system is well illustrated in this illustration, and in simplified form it is possible to trace the passage of air from the cowl down the ventilation trunk and to the Boiler Room ducts via the large fan at Platform Deck level.

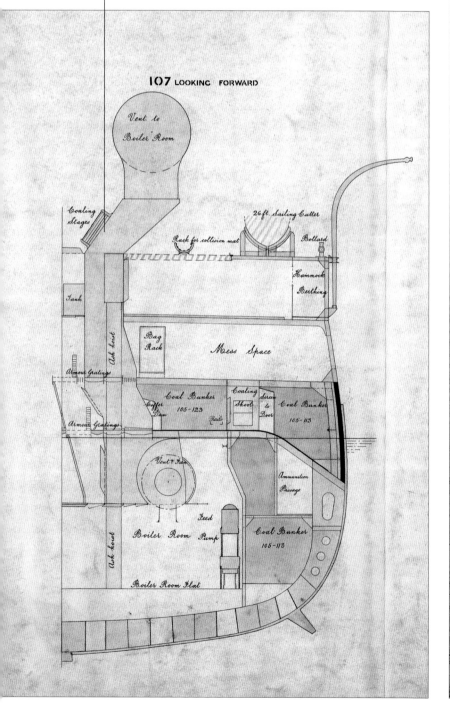

FRAME 141 TO FRAME 63

This large area of *Cressy*'s hull was taken up primarily by her propulsive machinery and the coal bunkers required to sustain it. A significant amount of space was also necessarily absorbed by the large funnel uptakes. Nonetheless, there was still sufficient room for extensive if somewhat cramped mess areas and the amidships 6-inch casemates on the Main Deck, as well as a lighter battery of 12-pounder guns on the Upper Deck.

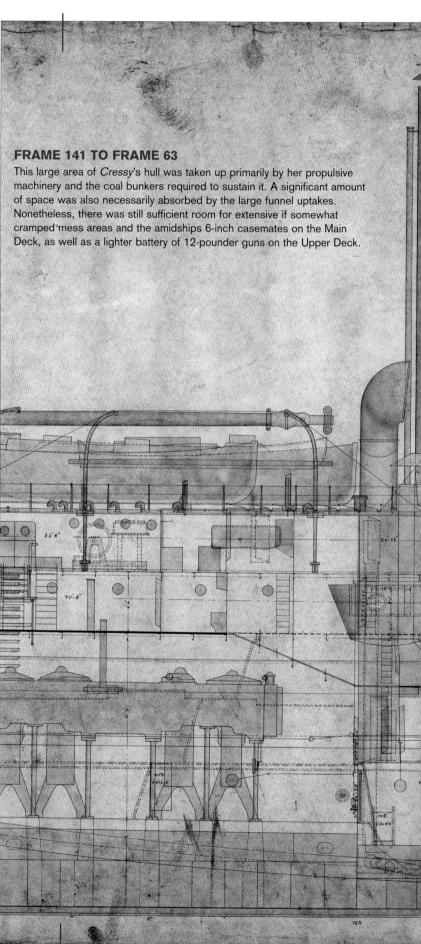

FRAME 141

FRAME 63 (LOOKING FORWARD)

Section through the forward boiler room and fore funnel, showing an outline view of the boilers and the surrounding coal bunkers. From this frame aft to Frame 141 almost the entirety of the Protective Deck was devoted to bunker space. The Main and Upper Decks comprised mess space and other crew amenities, with limited storage space on the Boat Deck for various items of equipment, some of which are illustrated here.

Bare, undecked beams, denoted by the hatched blue lines. These were strong enough to support a reasonable amount of weight, including as shown here a rail for use with the ash shoots and a Temperley transporter overhead crane in its stowed position. The bipod structure on the other side of the inboard guardrail is a stand for an electric wire drum.

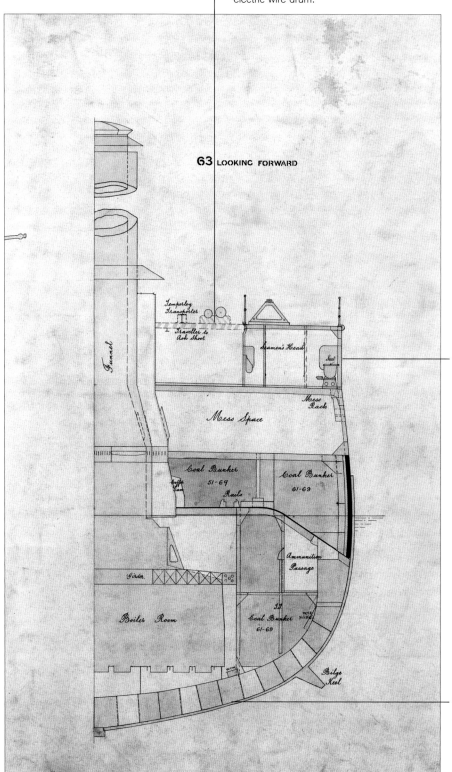

Seamen's Heads. A convention of late Victorian warship design was the habit of placing the seamen's heads in or close by the forward part of the superstructure. This section shows the Seamen's Head in some detail, illustrating the urinals to the left and toilets to the right.

The cellular double bottom. A significant percentage of this space was used to house reserve feed water for the boilers. *Cressy* had the capacity to store 98 tons in this manner.

FRAME 63 TO FRAME 38

This area comprises the forward end of the Boat Deck between the fore funnel and the break of the forecastle. Like the shelter deck aft, the forecastle was constructed slightly higher than the level of the Boat Deck, forming what was known as a 'topgallant forecastle'. The Seamen's Heads and mess spaces slightly overlap the forward 6-inch casemates, while the machinery spaces below come to an end at Frame 51. Forward of this on the Protective Deck is the hoist machinery and ammunition passages serving the forward 6-inch guns in an arrangement which mirrors the system employed to serve the aft casemates. The area shaded grey in the Hold is a transverse coal bunker running across the front of the boiler room.

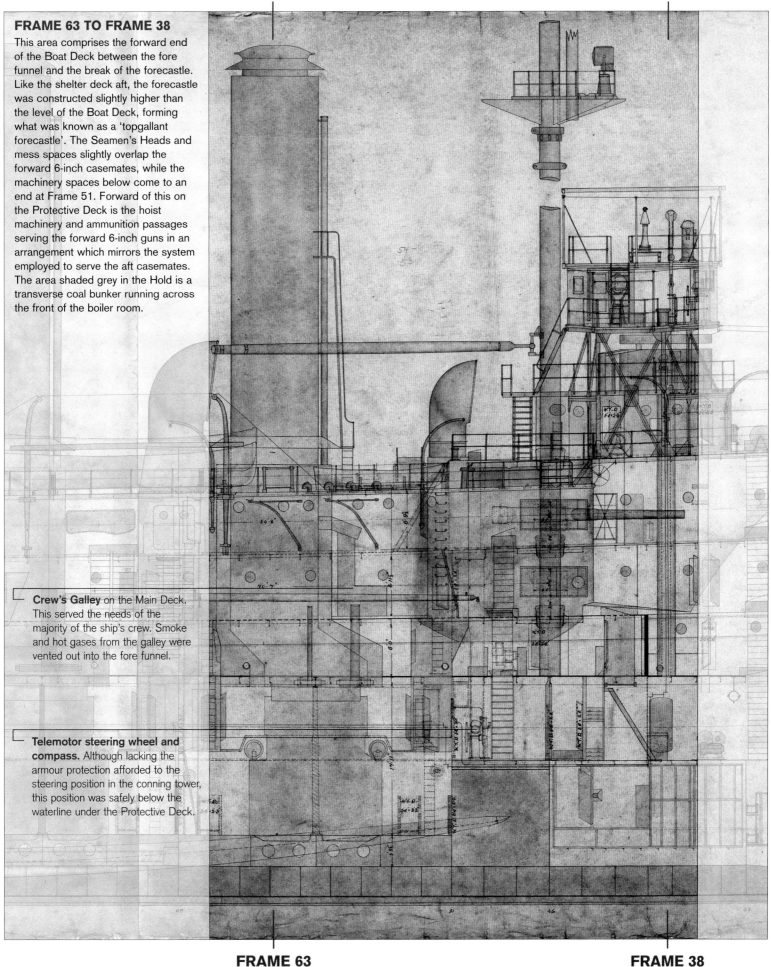

Crew's Galley on the Main Deck. This served the needs of the majority of the ship's crew. Smoke and hot gases from the galley were vented out into the fore funnel.

Telemotor steering wheel and compass. Although lacking the armour protection afforded to the steering position in the conning tower, this position was safely below the waterline under the Protective Deck.

FRAME 63

FRAME 38

FRAME 38 (LOOKING FORWARD)

This section emphasises the commanding height of the bridge and forward superstructure, an aspect subconsciously reinforced by the fact that it is a half-section. The most notable feature is the heavily armoured conning tower and the communication tube for the telemotor lead pipes running down to the

bottom of the Protective Deck. The surrounding compartments for the most part comprise mess spaces, crew amenities such as the Stokers' Wash Place and the Dispensary, and the Bread Room. The submerged torpedo room is shown above the magazines.

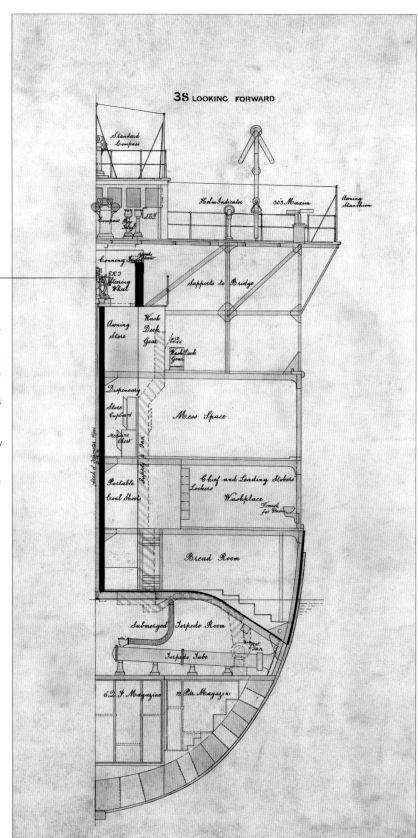

The armoured conning tower.
The concept behind this was that it could provide a secure command and control position for senior officers and the helmsman in battle. In reality, the space was very cramped, a fact made worse by the inclusion of the port and starboard torpedo directors in this small space. Another problem was the very limited field of vision, which could be affected by spray in heavy weather. By the First World War many captains preferred to eschew the safety of this position for the more vulnerable bridge or compass platform, from which they could enjoy better situational awareness.

FRAME 38 TO FRAME 27

This part shows the face of the forward superstructure up to roughly the centreline of the 9.2-inch gunhouse. The heavy armour of the citadel ended just before this point, giving way to the thinner 2in plates which protected the bow. The Upper and Main Decks comprised more mess spaces, clustered around the Sick Bay which was on the port side of the Upper Deck The submerged torpedo room and its magazine occupied the Platform Deck and Hold respectively.

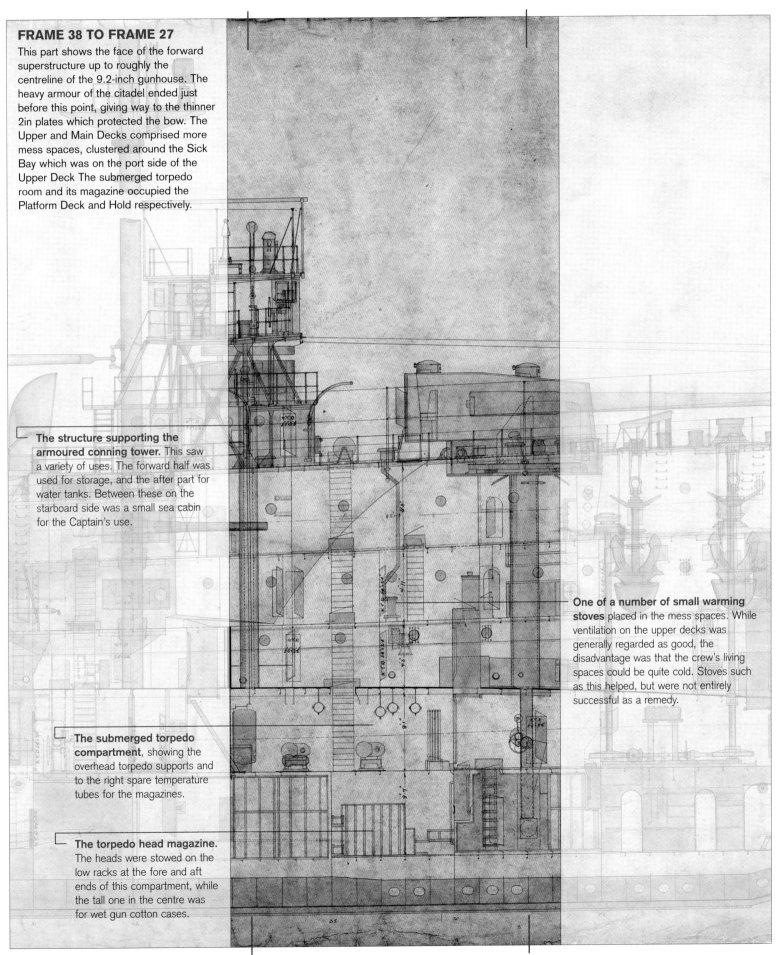

The structure supporting the armoured conning tower. This saw a variety of uses. The forward half was used for storage, and the after part for water tanks. Between these on the starboard side was a small sea cabin for the Captain's use.

One of a number of small warming stoves placed in the mess spaces. While ventilation on the upper decks was generally regarded as good, the disadvantage was that the crew's living spaces could be quite cold. Stoves such as this helped, but were not entirely successful as a remedy.

The submerged torpedo compartment, showing the overhead torpedo supports and to the right spare temperature tubes for the magazines.

The torpedo head magazine. The heads were stowed on the low racks at the fore and aft ends of this compartment, while the tall one in the centre was for wet gun cotton cases.

FRAME 38

FRAME 27

FRAME 27 (LOOKING FORWARD)

The interior of the forward 9.2-inch gunhouse is shown in some detail, as are the shell rooms and magazines that serve it. In keeping with the layout immediately aft of here the Upper and Main Decks contain mess spaces. These are built around the base of the barbette, the interior of which has been used for storage space. From Frames 27 to 24 the Protective Deck holds fresh water tanks with a combined capacity of 56½ tons.

The breech of the 9.2-inch gun.
This illustration also shows the top of the cordite hoist which is offset to the right. Interestingly, it bears a closer resemblance to the Vickers design drawing than Midshipman Leeke's sketch (pages 42–43). The mechanism for passing cordite charges up the armoured tube to the gunhouse is partially visible on the Platform Deck.

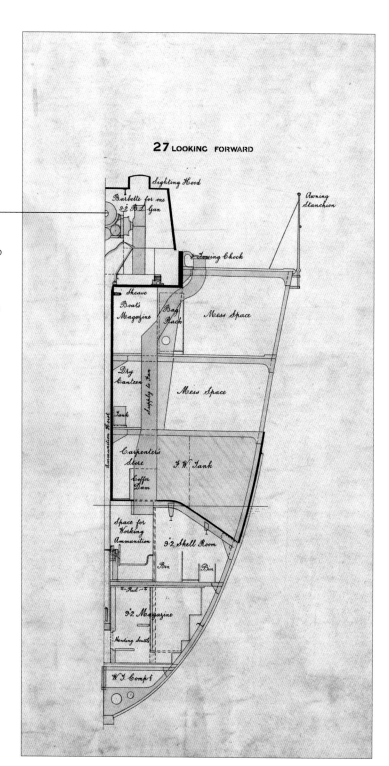

FRAME 27 TO FRAME 19

The area covered here runs from the forward half of the 9.2-inch gunhouse to a point in line with the capstans and the anchors. The extent of the armoured protection to the cordite hoist is shown more clearly here than is the case for its counterpart aft, as are more details of the interior layout of the gunhouse.

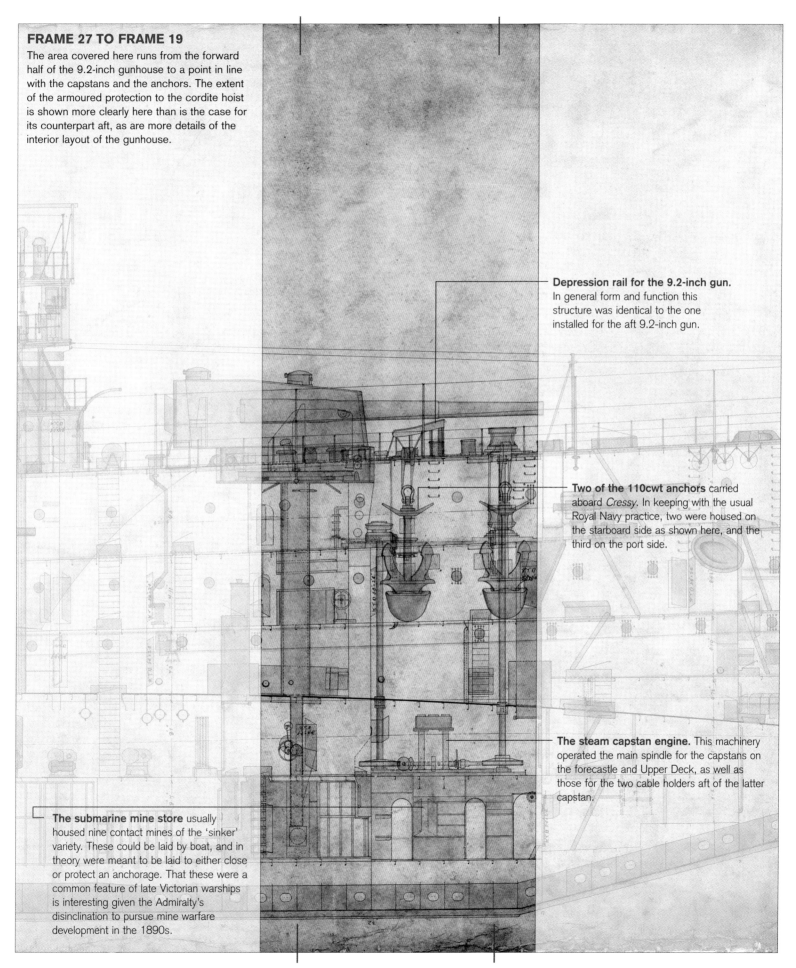

Depression rail for the 9.2-inch gun. In general form and function this structure was identical to the one installed for the aft 9.2-inch gun.

Two of the 110cwt anchors carried aboard *Cressy*. In keeping with the usual Royal Navy practice, two were housed on the starboard side as shown here, and the third on the port side.

The steam capstan engine. This machinery operated the main spindle for the capstans on the forecastle and Upper Deck, as well as those for the two cable holders aft of the latter capstan.

The submarine mine store usually housed nine contact mines of the 'sinker' variety. These could be laid by boat, and in theory were meant to be laid to either close or protect an anchorage. That these were a common feature of late Victorian warships is interesting given the Admiralty's disinclination to pursue mine warfare development in the 1890s.

FRAME 19 (LOOKING FORWARD)

The furthest forward of the hull sections on this plan, taken through the main capstan spindle. Slightly aft of this point the hull narrows to a degree that made it impractical for mess spaces, but the compartments can still be utilised for storage. Much of the space is dominated by the apparatus for operating the anchors and stowing the cables, and the empty Main Deck compartment shown here housed the bower and sheet cable deck pipes leading to the cable lockers one deck below.

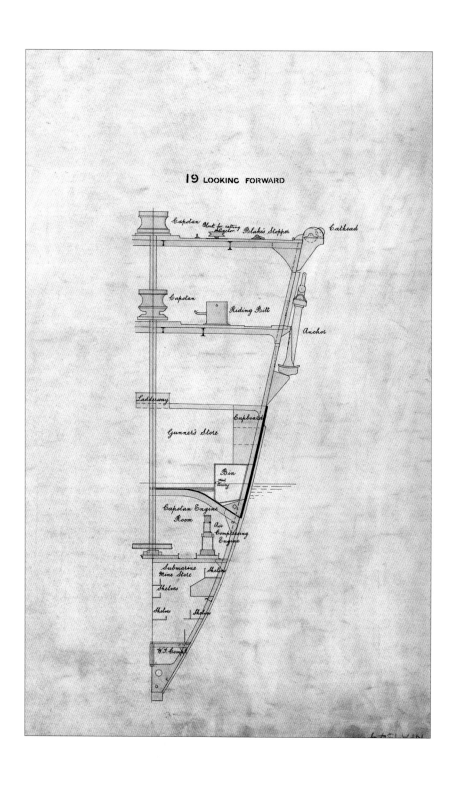

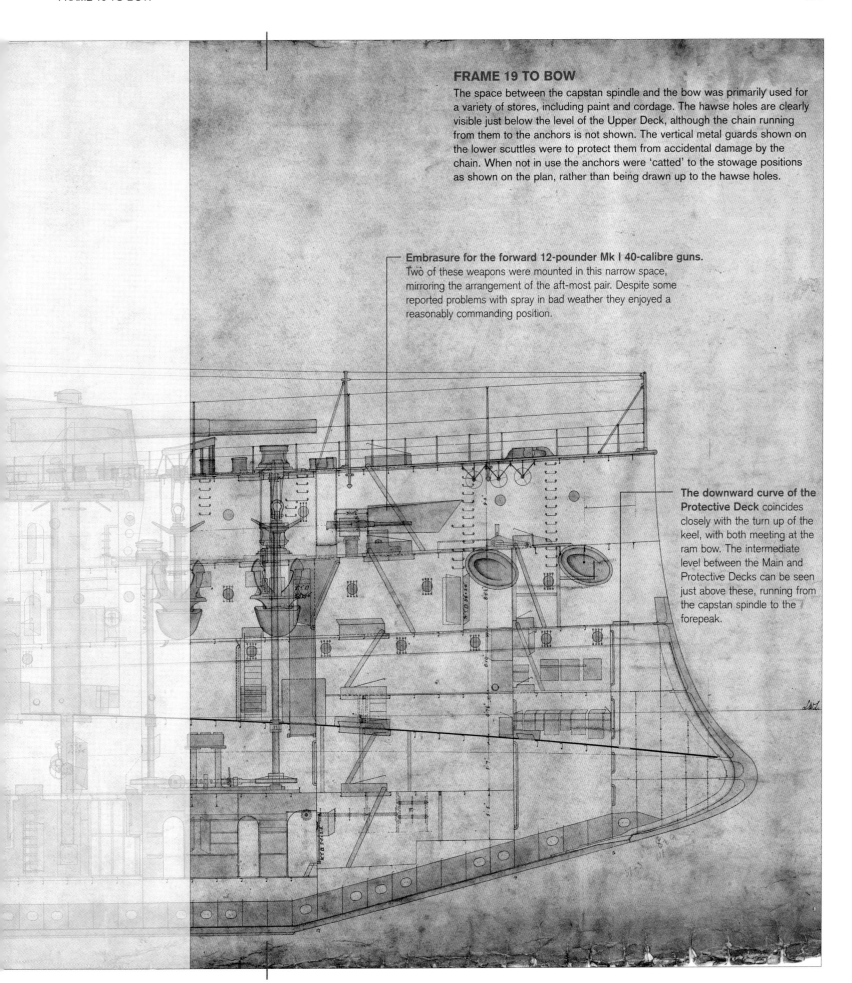

FRAME 19 TO BOW

The space between the capstan spindle and the bow was primarily used for a variety of stores, including paint and cordage. The hawse holes are clearly visible just below the level of the Upper Deck, although the chain running from them to the anchors is not shown. The vertical metal guards shown on the lower scuttles were to protect them from accidental damage by the chain. When not in use the anchors were 'catted' to the stowage positions as shown on the plan, rather than being drawn up to the hawse holes.

Embrasure for the forward 12-pounder Mk I 40-calibre guns. Two of these weapons were mounted in this narrow space, mirroring the arrangement of the aft-most pair. Despite some reported problems with spray in bad weather they enjoyed a reasonably commanding position.

The downward curve of the Protective Deck coincides closely with the turn up of the keel, with both meeting at the ram bow. The intermediate level between the Main and Protective Decks can be seen just above these, running from the capstan spindle to the forepeak.

FRAME 19

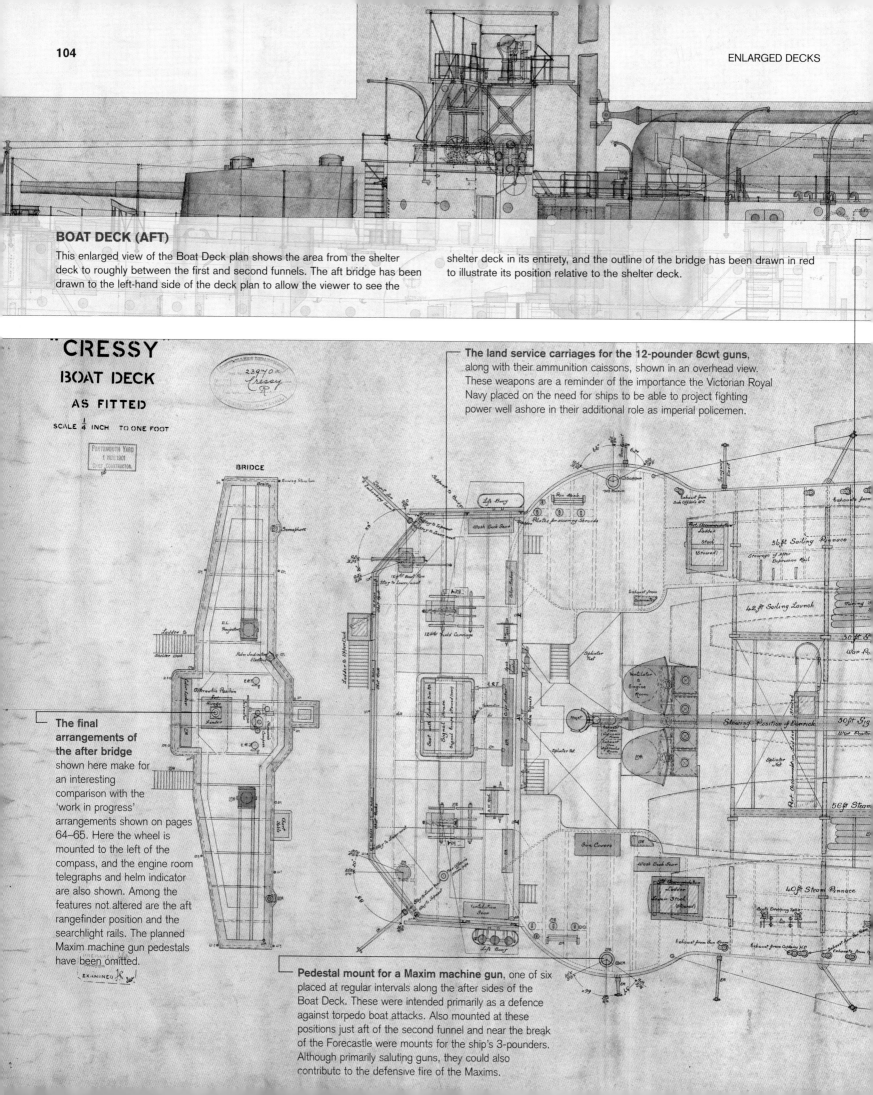

BOAT DECK (AFT)

This enlarged view of the Boat Deck plan shows the area from the shelter deck to roughly between the first and second funnels. The aft bridge has been drawn to the left-hand side of the deck plan to allow the viewer to see the shelter deck in its entirety, and the outline of the bridge has been drawn in red to illustrate its position relative to the shelter deck.

"CRESSY

BOAT DECK

AS FITTED

SCALE 1/4 INCH TO ONE FOOT

The land service carriages for the 12-pounder 8cwt guns, along with their ammunition caissons, shown in an overhead view. These weapons are a reminder of the importance the Victorian Royal Navy placed on the need for ships to be able to project fighting power well ashore in their additional role as imperial policemen.

The final arrangements of the after bridge shown here make for an interesting comparison with the 'work in progress' arrangements shown on pages 64–65. Here the wheel is mounted to the left of the compass, and the engine room telegraphs and helm indicator are also shown. Among the features not altered are the aft rangefinder position and the searchlight rails. The planned Maxim machine gun pedestals have been omitted.

Pedestal mount for a Maxim machine gun, one of six placed at regular intervals along the after sides of the Boat Deck. These were intended primarily as a defence against torpedo boat attacks. Also mounted at these positions just aft of the second funnel and near the break of the Forecastle were mounts for the ship's 3-pounders. Although primarily saluting guns, they could also contribute to the defensive fire of the Maxims.

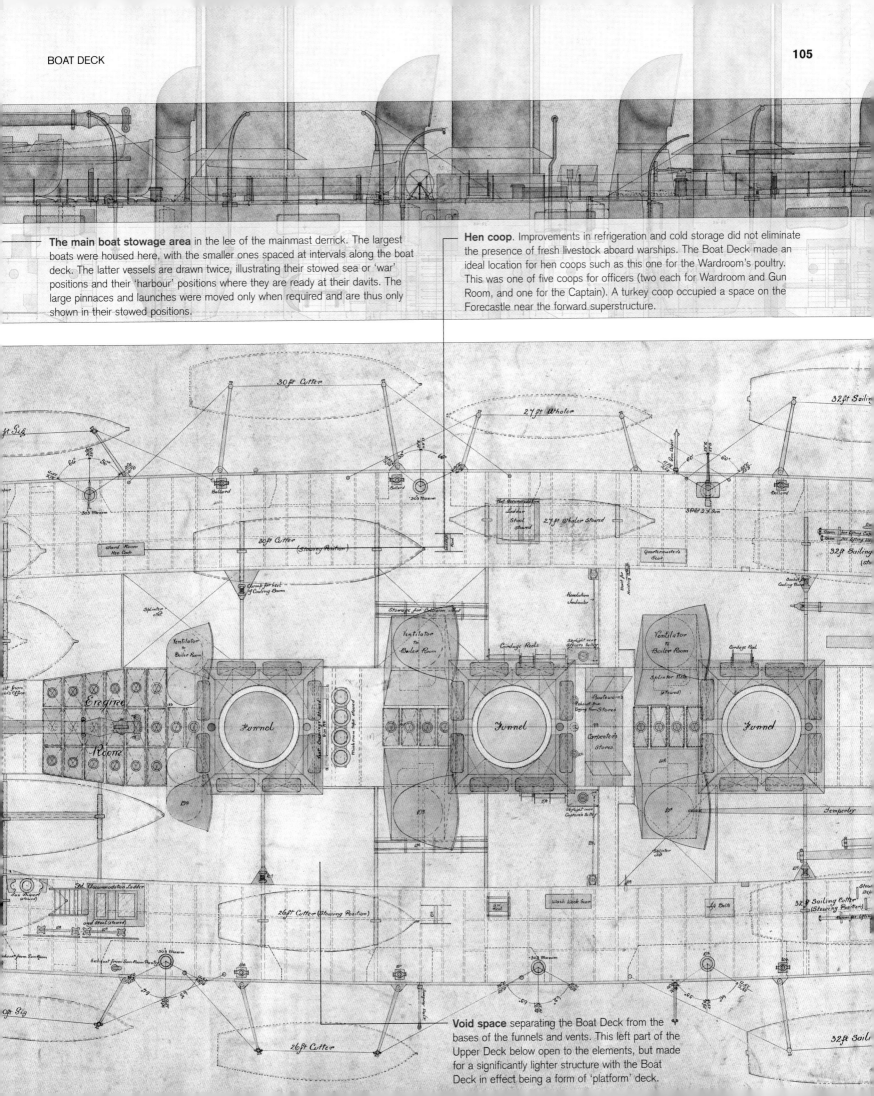

The main boat stowage area in the lee of the mainmast derrick. The largest boats were housed here, with the smaller ones spaced at intervals along the boat deck. The latter vessels are drawn twice, illustrating their stowed sea or 'war' positions and their 'harbour' positions where they are ready at their davits. The large pinnaces and launches were moved only when required and are thus only shown in their stowed positions.

Hen coop. Improvements in refrigeration and cold storage did not eliminate the presence of fresh livestock aboard warships. The Boat Deck made an ideal location for hen coops such as this one for the Wardroom's poultry. This was one of five coops for officers (two each for Wardroom and Gun Room, and one for the Captain). A turkey coop occupied a space on the Forecastle near the forward superstructure.

Void space separating the Boat Deck from the bases of the funnels and vents. This left part of the Upper Deck below open to the elements, but made for a significantly lighter structure with the Boat Deck in effect being a form of 'platform' deck.

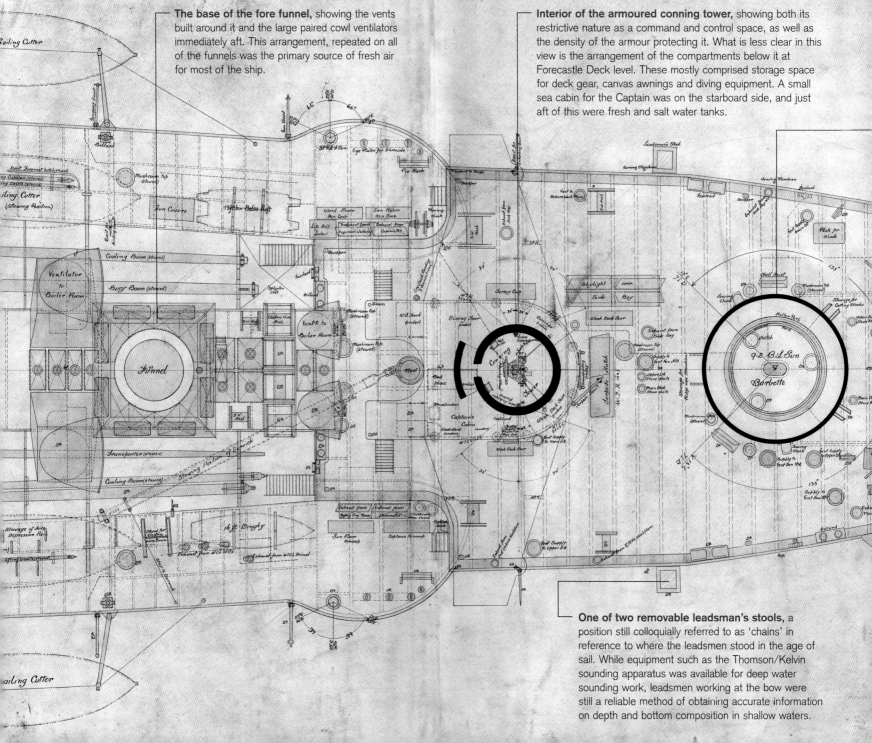

The base of the fore funnel, showing the vents built around it and the large paired cowl ventilators immediately aft. This arrangement, repeated on all of the funnels was the primary source of fresh air for most of the ship.

Interior of the armoured conning tower, showing both its restrictive nature as a command and control space, as well as the density of the armour protecting it. What is less clear in this view is the arrangement of the compartments below it at Forecastle Deck level. These mostly comprised storage space for deck gear, canvas awnings and diving equipment. A small sea cabin for the Captain was on the starboard side, and just aft of this were fresh and salt water tanks.

One of two removable leadsman's stools, a position still colloquially referred to as 'chains' in reference to where the leadsmen stood in the age of sail. While equipment such as the Thomson/Kelvin sounding apparatus was available for deep water sounding work, leadsmen working at the bow were still a reliable method of obtaining accurate information on depth and bottom composition in shallow waters.

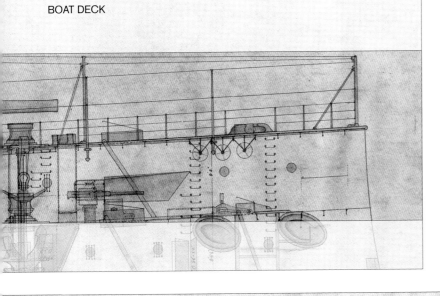

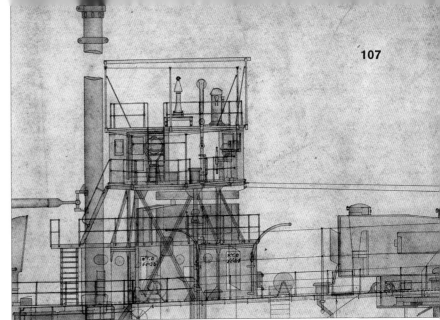

BOAT DECK (FORWARD)

Although treated as a part of the Boat Deck on the plan, the Forecastle was different in being more strongly constructed to help bear the weight of the armoured structures of the conning tower and 9.2-inch gunhouse. It was also noticeably less cluttered as the Boat Deck was better suited for the stowage of deck gear and other equipment such as coaling booms and accommodation ladders.

The fore bridge and compass platform have been 'unstacked' and drawn to the right of the Boat Deck plan in a manner which mirrors the left hand side of the drawing. As with the illustration of the after bridge, the arrangements here show the same sort of variation from the plans on pages 62–63.

The 9.2-inch barbette, illustrating the layout of the interior behind the armour plating. The inner circle represents the roller path for the mounting, with the opening for the ammunition hoist in the centre. The three circular hatches permitted access to the hydraulic mechanisms at the base of the barbette.

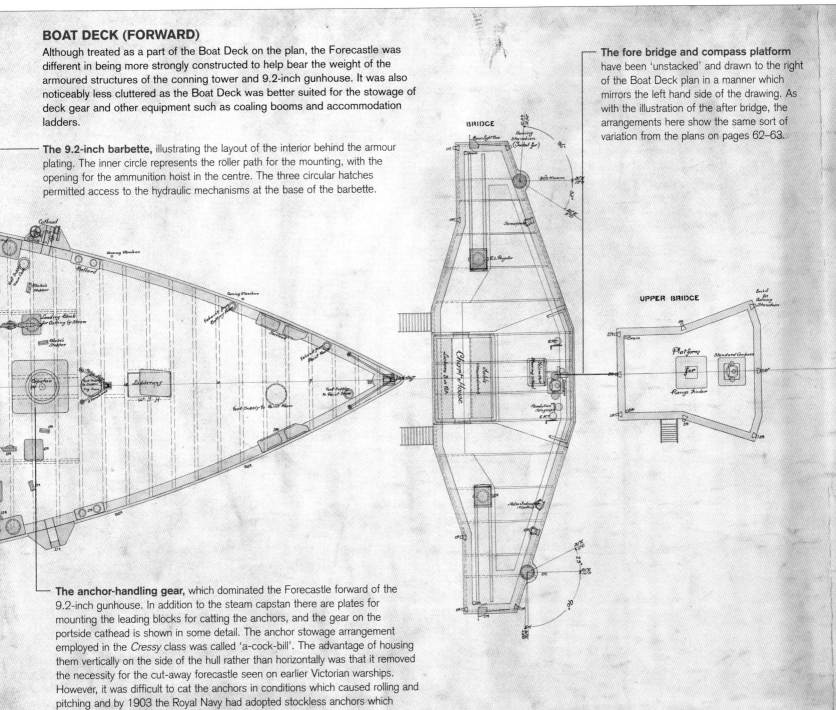

The anchor-handling gear, which dominated the Forecastle forward of the 9.2-inch gunhouse. In addition to the steam capstan there are plates for mounting the leading blocks for catting the anchors, and the gear on the portside cathead is shown in some detail. The anchor stowage arrangement employed in the *Cressy* class was called 'a-cock-bill'. The advantage of housing them vertically on the side of the hull rather than horizontally was that it removed the necessity for the cut-away forecastle seen on earlier Victorian warships. However, it was difficult to cat the anchors in conditions which caused rolling and pitching and by 1903 the Royal Navy had adopted stockless anchors which could be brought up to the hawse holes.

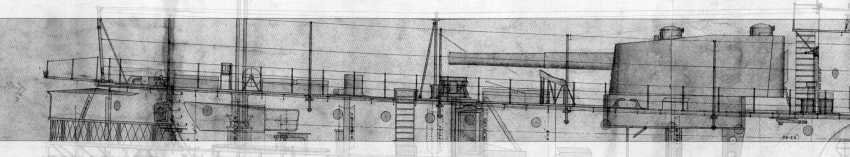

UPPER DECK (AFT)

The Upper Deck aft of Frame 166 was often referred to as the 'quarterdeck' in deference to the conventions of the sailing navy. In keeping with the traditions inherited from that era it was very much the preserve of officers, albeit not to the degree that other ranks were entirely excluded. It was the only part of this deck completely exposed to the elements; the remainder of the Upper Deck was enclosed at the sides but not entirely from above.

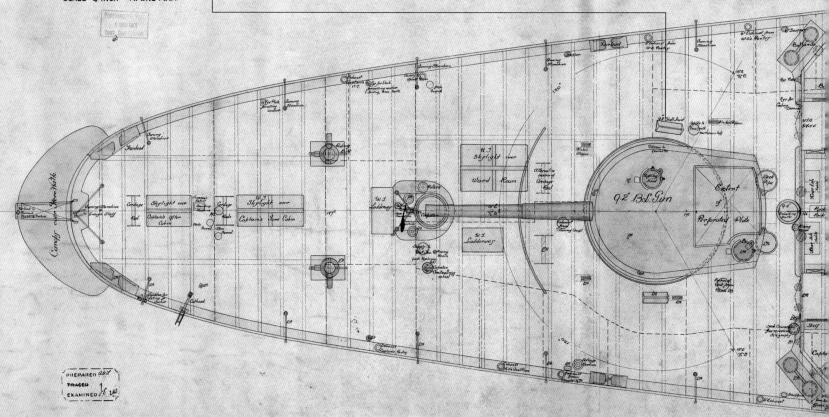

Interior of the upper 6-inch casemate on the starboard quarter. This one is shown in less detail than its counterpart on the opposite page, but it does allow for a clearer appreciation of the structural framing supporting it. The curved line shows where the deck planking ends near the base of the gun mounting.

The top of one of the two 9.2-inch hydraulic shell hoists. These were placed on the port and starboard sides of the barbettes, but neither the fore nor aft ones were arranged symmetrically. Given the awkwardness this system would impose in a combat situation, it is likely that the forty ready-use rounds in the gunhouse and barbette were regarded as sufficient for a single engagement.

"CRESSY"
UPPER DECK
AS FITTED
SCALE 1/4 INCH TO ONE FOOT

Cabins for senior officers occupied the space immediately forward of the mainmast, with three reserved specifically for the use of the Captain, Commander and Navigating Officer. The Captain's cabin was in effect a spare, to be used in such instances as *Cressy* embarking a more senior officer.

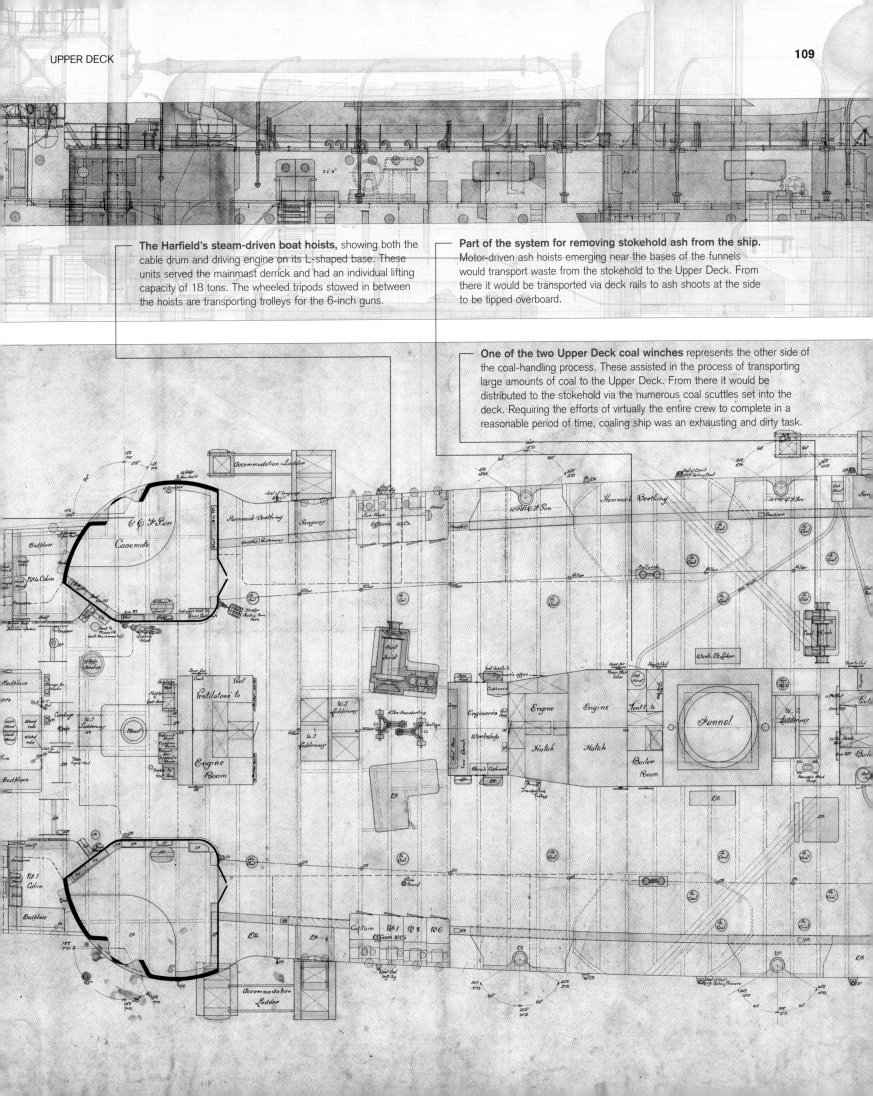

The Harfield's steam-driven boat hoists, showing both the cable drum and driving engine on its L-shaped base. These units served the mainmast derrick and had an individual lifting capacity of 18 tons. The wheeled tripods stowed in between the hoists are transporting trolleys for the 6-inch guns.

Part of the system for removing stokehold ash from the ship. Motor-driven ash hoists emerging near the bases of the funnels would transport waste from the stokehold to the Upper Deck. From there it would be transported via deck rails to ash shoots at the side to be tipped overboard.

One of the two Upper Deck coal winches represents the other side of the coal-handling process. These assisted in the process of transporting large amounts of coal to the Upper Deck. From there it would be distributed to the stokehold via the numerous coal scuttles set into the deck. Requiring the efforts of virtually the entire crew to complete in a reasonable period of time, coaling ship was an exhausting and dirty task.

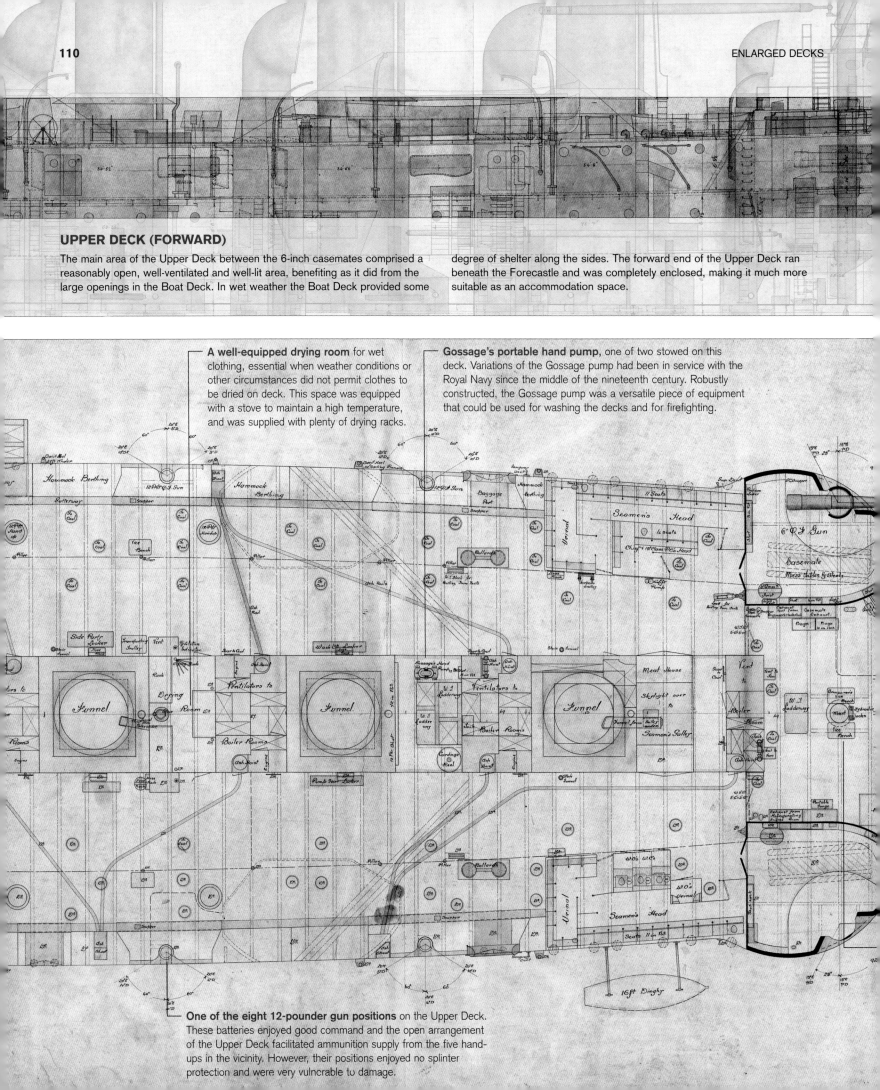

UPPER DECK (FORWARD)

The main area of the Upper Deck between the 6-inch casemates comprised a reasonably open, well-ventilated and well-lit area, benefiting as it did from the large openings in the Boat Deck. In wet weather the Boat Deck provided some degree of shelter along the sides. The forward end of the Upper Deck ran beneath the Forecastle and was completely enclosed, making it much more suitable as an accommodation space.

A well-equipped drying room for wet clothing, essential when weather conditions or other circumstances did not permit clothes to be dried on deck. This space was equipped with a stove to maintain a high temperature, and was supplied with plenty of drying racks.

Gossage's portable hand pump, one of two stowed on this deck. Variations of the Gossage pump had been in service with the Royal Navy since the middle of the nineteenth century. Robustly constructed, the Gossage pump was a versatile piece of equipment that could be used for washing the decks and for firefighting.

One of the eight 12-pounder gun positions on the Upper Deck. These batteries enjoyed good command and the open arrangement of the Upper Deck facilitated ammunition supply from the five hand-ups in the vicinity. However, their positions enjoyed no splinter protection and were very vulncrable to damage.

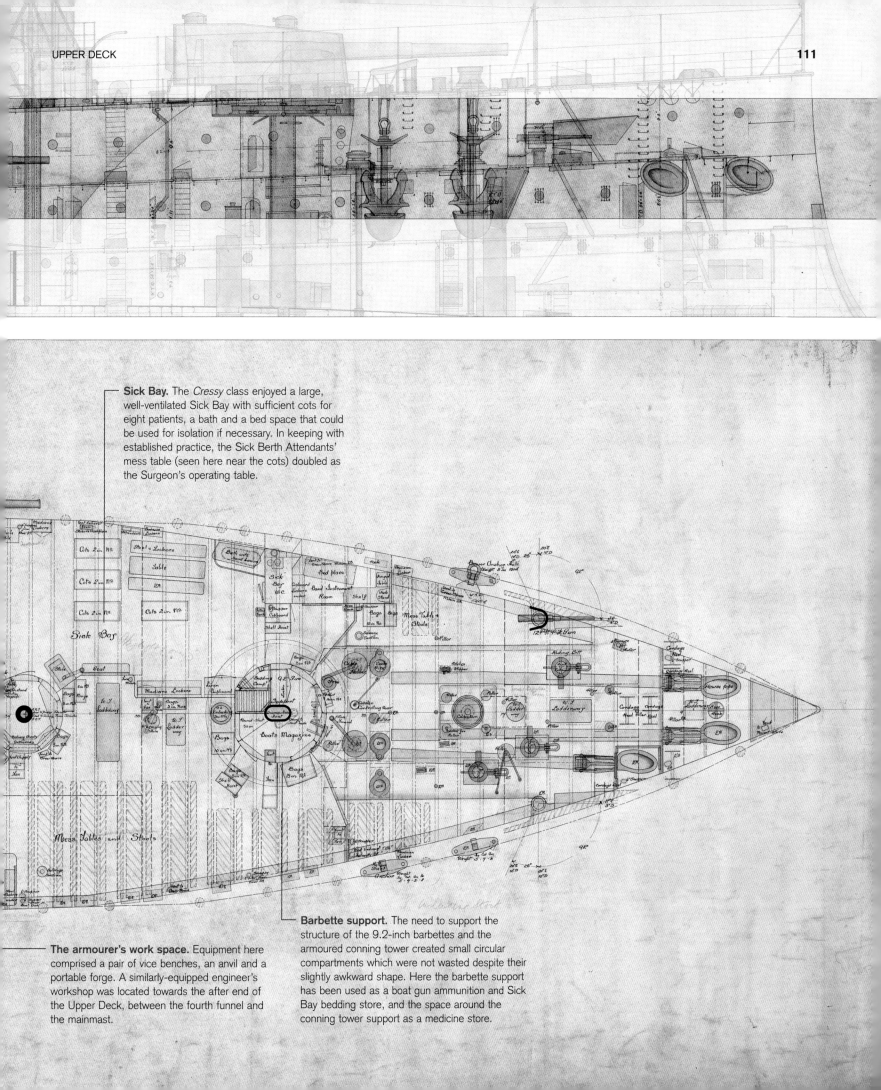

Sick Bay. The *Cressy* class enjoyed a large, well-ventilated Sick Bay with sufficient cots for eight patients, a bath and a bed space that could be used for isolation if necessary. In keeping with established practice, the Sick Berth Attendants' mess table (seen here near the cots) doubled as the Surgeon's operating table.

Barbette support. The need to support the structure of the 9.2-inch barbettes and the armoured conning tower created small circular compartments which were not wasted despite their slightly awkward shape. Here the barbette support has been used as a boat gun ammunition and Sick Bay bedding store, and the space around the conning tower support as a medicine store.

The armourer's work space. Equipment here comprised a pair of vice benches, an anvil and a portable forge. A similarly-equipped engineer's workshop was located towards the after end of the Upper Deck, between the fourth funnel and the mainmast.

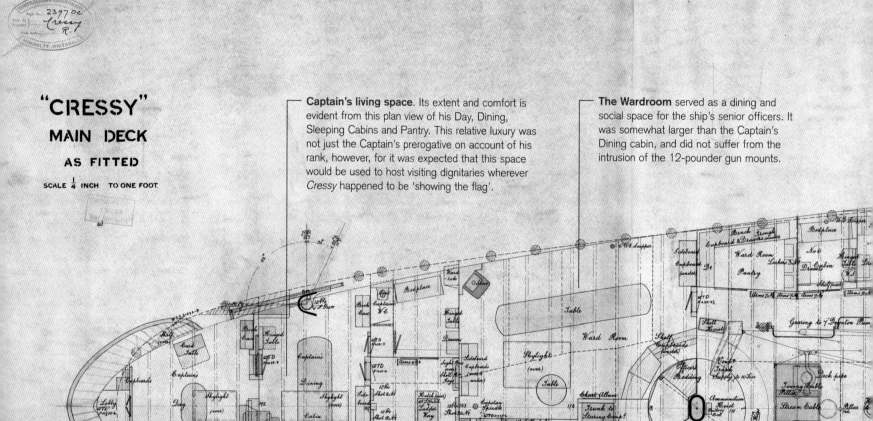

MAIN DECK (AFT)

With the exception of the space allocated to the majority of the 6-inch guns, the Main Deck's primary function was accommodation space for most of the ship's crew. The layout of the living spaces broadly followed the tradition of senior officers right aft, junior officers slightly forward of them and other ranks in the remaining spaces amidships and forward. The amount of space enjoyed by officers was significantly greater, and as the plan on this page shows officers' accommodation occupied nearly half of the Main Deck.

"CRESSY"
MAIN DECK
AS FITTED

SCALE $\frac{1}{4}$ INCH TO ONE FOOT.

Captain's living space. Its extent and comfort is evident from this plan view of his Day, Dining, Sleeping Cabins and Pantry. This relative luxury was not just the Captain's prerogative on account of his rank, however, for it was expected that this space would be used to host visiting dignitaries wherever *Cressy* happened to be 'showing the flag'.

The Wardroom served as a dining and social space for the ship's senior officers. It was somewhat larger than the Captain's Dining cabin, and did not suffer from the intrusion of the 12-pounder gun mounts.

Wireless Telegraphy Office. Although no documentation survives to this effect, it has the appearance of a cabin that has been converted to a new purpose, an interesting reminder of the changes taking place in the Royal Navy while *Cressy* was being built. The W/T set cables were connected to the mainmast, passing from this room through an aperture in the Upper Deck near the after superstructure.

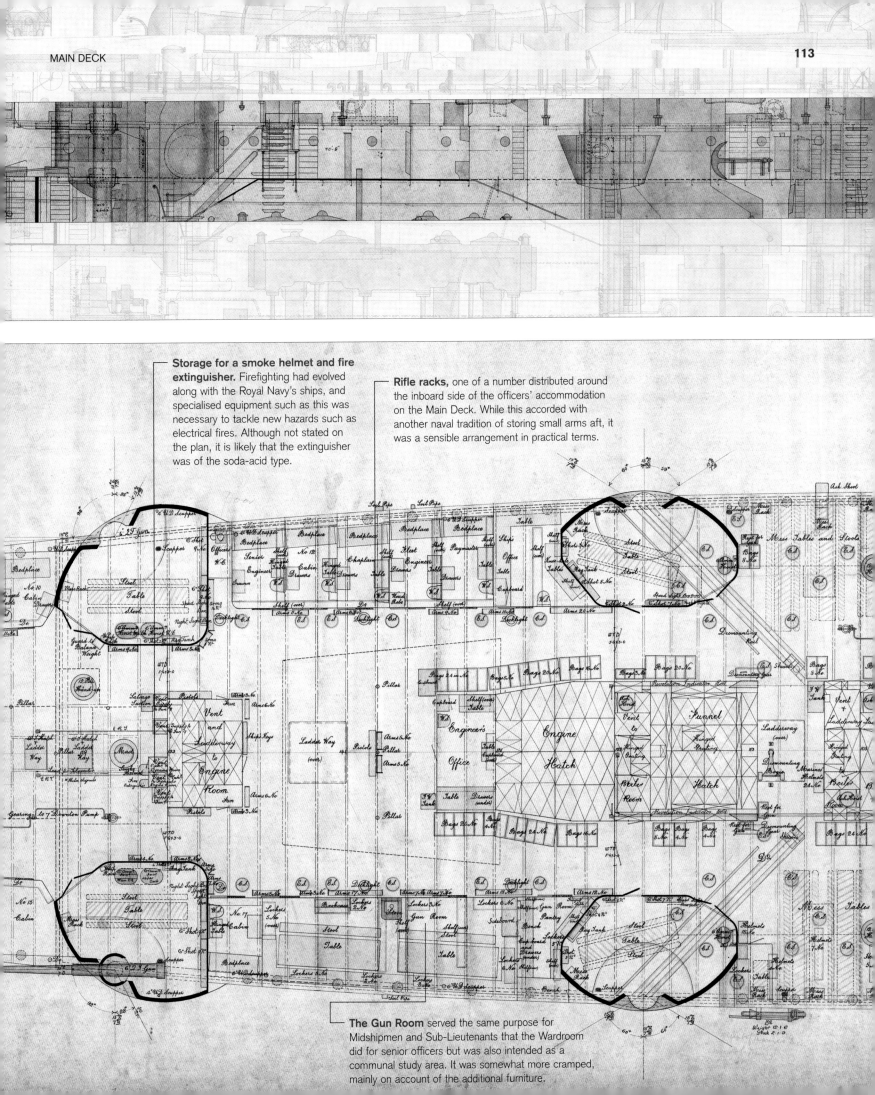

Storage for a smoke helmet and fire extinguisher. Firefighting had evolved along with the Royal Navy's ships, and specialised equipment such as this was necessary to tackle new hazards such as electrical fires. Although not stated on the plan, it is likely that the extinguisher was of the soda-acid type.

Rifle racks, one of a number distributed around the inboard side of the officers' accommodation on the Main Deck. While this accorded with another naval tradition of storing small arms aft, it was a sensible arrangement in practical terms.

The Gun Room served the same purpose for Midshipmen and Sub-Lieutenants that the Wardroom did for senior officers but was also intended as a communal study area. It was somewhat more cramped, mainly on account of the additional furniture.

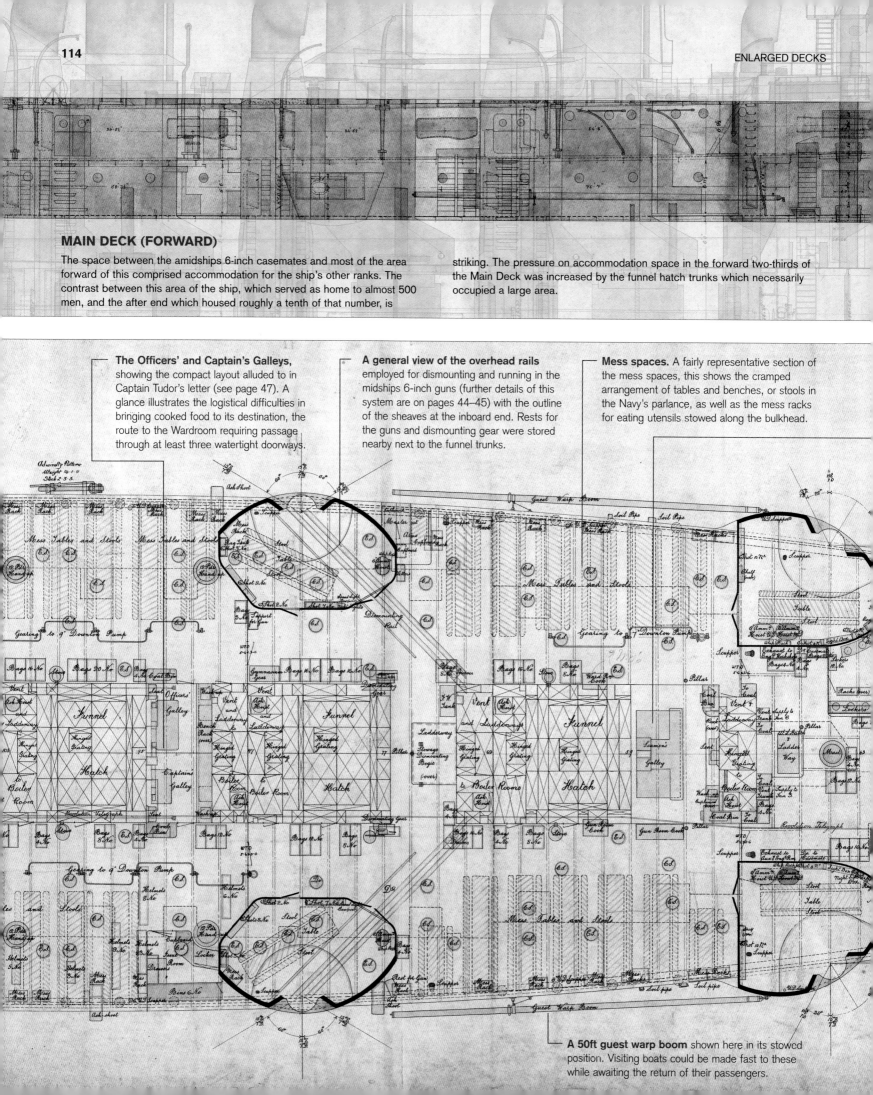

MAIN DECK (FORWARD)

The space between the amidships 6-inch casemates and most of the area forward of this comprised accommodation for the ship's other ranks. The contrast between this area of the ship, which served as home to almost 500 men, and the after end which housed roughly a tenth of that number, is striking. The pressure on accommodation space in the forward two-thirds of the Main Deck was increased by the funnel hatch trunks which necessarily occupied a large area.

The Officers' and Captain's Galleys, showing the compact layout alluded to in Captain Tudor's letter (see page 47). A glance illustrates the logistical difficulties in bringing cooked food to its destination, the route to the Wardroom requiring passage through at least three watertight doorways.

A general view of the overhead rails employed for dismounting and running in the midships 6-inch guns (further details of this system are on pages 44–45) with the outline of the sheaves at the inboard end. Rests for the guns and dismounting gear were stored nearby next to the funnel trunks.

Mess spaces. A fairly representative section of the mess spaces, this shows the cramped arrangement of tables and benches, or stools in the Navy's parlance, as well as the mess racks for eating utensils stowed along the bulkhead.

A 50ft guest warp boom shown here in its stowed position. Visiting boats could be made fast to these while awaiting the return of their passengers.

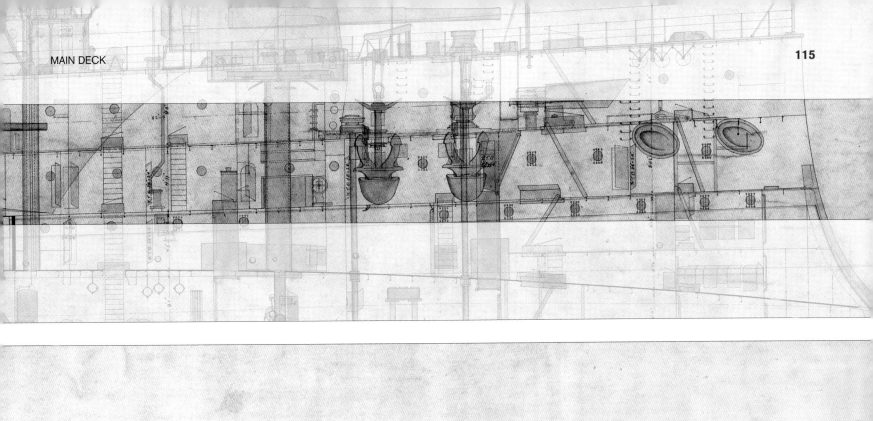

The Seamen's Galley occupied the same amount of space as the Officers' and Captain's Galleys and had a significantly larger if less versatile cooking range. However, any advantage of this was offset by the number of meals that had to be cooked here.

Wash places for stokers and engine room artificers. The dirty nature of their duties made provision of dedicated facilities essential. The arrangements shown here provided enough space for the boiler and engine room personnel coming off watch, but the water supply system was not very efficient.

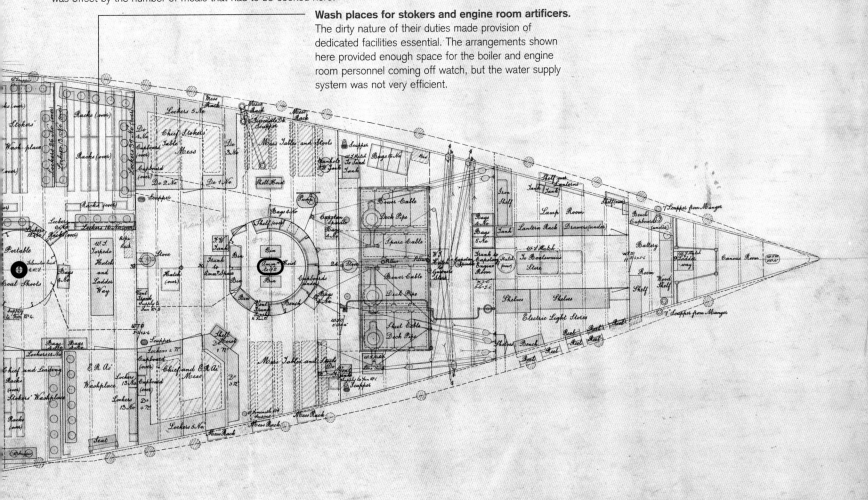

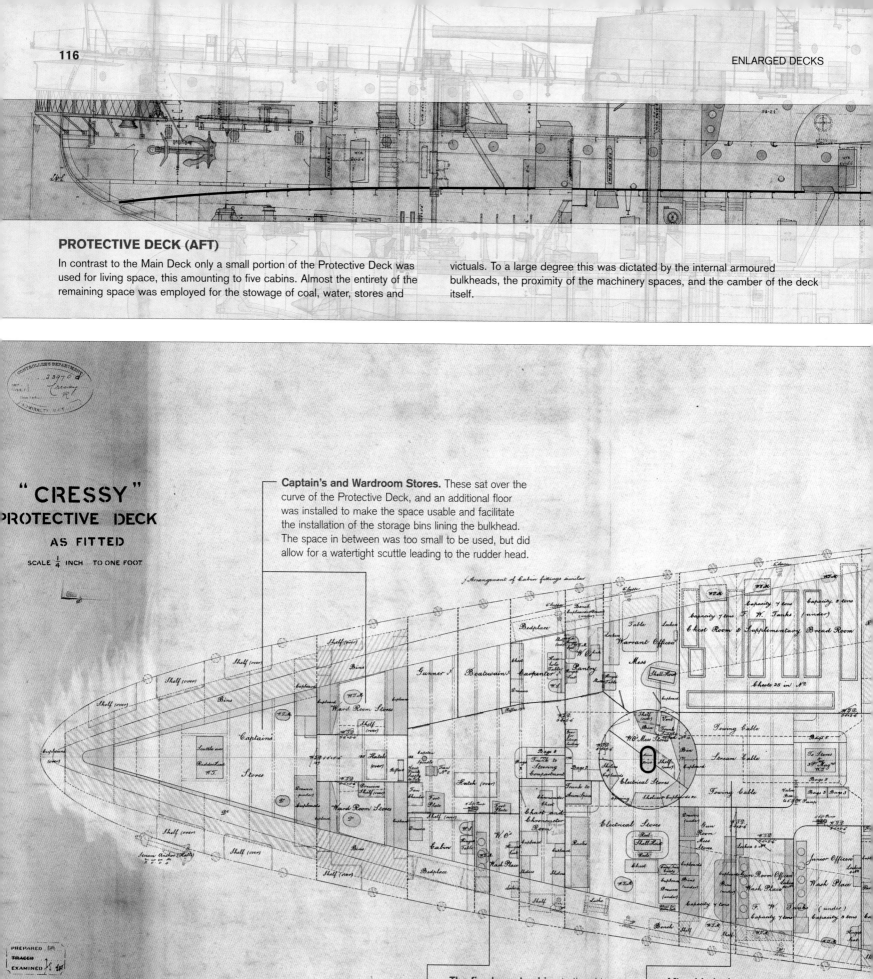

PROTECTIVE DECK (AFT)

In contrast to the Main Deck only a small portion of the Protective Deck was used for living space, this amounting to five cabins. Almost the entirety of the remaining space was employed for the stowage of coal, water, stores and victuals. To a large degree this was dictated by the internal armoured bulkheads, the proximity of the machinery spaces, and the camber of the deck itself.

"CRESSY"
PROTECTIVE DECK
AS FITTED

SCALE $\frac{1}{4}$ INCH TO ONE FOOT

Captain's and Wardroom Stores. These sat over the curve of the Protective Deck, and an additional floor was installed to make the space usable and facilitate the installation of the storage bins lining the bulkhead. The space in between was too small to be used, but did allow for a watertight scuttle leading to the rudder head.

The five lowest cabins in the ship were allocated to the Warrant Officers, including the Boatswain, Carpenter and Gunner. In terms of amenities they were similar to the cabins for more senior officers, and the occupants also had their own Mess adjacent to the three portside cabins.

Aft cable lockers, mirroring the arrangements at the forward end of the ship. Unlike their counterparts forward, only one of these contained anchor cable, in this case for a stream anchor. The other two contained towing cable.

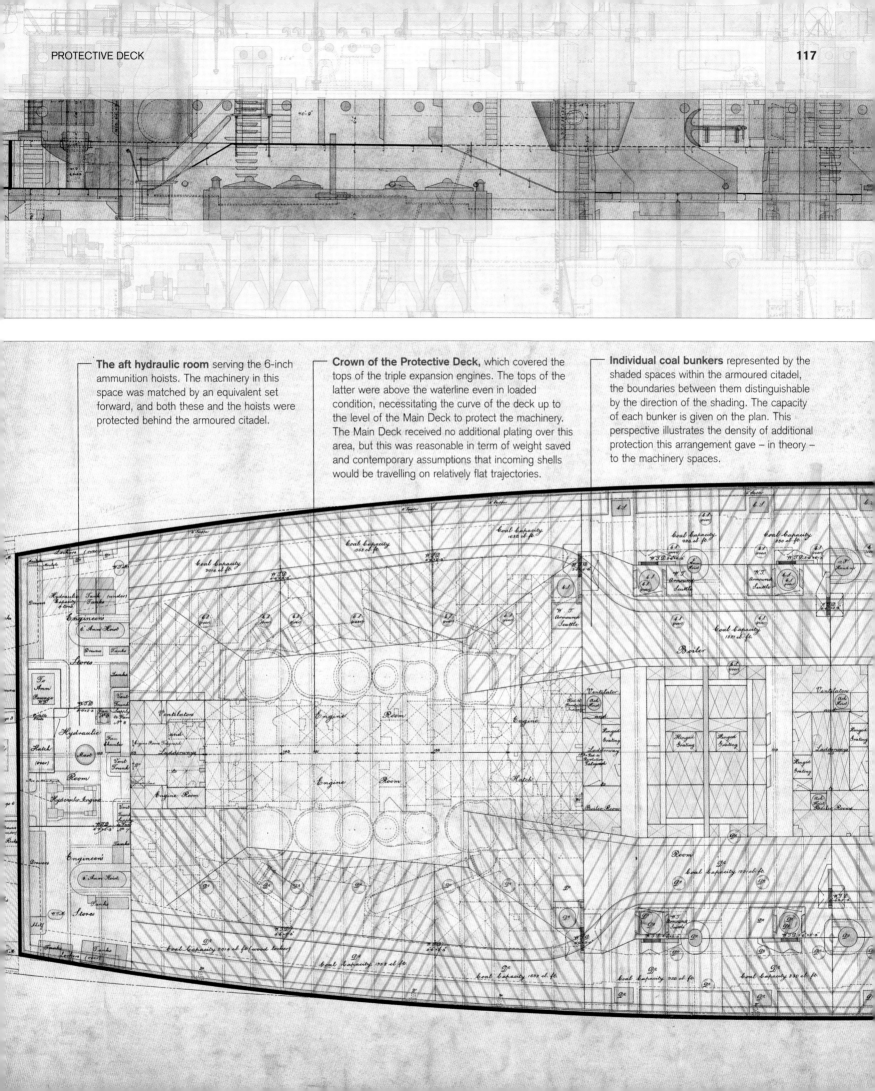

The aft hydraulic room serving the 6-inch ammunition hoists. The machinery in this space was matched by an equivalent set forward, and both these and the hoists were protected behind the armoured citadel.

Crown of the Protective Deck, which covered the tops of the triple expansion engines. The tops of the latter were above the waterline even in loaded condition, necessitating the curve of the deck up to the level of the Main Deck to protect the machinery. The Main Deck received no additional plating over this area, but this was reasonable in term of weight saved and contemporary assumptions that incoming shells would be travelling on relatively flat trajectories.

Individual coal bunkers represented by the shaded spaces within the armoured citadel, the boundaries between them distinguishable by the direction of the shading. The capacity of each bunker is given on the plan. This perspective illustrates the density of additional protection this arrangement gave – in theory – to the machinery spaces.

PROTECTIVE DECK (FORWARD)

The different armour and protective arrangements are clearly shown on this plan in solid black lines. An interesting feature of the armoured citadel is the absence of any access from the compartments fore and aft of it at Protective Deck level, although access from above and below was possible via hatches in the spaces immediately adjacent to the coal bunkers. Forward of the citadel is the armoured communication tube for the telegraph cables and telemotor steering leads from the forward superstructure, and ahead of that the armoured cordite hoist tube. Running forward from the citadel is the thinner bow side plating.

The funnel uptakes represented a necessary weakness in the arrangement of the Protective Deck, particularly with regards the danger of splinters penetrating to the vulnerable machinery spaces below. The solution adopted was the installation of armoured gratings, marked here with blue lines.

Rails for coal trollies ran for almost the entire length of the coal bunker spaces. The function of the ones on this deck was to make 'trimming' and distribution of coal simpler, but the arrangement of watertight compartmentation complicated this task, with six watertight doors separating one end of the bunker spaces from the other.

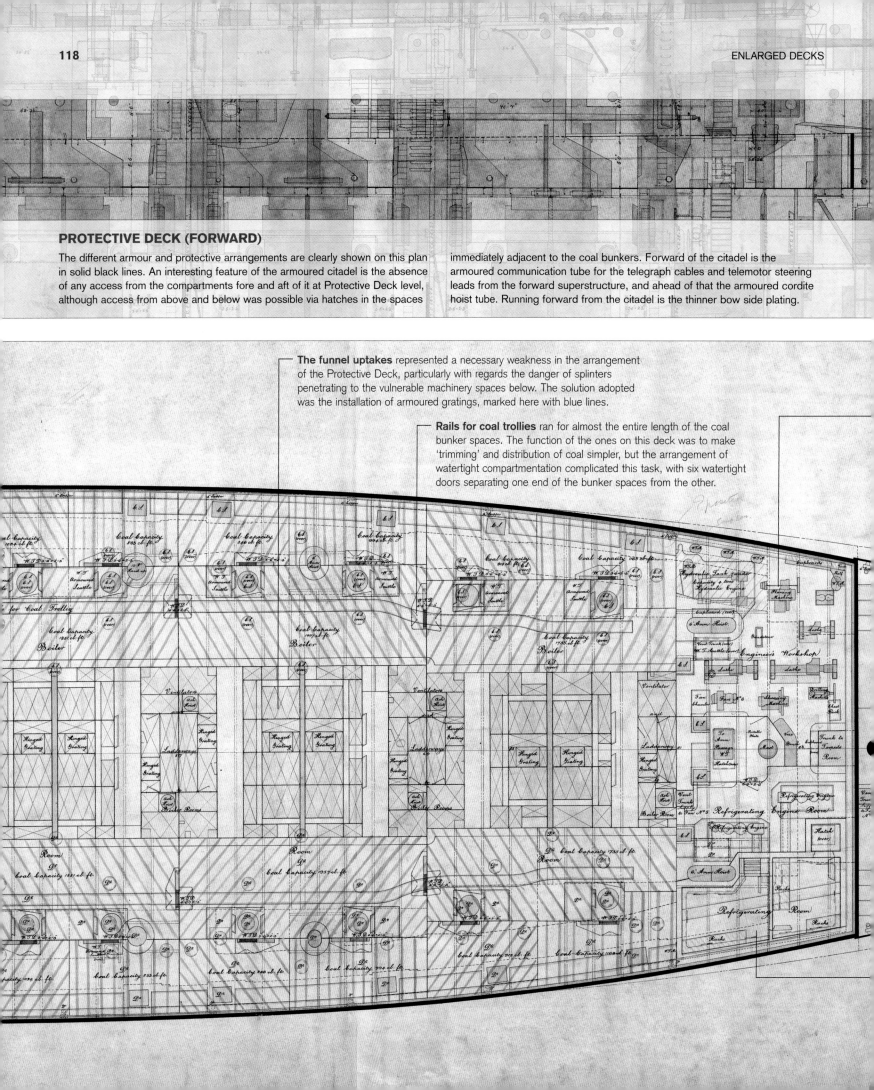

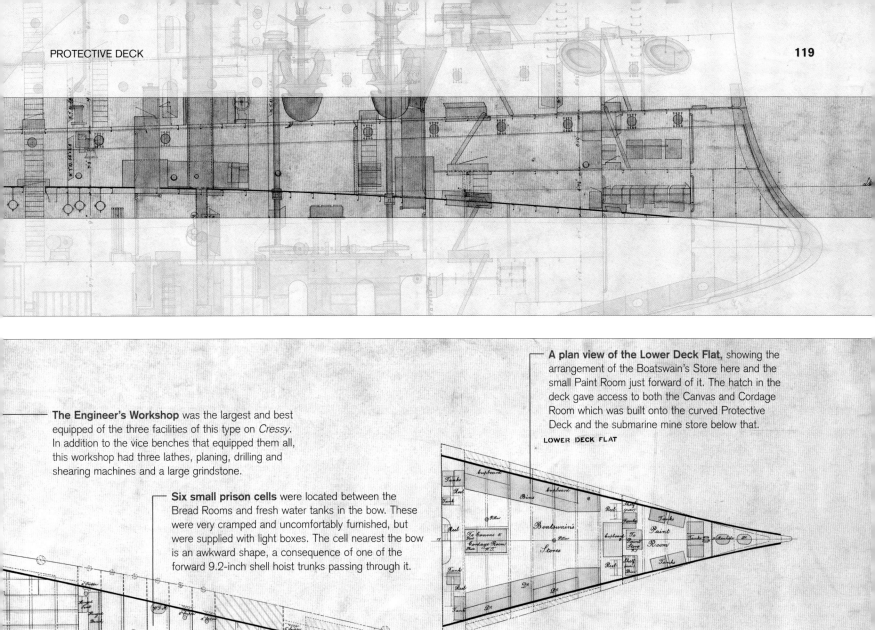

A plan view of the Lower Deck Flat, showing the arrangement of the Boatswain's Store here and the small Paint Room just forward of it. The hatch in the deck gave access to both the Canvas and Cordage Room which was built onto the curved Protective Deck and the submarine mine store below that.

LOWER DECK FLAT

The Engineer's Workshop was the largest and best equipped of the three facilities of this type on *Cressy*. In addition to the vice benches that equipped them all, this workshop had three lathes, planing, drilling and shearing machines and a large grindstone.

Six small prison cells were located between the Bread Rooms and fresh water tanks in the bow. These were very cramped and uncomfortably furnished, but were supplied with light boxes. The cell nearest the bow is an awkward shape, a consequence of one of the forward 9.2-inch shell hoist trunks passing through it.

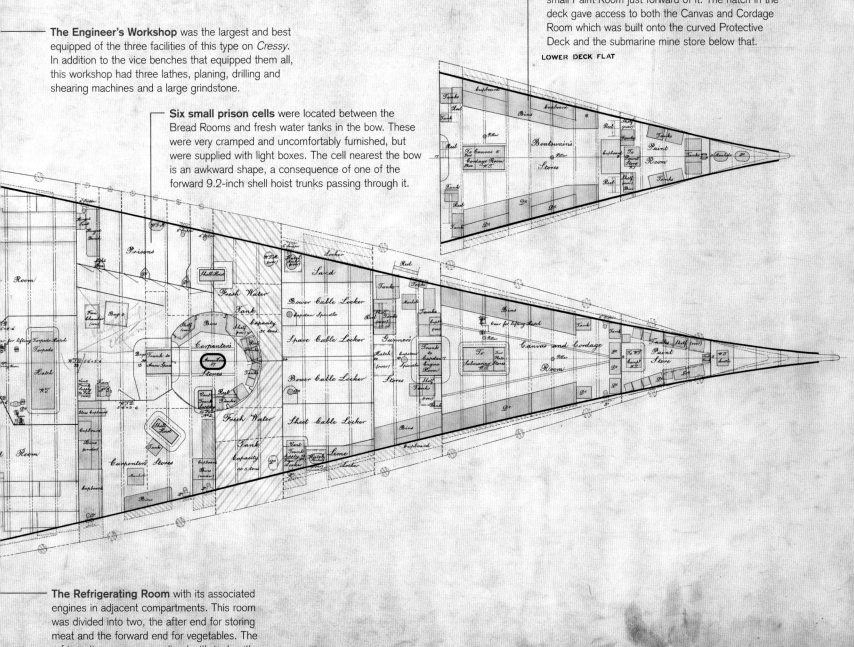

The Refrigerating Room with its associated engines in adjacent compartments. This room was divided into two, the after end for storing meat and the forward end for vegetables. The refrigeration spaces were lined with teak with silicate cotton insulation.

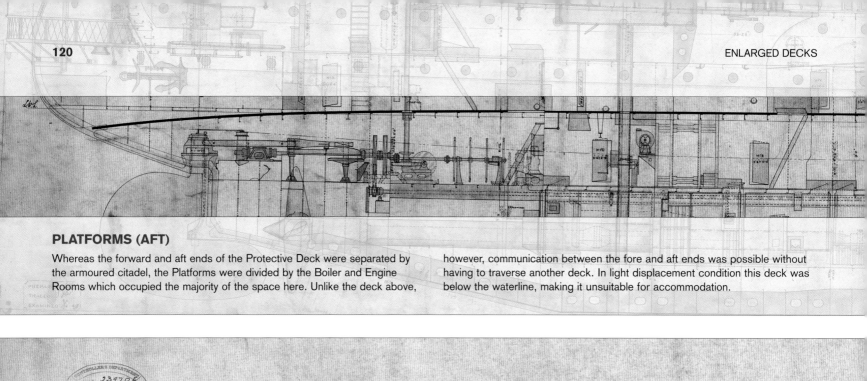

PLATFORMS (AFT)

Whereas the forward and aft ends of the Protective Deck were separated by the armoured citadel, the Platforms were divided by the Boiler and Engine Rooms which occupied the majority of the space here. Unlike the deck above, however, communication between the fore and aft ends was possible without having to traverse another deck. In light displacement condition this deck was below the waterline, making it unsuitable for accommodation.

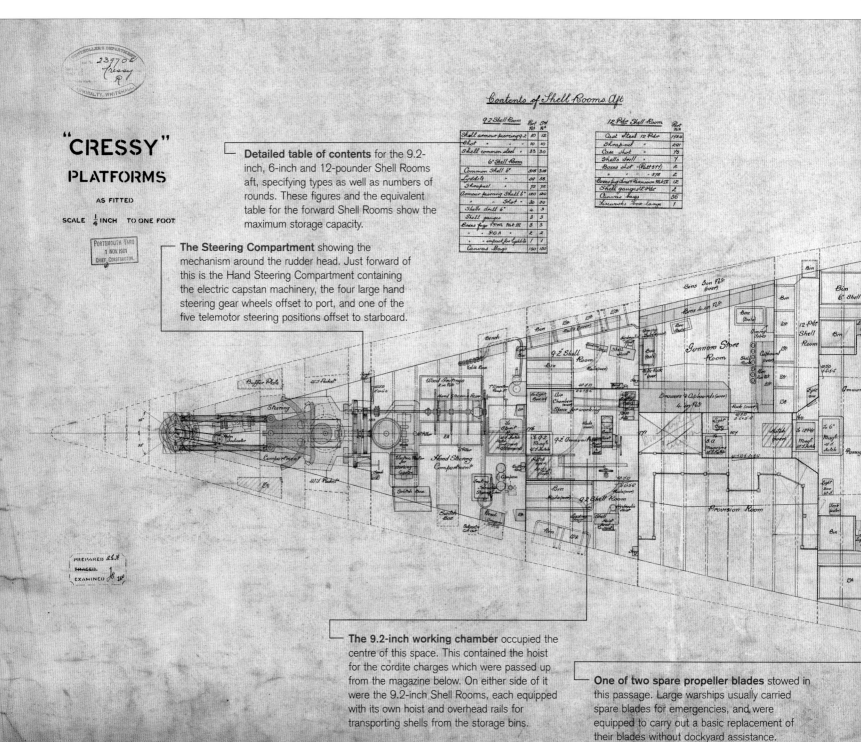

"CRESSY"
PLATFORMS
AS FITTED

SCALE 1/4 INCH TO ONE FOOT

Detailed table of contents for the 9.2-inch, 6-inch and 12-pounder Shell Rooms aft, specifying types as well as numbers of rounds. These figures and the equivalent table for the forward Shell Rooms show the maximum storage capacity.

Contents of Shell Rooms Aft

The Steering Compartment showing the mechanism around the rudder head. Just forward of this is the Hand Steering Compartment containing the electric capstan machinery, the four large hand steering gear wheels offset to port, and one of the five telemotor steering positions offset to starboard.

The 9.2-inch working chamber occupied the centre of this space. This contained the hoist for the cordite charges which were passed up from the magazine below. On either side of it were the 9.2-inch Shell Rooms, each equipped with its own hoist and overhead rails for transporting shells from the storage bins.

One of two spare propeller blades stowed in this passage. Large warships usually carried spare blades for emergencies, and were equipped to carry out a basic replacement of their blades without dockyard assistance.

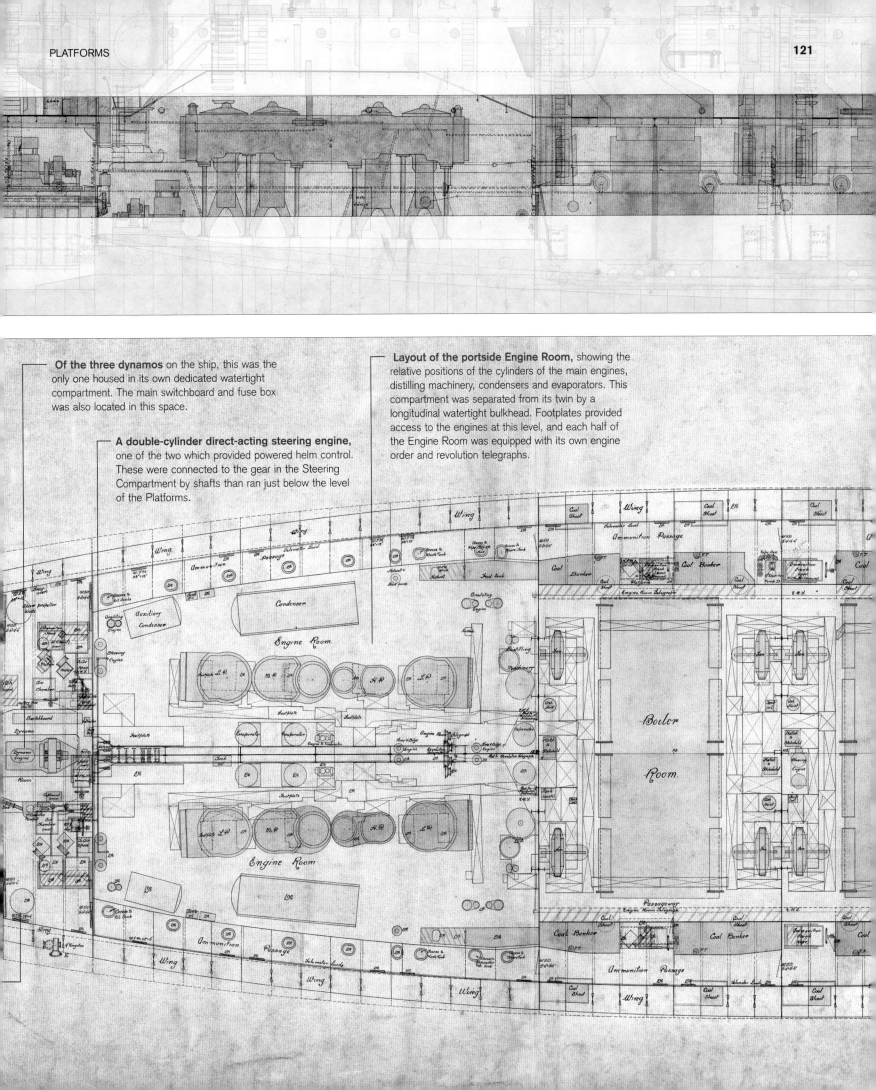

Of the three dynamos on the ship, this was the only one housed in its own dedicated watertight compartment. The main switchboard and fuse box was also located in this space.

A double-cylinder direct-acting steering engine, one of the two which provided powered helm control. These were connected to the gear in the Steering Compartment by shafts than ran just below the level of the Platforms.

Layout of the portside Engine Room, showing the relative positions of the cylinders of the main engines, distilling machinery, condensers and evaporators. This compartment was separated from its twin by a longitudinal watertight bulkhead. Footplates provided access to the engines at this level, and each half of the Engine Room was equipped with its own engine order and revolution telegraphs.

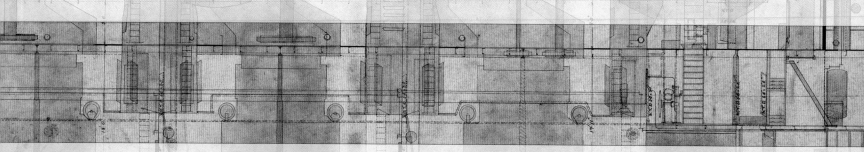

PLATFORMS (FORWARD)

The spaces fore and aft of the Engine and Boiler Rooms and the ammunition passages that ran alongside them essentially created a 'gallery' deck around compartments that were two storeys in height. As part of the system of watertight subdivision, the machinery spaces at this level were completely isolated from the rest of the deck.

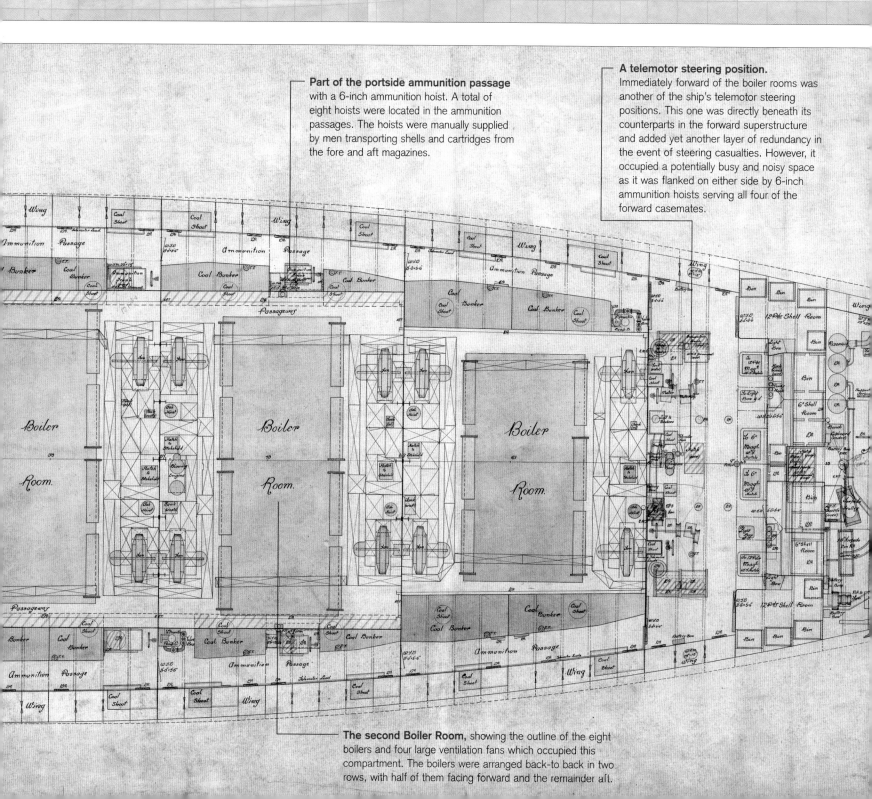

Part of the portside ammunition passage with a 6-inch ammunition hoist. A total of eight hoists were located in the ammunition passages. The hoists were manually supplied by men transporting shells and cartridges from the fore and aft magazines.

A telemotor steering position. Immediately forward of the boiler rooms was another of the ship's telemotor steering positions. This one was directly beneath its counterparts in the forward superstructure and added yet another layer of redundancy in the event of steering casualties. However, it occupied a potentially busy and noisy space as it was flanked on either side by 6-inch ammunition hoists serving all four of the forward casemates.

The second Boiler Room, showing the outline of the eight boilers and four large ventilation fans which occupied this compartment. The boilers were arranged back-to back in two rows, with half of them facing forward and the remainder aft.

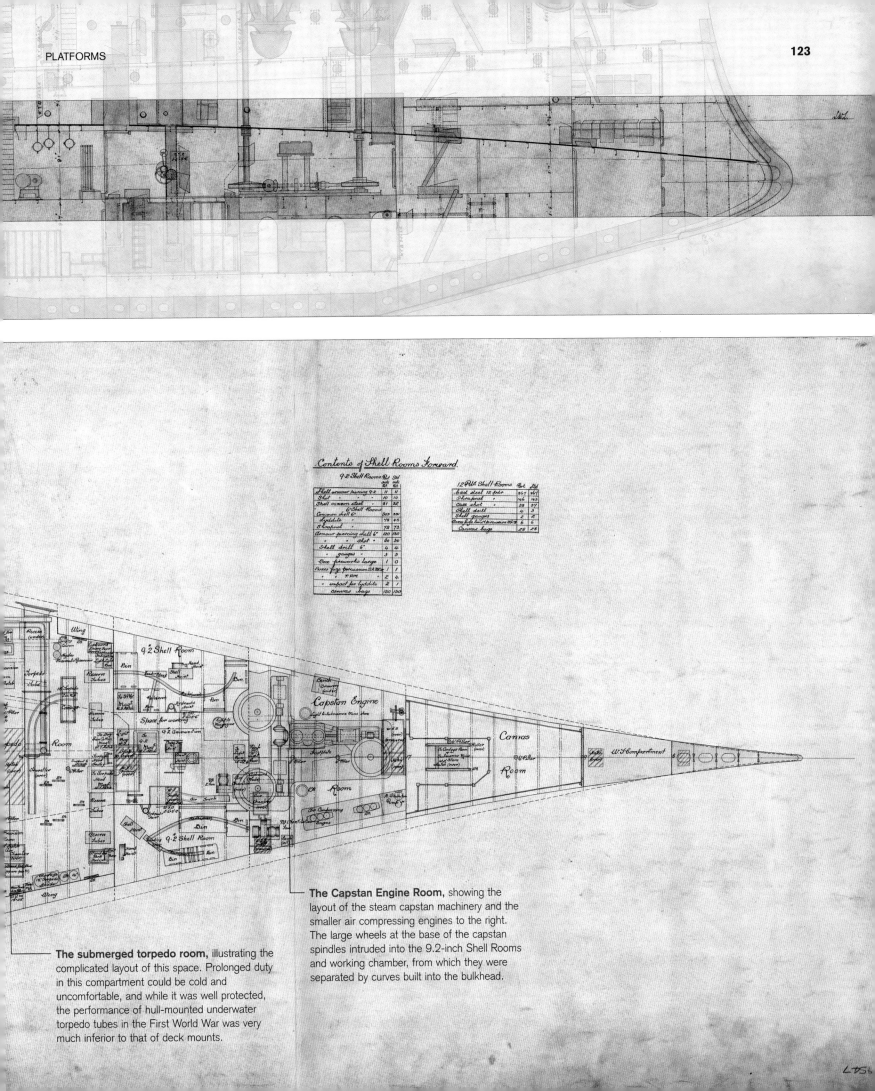

Contents of Shell Rooms Forward.

9.2 Shell Rooms	Port	Std
Shell armour piercing 9.2	11	11
Shot	10	10
Shell common steel	31	32
6" Shell Rooms		
Common shell 6"	303	331
Lyddite	75	45
Shrapnel	72	73
Armour piercing shell 6"	120	120
" Shot	60	30
Shell drill 6"	4	4
" gauges	3	3
Box fireworks large	1	0
Boxes fuze percussion QA Mk II	1	1
T.D.M.	2	4
impact for lyddite	2	1
canvas bags	150	150

12 Pdr Shell Rooms	Port	Std
Cast steel 12 pdr	354	357
Shrapnel	146	143
Case shot	33	34
Shell drill	2	3
Shell gauges	2	2
Boxes fuze late percussion Mk II	6	6
Canvas bags	28	28

The submerged torpedo room, illustrating the complicated layout of this space. Prolonged duty in this compartment could be cold and uncomfortable, and while it was well protected, the performance of hull-mounted underwater torpedo tubes in the First World War was very much inferior to that of deck mounts.

The Capstan Engine Room, showing the layout of the steam capstan machinery and the smaller air compressing engines to the right. The large wheels at the base of the capstan spindles intruded into the 9.2-inch Shell Rooms and working chamber, from which they were separated by curves built into the bulkhead.

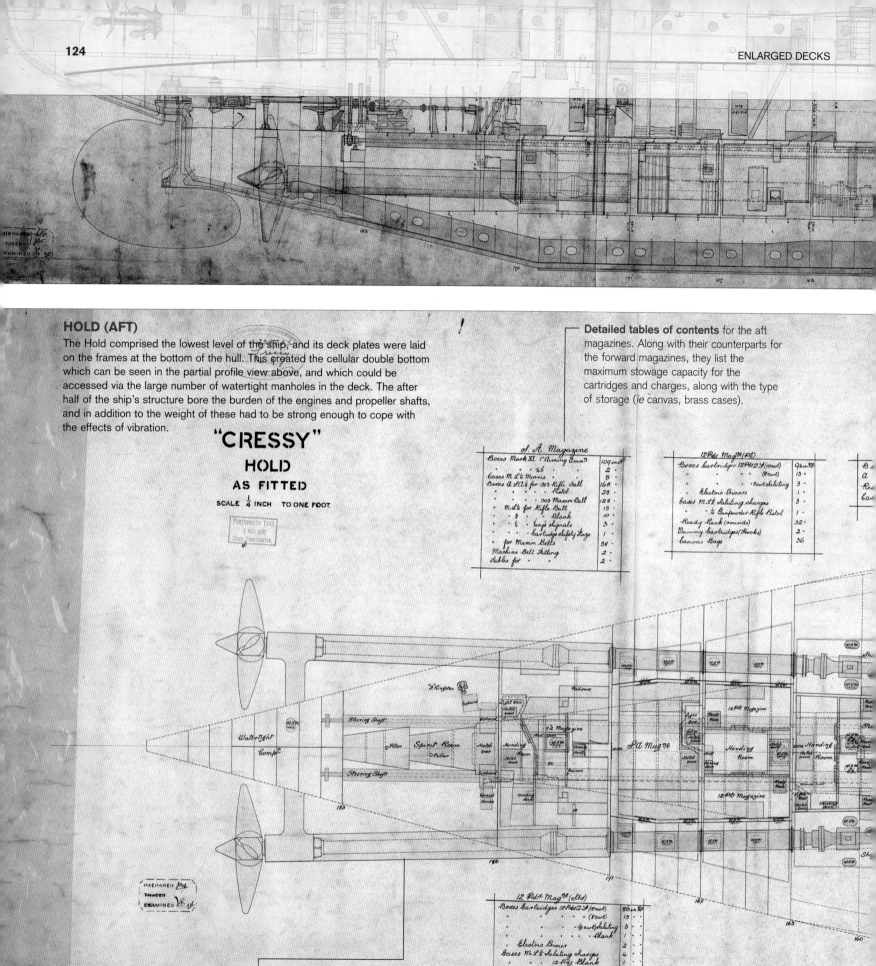

HOLD (AFT)

The Hold comprised the lowest level of the ship, and its deck plates were laid on the frames at the bottom of the hull. This created the cellular double bottom which can be seen in the partial profile view above, and which could be accessed via the large number of watertight manholes in the deck. The after half of the ship's structure bore the burden of the engines and propeller shafts, and in addition to the weight of these had to be strong enough to cope with the effects of vibration.

Detailed tables of contents for the aft magazines. Along with their counterparts for the forward magazines, they list the maximum stowage capacity for the cartridges and charges, along with the type of storage (ie canvas, brass cases).

"CRESSY"
HOLD
AS FITTED
SCALE ¼ INCH TO ONE FOOT

Detailed plan view of the propeller shafts, illustrating in addition to their physical arrangement the fact that they are splayed outboard 5° off the centre line. This arrangement slightly increased the propulsive power generated by the action of the screws.

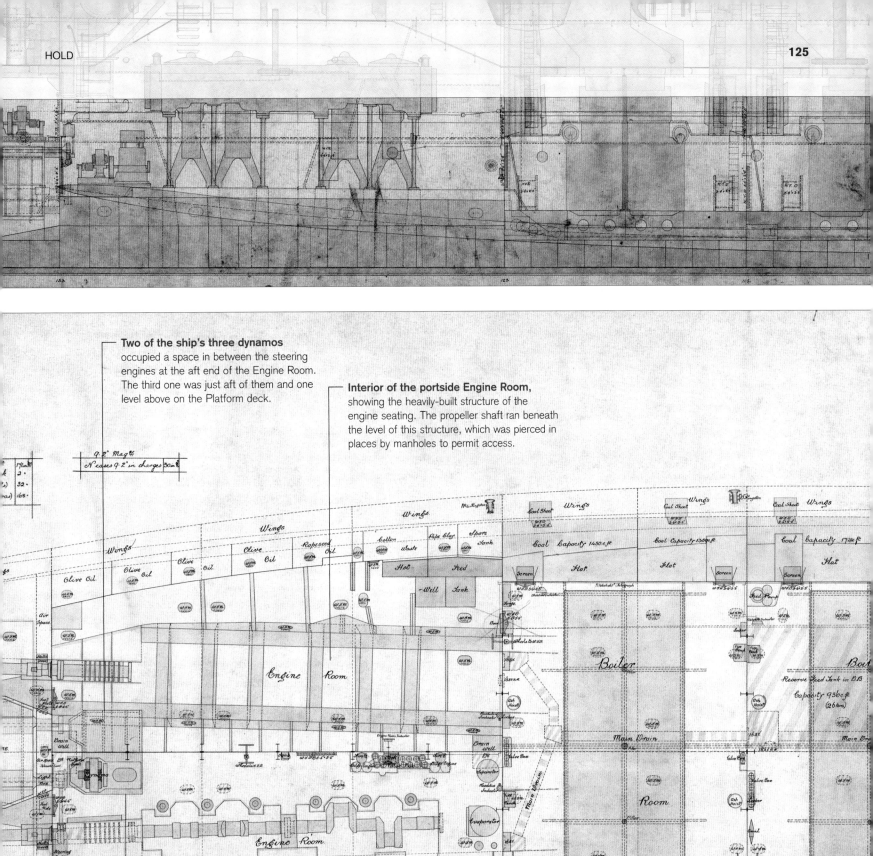

Two of the ship's three dynamos occupied a space in between the steering engines at the aft end of the Engine Room. The third one was just aft of them and one level above on the Platform deck.

Interior of the portside Engine Room, showing the heavily-built structure of the engine seating. The propeller shaft ran beneath the level of this structure, which was pierced in places by manholes to permit access.

Interior of the starboard Engine Room, showing the outline of the base of the engine and the arrangement of the crankshaft and the four crankpin bearings. *Cressy's* engines were classed as triple expansion despite having four cylinders because the two low pressure engines were of equal size and worked to identical specifications.

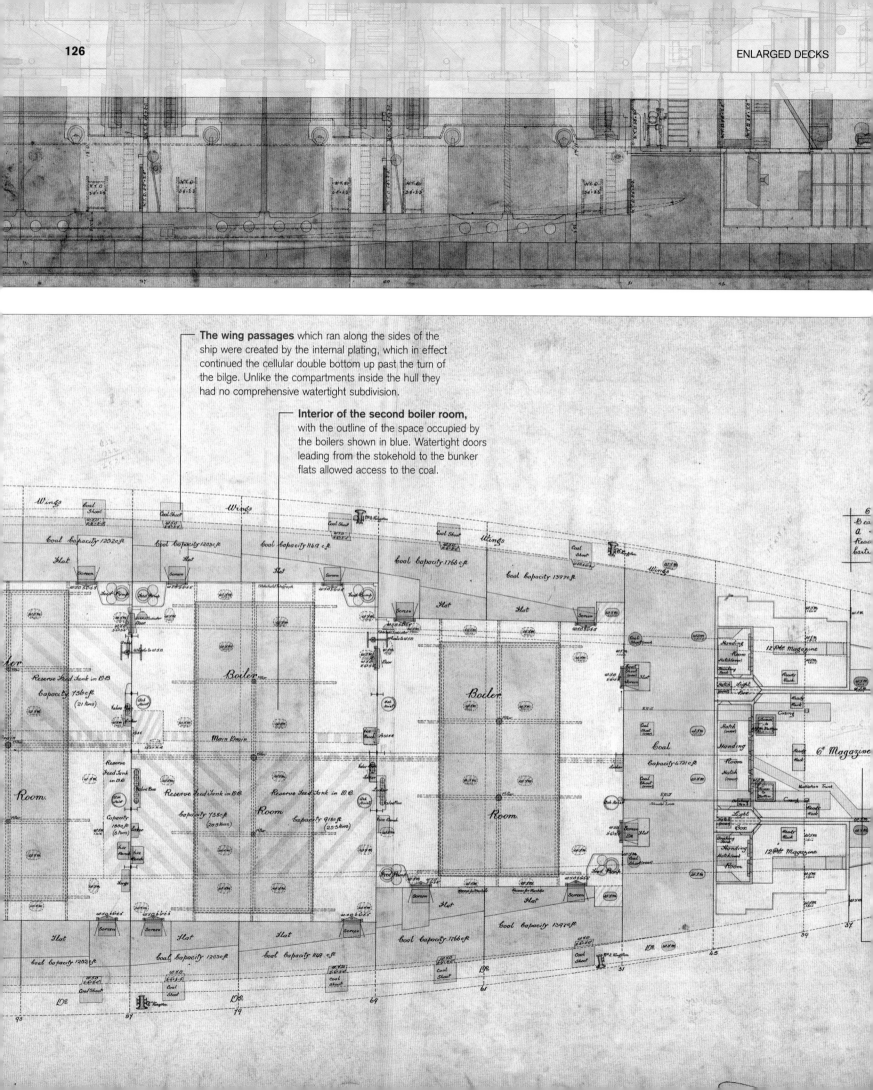

The wing passages which ran along the sides of the ship were created by the internal plating, which in effect continued the cellular double bottom up past the turn of the bilge. Unlike the compartments inside the hull they had no comprehensive watertight subdivision.

Interior of the second boiler room, with the outline of the space occupied by the boilers shown in blue. Watertight doors leading from the stokehold to the bunker flats allowed access to the coal.

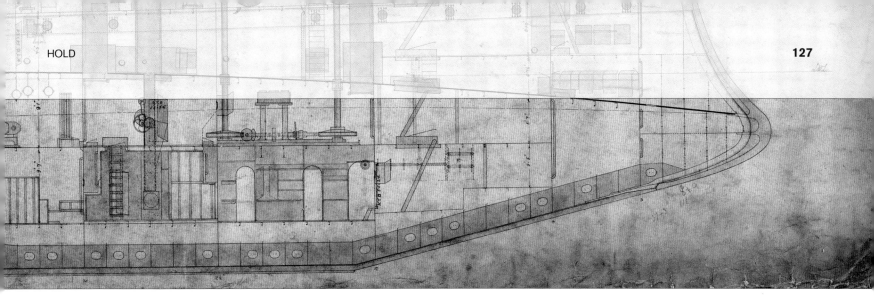

HOLD (FORWARD)

Outside of the machinery spaces and their associated coal bunkers, the majority of the space in the Hold was home to the ship's magazines. These were generally concentrated forward and aft of the ship's propulsive machinery, with the arrangement of the aft ones slightly complicated by the run of the propeller shafts. Another form of hazardous but arguably necessary material was housed right aft in the Spirit Room.

One of the ten Kingston valves placed in the Hold. Their primary purpose was to keep the salt water tanks topped up but they could also be used for controlled flooding when circumstances required. Each was assigned a number or letter, but the arrangement of these confusingly alternated between port and starboard side. Therefore, the sequence of valves running from the port bow towards the stern would be '1', 'B', '3', 'D' and so on.

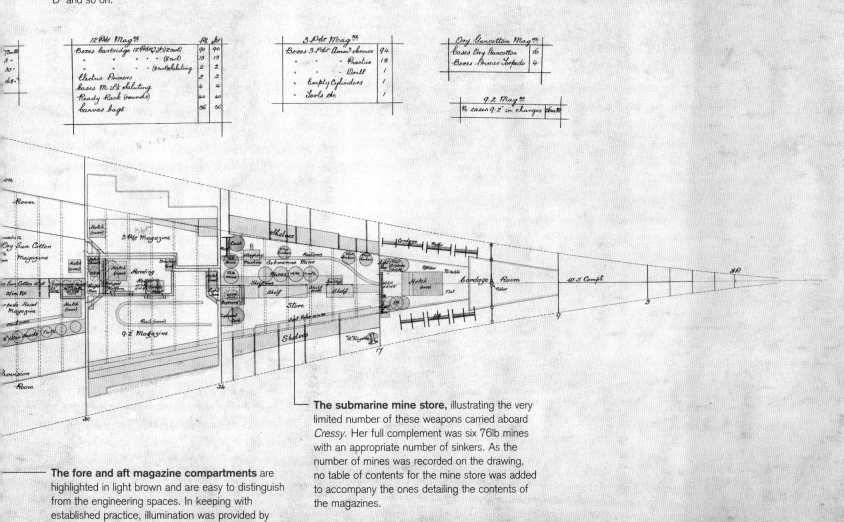

The fore and aft magazine compartments are highlighted in light brown and are easy to distinguish from the engineering spaces. In keeping with established practice, illumination was provided by sealed light boxes and the magazines were separated from the working chambers above by Handing Rooms. Each magazine was a self-contained unit with no direct communication with its neighbours.

The submarine mine store, illustrating the very limited number of these weapons carried aboard *Cressy*. Her full complement was six 76lb mines with an appropriate number of sinkers. As the number of mines was recorded on the drawing, no table of contents for the mine store was added to accompany the ones detailing the contents of the magazines.

SOURCES

OFFICIAL & UNPUBLISHED SOURCES

Documents in the National Archives (Kew)

ADM116/446: *Cressy* Class Twin Screw Armoured Cruisers, 1898

ADM226/10/15: *Cressy* Speed Trials: Analysis of Results, 1901

ADM226/11/19: *Cressy* Rudder Experiments; Full Report, 1902

ADM1/8396/356: Court of Enquiry. Loss of *Aboukir*, *Cressy* and *Hogue* on 22 Sept 1914

Documents at the National Maritime Museum
Caird Library (Greenwich)

623.94: 623.422.24 GRE B9220: Admiralty Handbook for the 6in QF Gun, 1906

LOG/N/13/1: Log Book of Midshipman W H Leeke (HMS *Cressy*), 1901–1903

Brass Foundry (Woolwich)

ADM/SC/157 – 157A: Ships' Covers for the *Cressy* Class

ADMB0715: Specifications for the hull, machinery, masts and derricks for the *Cressy* Class, 1898

ADMB1654: Rigging warrant for the *Cressy* Class, 1899

ADMB1925: Description of fresh and salt water services for HMS *Cressy*, 1901

ADMB1895: Description of ventilation arrangements for HMS *Cressy*, 1901

PUBLISHED SOURCES

Attwood, E, *War-Ships* (Longmans, 1904)

Boursnell, D, *Forging the Fleet* (Sheffield Industrial Museum Trust, 2016)

Brassey, T (editor), *The Naval Annual*, volumes for 1896–1903 (Simpkin, Marshall & Co.)

Brown, D, *Warrior to Dreadnought* (Chatham Publishing, 1997)

Brown, D, *The Grand Fleet* (Chatham Publishing, 1999)

Coles, A, *Three Before Breakfast* (Kenneth Mason, 1979)

Dodson, A, *Before the Battlecruiser* (Seaforth Publishing, 2018)

Friedman, N, *British Cruisers of the Victorian Era* (Seaforth Publishing, 2012)

Friedman, N, *Naval Weapons of World War One* (Seaforth Publishing, 2011)

Manning, F, *The Life of Sir William White* (J Murray, 1923)

Massie, R, *Castles of Steel* (Vintage, 2007)

McKee, C, *Sober Men and True* (Harvard University Press, 2002)

Parkinson, R, *The Late Victorian Navy* (Boydell & Brewer, 2013)

Perkins, R, *British Warship Recognition Volume III: Cruisers 1865-1939 Part 1* (Seaforth Publishing, 2017)

Warren, K, *Armstrongs of Elswick* (Palgrave Macmillan, 1989)

ORIGINAL PLANS USED IN THIS BOOK

HMS *ARIADNE* (1898)

Inboard profile as fitted	M1757

CRESSY CLASS DESIGN

Outline Design for New Armoured Cruiser	M1573
Sheer drawing	M1761
Sketch of rig as designed 1898	M1758
HMS *Sutlej* fore end sections	M1575
HMS *Sutlej* aft end sections	M1576

HMS *CRESSY* GENERAL ARRANGEMENTS 'AS FITTED' 1901

Profile	M0189
Boat Deck	M0190
Upper Deck	M0191
Main Deck	M0192
Protective Deck	M0193
Platforms	M0194
Hold	M0195
Sections	M0196
Sketch of Rig	M1759

CRESSY CLASS DETAILS

HMS *Cressy* watertight arrangements, 1901	M1760
HMS *Euryalus* propeller erosion	M1579
HMS *Aboukir* propeller erosion	M1583
HMS *Cressy* and HMS *Aboukir* citadel armour	M0197
Proposed arrangement of 9.2-inch gun mounting	M1584
HMS *Sutlej* arrangement of belt armour	M1574
HMS *Cressy* and HMS *Aboukir* arrangement of forward bridge	M0198
HMS *Cressy* and HMS *Aboukir* arrangement of after bridge	M0199
HMS *Cressy* and HMS *Aboukir* arrangement of wood, corticene etc decks	
Forecastle, Boat Deck	M1580
Upper Deck, Main Deck	M1581
Protective & Lower Decks, Platform Deck	M1582
HMS *Cressy* arrangement of ventilation	
After sections	M1735
Sections 51 to 123	M1736
Forward sections	M1737

HMS *Euryalus* magazine cooling arrangements

Forward, as fitted	M1577
Aft, as fitted	M1578

HANDBOOK FOR THE 6-INCH QF GUN 1906

Plate XIX Between deck dismounting & housing gear	S5655

MIDSHIPMAN'S LOG OF W H LEEKE

Sketch of 24-inch Electric Light Projector	S5656-001
Diagram of warping *Cressy* into dock at Kowloon	S5656-002
Sketch of 9.2-inch gun mounting	S5656-003

National Maritime Museum ship plans

Exact scale colour prints of ship plans can be purchased online from **http://prints.rmg.co.uk** or please contact **pictures@rmg.co.uk** for scanning services.